THE
GRANDEST
OF LIVES
EYE TO EYE
WITH WHALES

DOUGLAS H. CHADWICK

SIERRA CLUB BOOKS
San Francisco

For Bop (Teal Iris) from Pop

The Sierra Club, founded in 1892 by author and conservationist John Muir, is the oldest, largest, and most influential grassroots environmental organization in the United States. With more than a million members and supporters—and some sixty chapters across the country—we are working hard to protect our local communities, ensure an enduring legacy for America's wild places, and find smart energy solutions to stop global warming. To learn how you can participate in the Sierra Club's programs to explore, enjoy, and protect the planet, please address inquiries to Sierra Club, 85 Second Street, San Francisco, California 94105, or visit our website at www.sierraclub.org.

The Sierra Club's book publishing division, Sierra Club Books, has been a leading publisher of titles on the natural world and environmental issues for nearly half a century. We offer books to the general public as a nonprofit educational service in the hope that they may enlarge the public's understanding of the Sierra Club's concerns and priorities. The point of view expressed in each book, however, does not necessarily represent that of the Sierra Club. For more information on Sierra Club Books and a complete list of our titles and authors, please visit www.sierraclub.org/books.

First Trade Paperback Edition 2008

Published by Sierra Club Books
85 Second Street, San Francisco, CA 94105

Sierra Club Books are published in association with Counterpoint (www.counterpointpress.com).

SIERRA CLUB, SIERRA CLUB BOOKS, and the Sierra Club design logos
are registered trademarks of the Sierra Club.

Book and cover design by Blue Design (www.bluedes.com)
Illustrations copyright © Pieter Folkens

Library of Congress Cataloging-in-Publication Data
Chadwick, Douglas H.
    The grandest of lives : eye to eye with whales / Douglas H. Chadwick.–1st ed.
        p. cm.
    ISBN 10: 1-57805-147-9
    ISBN 13: 978-1-57805-147-2
        1. Whales. I. Title.
QL737.C4C397 2006
599.5—dc22   2005056341

Printed in the United States of America on New Leaf Ecobook 50 acid-free paper, which contains a minimum of 50 percent post-consumer waste, processed chlorine free. Of the balance, 25 percent is Forest Stewardship Council certified to contain no old-growth trees and to be pulped totally chlorine free.

Distributed to the trade by Publishers Group West
12 11 10 09 08
10 9 8 7 6 5 4 3 2 1

CONTENTS

ACKNOWLEDGMENTS

I'm eager to thank the following folks for helping me learn, write, and spread fresh news about whales: First come Jim and Mary Borrowman, owner-operators of Stubbs Island Charters, who for no good reason in particular let me on their whale-watching boat to spend time with orcas in Johnstone Strait, British Columbia, whenever I had the urge. As they have done for the researchers working in the area for, well, decades now, the Borrowmans educated and informed me, fed me fresh salmon, provided a soft bed on shore, and warmed many a gray, rainy coastal day with their companionship. Next, my appreciation goes out to Art Sutch and Pete Metcalfe, a pair of Alaskan gentlemen, consummate fishermen, and scuba divers, who not only helped with fieldwork but also carried out a midnight rescue from a lonesome cove when the ship I was on became disabled. My sincere gratitude goes to two other Alaskans as well, Kim and Melanie Heacox, for wonderful hospitality in the little port of Gustavus; to Koji and Miyuki Nakamura for extending the same kindness in Tokyo; and to my friends Flip Nicklin and Jason Sturgis for letting me continue to mooch food and shelter in Hawaii during one humpback whale breeding season after another. Official thanks go to members of the National Marine Fisheries Service and National Marine Sanctuary System for information, assistance, and boat time. More informal thanks are due a wild-eyed whale-lover named Bill Graves, whose day job was as the chief editor of *National Geographic* magazine; Jennifer Reek, my longtime, talented, and endlessly tolerant articles editor at that venerable institution; Robert. M. Poole, former *Geographic* executive editor; and Bernard Ohanian, a former associate editor there. This part can't close without a nod to Linda Gunnarson, an editor at Sierra Club Books, who has to deal with the quirks, qualms, testiness, and outright tantrums all-too-typical of writers. I am no exception. But Linda, with her reserves of sympathy and goodwill, is. Thank you.

Finally, the many scientists and field crews mentioned in this book all helped bring it to life through their willingness to share hard-won information. I count their drive and curiosity among the planet's natural wonders. Jim Darling, Volker Deecke, John Calambokidis, Jon Stern, Bruce Mate, Richard Sears, Sascha Hooker, Hal Whitehead, Craig Matkin, and Eva Saulitis, top-notch, busy researchers all, kindly took time to review portions of the manuscript for accuracy. I am in their debt. Of course, we all know the responsibility for inaccuracies rests on my shoulders alone.

Introduction
The Grandest
of Lives

Whales sometimes leap from the sea, heaving heavenward the greatest masses of flesh ever formed on Earth. No one knows why. The behavior is called breaching. Since falling back onto the ocean surface smacks away layers of dead skin along with hitchhiking barnacles and sea lice, some think this is how an animal deals with hundreds of square feet of itchy hide when it has no hands, feet, horns, or even a flexible neck to scratch with. That doesn't explain why a jump by one member of a group often seems to spark jumping by others. Breaching might express excitement or aggression triggered by social interactions beneath the waves. It could be a way to send out a signal, for the splashdown resounds like a cannon shot. Possibly the animals are just playing or—if you'll grant them the capacity—jumping for joy. Or maybe whales erupt from the water for all of the above reasons, and more.

Incomparable strength lies within those rounded bodies with no visible musculature. Just three or four beats of the broad, horizontal tail fins, or flukes, are enough to launch a breach. In water, remember, even the most ponderous-looking whales are virtually weightless, liberated from the lifelong constraints gravity places upon us. They fly through the ocean as flexible tubes, all tapered ends and smooth edges offering little resistance and an abundance of grace. And yet these highly specialized hydrodynamic forms are fellow mammals. If they hurl themselves out into the sky, they can breathe as much of it as they please.

Where we exchange 15 to 20 percent of the air in our lungs with each breath, whales are thought to exchange 80 to 90 percent. Blood makes up a larger proportion of total body weight in whales than it does in other animals—10 to 15 percent as opposed to 7 percent in humans, for instance. Awash in their own crimson sea, the giants' tissues fairly sizzle with oxygen flooding in from the lungs via rich capillary networks. Their muscle fibers are loaded with myoglobin, an iron-containing protein that grabs and stores the oxygen, then releases it to cells as needed, making possible the whales' long dives and other underwater exertions.

Maybe whales don't go skyborne for any particular purpose or pleasure so much as because they can and have no reason not to. Maybe in their hot-blooded, breath-holding mastery of a liquid environment, they enjoy a level of vitality beyond our reckoning and breach just as part of being so powerfully *alive.* That was my impression while watching killer whales, or orcas, in a glacial fjord along the Alaska coast one morning. The theory might not have been very solid, but the possibility was a delight to think about. It still is.

This is a water planet. Seen from space, the whole sphere glows blue. The vast majority of Earthly life takes place in marine ecosystems. If you're going to call yourself a naturalist, which I did, you should know at least a little about what goes on out there, down there, which I didn't for quite a long time. Then I teamed up with a photographer named Flip Nicklin on a *National Geographic* story about America's National Marine Sanctuary System, and my own life underwent a sea change. Soon, I was aboard one boat or another for days on end, starting to learn about oceans at last. And I realized that not even a lifetime of using the word *whale* as a synonym for *colossal* prepares anybody for the first encounter close enough to hear air rushing in and out of blowholes like blasts through an industrial pipe while mist from the exhalations carries across on the breeze to dampen your face and this flexing island-that-is-a-creature rises from the water and widens and rises more and lengthens . . . Whales are almost too big to get your mind around.

Flip grew up swimming, surfing, and working as a scuba instructor for his family's dive shop in San Diego. Able to free-dive to eighty feet without a tank for a look around, he quite possibly qualifies as some sort of marine mammal himself by now. After I got certified for scuba, he guided me down to explore the seafloors of several marine sanctuaries. We weren't looking for whales. But, submerged sometimes for two or three hours a day, I was able to sense for the first time what existence is like in an environment where you detect nearby movements as pressure waves on your skin, hear sounds directly through your skull, and move with equal ease in three dimensions with the flutter of a flipper.

Part of the North Pacific population of humpback whales travels each winter to the warm, clear waters around the Hawaiian Islands, gathering to breed and give birth. Flip had been photographing the leviathans there for years while his longtime friend and colleague, Jim Darling, director of the West Coast Whale Research Foundation, studied their activities. Eventually, Flip took on the role of full research partner, bringing his cameras into play primarily to identify individual animals and record their behavior. Before the National Marine Sanctuary System story wound down, he was proposing an article based on new information about the natural history of humpback whales to *National Geographic*. The editors approved and assigned me to write it.

One of the first things I learned was that collecting data on whales is slow, slow, wave-beaten work. Observers get weathered out more often than not. On many days when the winds and waters cooperate, the whales don't. And no matter what the weather, at least 90 percent of their activities take place below the surface. In addition to that, the animals may move hundreds of miles in a week. Studying them is a little like bobbing around in a tub hoping to learn all about submarines. Which helps explain why we know less about whales today than we knew about most land mammals a century or two ago.

Flip and Jim had a routine of heading out from the harbor at Lahaina on Maui's northwest coast shortly after dawn. The eight-mile-wide Au'au Channel between Maui and Lanai tends to be calmest in the morning hours. A minimum of wind, waves, and throbbing boat engines makes it easier for Jim to pursue his chief interest, which is the humpback's long, elaborate, strangely beautiful, and continually changing song. While the whales may be out of view at times, they are seldom out of hearing. Wade into the ocean from any beach facing the Au'au Channel, duck underwater, and humpback voices will fill your ears: sequences of squeaks, ribbits, trumpet blasts, trombone-slide groans, and pulsating rumbles flowing in from near and far. Dive a bit deeper, below the noises from rolling surf, and the songs swell in volume and number until you begin to feel serenaded by an otherworldly chorus. Drop a hydrophone thirty feet down over the side of a boat, and, like Jim Darling, you could start to pick out individual singers in the vicinity, find your way closer to the nearest one by moving in the direction of the loudest sounds, and document the animal's tunes with a recording device.

A Canadian scientist with a doctoral degree, Jim was able to offer impressive analyses of the notes' wavelengths and harmonics. He could identify rhythms and tell you how themes sung by the population change over time. But, as with breaching, he couldn't say why the whales were singing in the first place. His goal was to find an answer. At the time I showed up, he had already been probing the subject for eighteen years.

During one of my first days on Jim's twenty-four-foot speedboat, the good ship *Never Satisfied,* we went well out in the channel and drifted while the sounds caught by the hydrophone played through a speaker on deck. Clouds wreathed the islands' volcanic peaks above steep slopes that glowed green in the morning light. As the sun rose higher, the channel kept turning more blue and at the same time more transparent, until it was like a second sky. Jim located a singer and gradually homed in on its location, until the notes came rising up through the water around us and reverberated in the hull. Moments later, we could make out the animal itself suspended about fifty feet below.

(Federal regulations prohibit disrupting the activities of marine mammals by going too near. In addition, the Endangered Species Act makes it unlawful to disturb an imperiled life-form, and almost all the large whale species, having been devastated by commercial whaling, are still listed as threatened or endangered.

Whale-watching boats and other craft are required to maintain a minimum distance of one hundred yards. In Hawaii, as elsewhere in humpback range, the scientists I accompanied operated under hard-to-get permits that allowed them to be closer when necessary. Since I assisted with logistics, made sightings, and recorded data, I was covered under the permits too.)

Jim was recording a superb acoustic sequence on tape when the equipment sputtered and quit. Given saltwater corrosion on top of the abuse that electronic components take day after day on a boat jolting through waves, this was not a completely unexpected event. Just the same, he was muttering scurvy pirate curses as he started to pull in the hydrophone by its cable. Some minuscule metal part had just turned to junk and shot a promising morning all to hell, spreading disappointment fore and aft. Then Jim leaned over the side to peer down into the vitreous blue and announced that the whale was coming up. Close.

The humpback cruised right next to the *Never Satisfied* several times and stopped, hovering with a barnacle-stippled nose thrust out of the water. Then it continued making slow passes, singing during some of them. Our visitor paused to croon directly beneath the boat, investigated the hydrophone, put its head right next to the device as if auditioning, rubbed against the hydrophone, rose, and rubbed gently against the *Never Satisfied*. This meeting was turning into a mugging, which is how whale watchers describe incidents of an animal interacting closely with a boat. They don't occur all that often and seldom last long. For a singer to show so much interest was rarer still. The fascination was mutual. Jim and Flip hadn't encountered a humpback all season quite this curious or friendly or sexually attracted or whatever was in progress.

Surfacing by the boat again, the whale lifted its head high out of the water. It reversed position and lifted its tail above our heads. After slowly sinking back, the animal resumed making passes, rolling to bring an eye nearer the surface and stare up at us. Jim is a soft-spoken personality with a tendency to disengage from everyday dealings at times in favor of abstract thought. He is an even more reserved scientist, reluctant to draw conclusions, much less make sweeping pronouncements. But as the whale lingered on its side, moving its eye back and forth, taking us in, Jim turned from the gunwale and said, "This right here is the real reason humpbacks should never be hunted, and that's all I can say about it."

The whale stayed around so long that Flip eased into the water to see what he could make out through a face mask and try to photograph the animal's behavior. He motioned for me to follow as a safety diver. That meant assisting by keeping watch for sharks, incoming whales, or anything else someone concentrating on another subject in the water should be made aware of. Because scuba gear gives off noisy streams of bubbles, which can disturb humpbacks, we would be free-diving, relying solely on lung power. And that brought a slight but ever-present risk of shallow-water blackout by someone nearing the surface after spending time at depth—another good reason to practice a buddy system out there among the waves.

I passed from the gunwale into the Pacific, took a quick breath through the snorkel, and ducked my head under. Whereas I had barely been able to see 50 blurry feet into the water from the ship's deck, I suddenly had a crisp view stretching in every direction for 100 to 150 feet. It was an opalescent universe of borderless blue, gradually dimming toward gray in the distance.

And it was empty save for flecks of plankton drifting by. Then I looked past my feet.

The whale was suspended head down with its pectoral fins spread as if frozen in a swan dive, a pose often assumed by singers. Its music came straight through my flesh and played loudly in my bones. I felt strummed. After a while, the melody was replaced by a series of ascending whoops, and the whale came rising from the depths. I don't recall the exact sequence, but I know that this enormity, this sentient presence with a body about seven times my length and four hundred times my weight, approached very closely, eyeing me, and its passing took an achingly long time, and at one point a pectoral fin swept by inches over my head. I know the whale turned and came directly toward me once more, closing the distance much too fast for me to react. At the last instant, the nose began to pitch slightly down, and the rest of the head followed in an arc that left me four feet above it, awash in whale currents. Again the animal rolled onto a side and looked at me. Then it rolled farther until it was on its back, and the white, grooved belly slid on past and away.

Next came another approach straight at me. This time the humpback flared its pectoral fins and braked less than a yard from my face. We floated there nose to nose, scarcely moving. I rose slightly to look above the surface. There was nothing but more whale head in view. The thing was studded with tubercles— the stove-bolt-like knobs unique to humpback noses. Behind them stretched the long, flat plane formed by the upper part of the jaw, or rostrum, and dark, gray, wet skin gradually sloped up from that toward the animal's back like a hill. The whale tilted head-up, and a still wider expanse of whitish, pleated throat filled my view. I sank a few feet, and it was more whale all the way down; the animal's underside only broadened. Songs of other humpbacks came throbbing through me while my own blood pounded in my ears.

I felt wary and off balance but never really frightened. I was too overwhelmed, treading water slowly while facing a force so utterly beyond mine that I couldn't begin to make sense of the situation. There was simply no experience in my lifetime to use as a reference. I hadn't come with any preconceptions about whales being extraordinarily gentle or wise, but I somehow trusted that the force hovering before me was benign. This megamammal appeared able to keep track of exactly where I was and to fine-tune its movements accordingly. It showed no intention of doing anything except making inquiries after its fashion. I was before an intelligent, purposeful, immanent being. It had questions.

Maybe this is what an interview with God would be like. My mind should have been racing with profound ideas and possibilities, but I don't think I could have told you my name. I resisted the temptation to reach out and make actual contact. I only waited and watched and breathed, leaving everything up to the whale. Moments passed, and the interview was over. The animal continued on to the *Never Satisfied,* which was drifting nearby, and inspected the propeller and then the dangling hydrophone again. After that, it sank tail first until it was positioned straight up and down beneath the boat, which suddenly looked like a pool toy. The portion of the hull that showed below the waterline was scarcely one-third the length of the humpback perpendicular to it. That perspective made the whole enterprise of trying to study whales all the more amazing to me, and certainly more humbling.

For days after that meeting, I felt as if I were walking an inch or two off the ground. I was not the same man I had been before, and I knew that I would not be the same man again. Yet to be honest, when I had first clambered back aboard the ship, my first coherent thoughts were anything but enlightened. They ran more along the lines of: If the closest moment with the biggest animal in a career of watching wildlife just took place, that means I'll probably never be able to top it, right? So now what? This absurd internal dialogue lasted about a minute before I started to smile. Surely I was destined to be on a boat called the *Never Satisfied*. I coaxed my ego back into its cage and was quickly overtaken by a feeling of being the most fortunate novice whale observer to ever leave port.

Jim and Flip were as excited in their own way, because before our encounter ended, another whale had appeared and begun circling the first. The singer and the joiner, as Jim referred to the new arrival, spiraled around one another for some time before swimming off together and eventually merging with a larger group.

While humpbacks of both sexes make social noises, only the males are known to sing. Observers originally assumed that this whale "music" was like a bird's territorial call or an elk's rutting bugle, designed to announce a male's presence and attract receptive females. In a variation on this theory, Jim wondered if the song functioned somewhat like an acoustic version of the impressive antlers or horns many male hoofed animals carry to help advertise their status and fitness. Being able to hold your breath a long time while loudly belting out a tune might be a way of proclaiming, "I'm big and healthy with energy to spare!" which boils down to: "I carry fabulous genes!" However, Jim and Flip had been able today to determine the sex not only of the singer but also of the joiner. Both were male, and they didn't act like rivals. What did this mean?

Another twist in a compelling mystery had emerged as
I watched. Recalling the moment when a nagging inner voice
asked, Now what? I realized that I knew the answer: Why, more
humpbacks, of course. Then more whales and more oceans. And
always more questions. Good. The best adventures are propelled
by the desire to know the unknown.

So much about the natural world still exceeds ordinary understanding that the sooner you admit you're going to spend a lot of
time mystified, the sooner you'll feel free to plunge ahead anyway and keep trying to discover what you can. Lightning, fossils,
lodestones, pollination, epidemics, lunar eclipses, rainbows . . .
science has a long history of changing one generation's miracles
and confusions into the next generation's facts. Whales are somewhere in transition. Beasts so huge and rarely glimpsed come
with strong links to the realm of legend, and we haven't learned
enough about their ecology and behavior to place them firmly
within the context of real-world mammals. Not yet. But while it
could be said until fairly recently that we know more about how
to kill whales than about how they survive, the balance is finally
tipping in favor of insight into these grandest of lives.

Meanwhile, the manner in which whales are valued by society has already undergone a dramatic shift. The giants that were
sought for centuries as cheap sources of commodities such as
oil (for lamps, lubrication, and cosmetics) and meat (for human
consumption and pet food) turned into cherished icons of conservation. This was the driving force behind restrictions on commercial whaling, which began in the late 1960s and culminated in a
worldwide ban in 1986. Public sympathy for whales continues to
be strong, and it helps focus attention on the hard-pressed marine

environment as a whole, where whales now contend with wide-spread commercial overharvest of fish populations, entanglement in fishing nets and lines, increasing levels of chemical pollution and underwater noise pollution, and collisions with ever-increasing shipping traffic. At the same time, a growing number of nations, led by Japan, have found ways around the international hunting moratorium. They are increasing their harvest of whales every year and adding more species to the list, humpbacks being the latest. It becomes tremendously important for people to take a fresh look at the animals in order to judge for themselves what's at stake today.

To much of the public, whales are whales—big and wonderful maybe, but more or less alike. In reality, they encompass a mind-stretching assortment of lifestyles, adaptations, social relationships, and knowledge. The foremost whale photographer of his generation, Flip developed a plan for doing stories on several kinds of whales that, between them, represent a cross section of the group's diversity. *National Geographic* once again signed on and turned me loose as the writer. In addition to following humpback research, I soon hooked up with projects uncovering new information about the northern bottlenose whale, an obscure, squid-hunting roamer of the abyss; the killer whale, whose habits are shaped by learned information passed on within its tightly knit families and clans—in short, by its culture; the modest-sized, relatively abundant minke whale, currently the harpooners' principal target, on display in slabs at meat markets but otherwise poorly known; and the blue whale, the largest animal from any era in Earth's long history.

In my mind, these species became, respectively, the singer, the diver, the killer, the commoner, and the giant. This book is meant to be a vessel that carries you closer to each. I also hope you'll take pleasure in meeting some of the people who work glimpse by glimpse, through fair weather and foul, year after year, out on the rolling, whale-tracked sea to provide us with a clearer understanding. But some background on the origins and current classification of these creatures is called for first.

> *And God made great whales. . . . And God*
> *blessed them, saying, Be fruitful, and multiply,*
> *and fill the waters in the seas.*
> —*Genesis 1:21–22*

> *Then the whole world was the whale's; and,*
> *king of creation, he left his wake.*
> —Herman Melville, *Moby Dick*

Whales, dolphins, and porpoises make up the order of mammals known as the Cetacea (from ketos, the Greek word for sea monster). So thoroughly have these animals modified the basic mammalian body plan to suit an ocean existence, scientists couldn't decide for a long time which group gave rise to them. The oldest known fossils of ancient cetaceans, termed archaeocetes, shed little light on the problem, because they had already taken on the basic appearance of whales. Then a recent spate of discoveries among foothills at the base of the Himalayas turned up ancestral whales between 50 and 55 million years old in what were once the deltas of streams and rivers flowing into the prehistoric Tethys Sea. The riddle was solved at last, the experts declared: based on similarities in teeth and skull anatomy, whales were descended from mesonychians, a curious line of meat-eating ungulates that looked something like heavy-jawed coyotes or wolves with hoofs.

· TYPICAL LENGTHS OF FIVE WHALE SPECIES ·

Blue, *Balaenoptera musculus*, 80 to 100 feet

Humpback, *Megaptera novaeangliae*, 40 to 50 feet

Orca, *Orcinus orca*, 18 to 33 feet

Minke, *Balaenoptera acutorostrata*, 22 to 33 feet

Northern Bottlenose, *Hyperoodon ampullatus*, 23 to 29 feet

It made a kind of sense, for although people commonly speak of whales grazing on plankton and call the males bulls and the females cows, every cetacean large and small is carnivorous—a full-time predator; it's just that some specialize in scooping up masses of very small prey such as fish fry and shrimp.

But new technology yielded a different answer. While the part about cetaceans being descended from ungulates was accurate—modern whales still have multichambered stomachs just as cattle and deer do—studies of molecular sequences in DNA strands just recently revealed the closest living relatives of cetaceans to be hippos. This means the two groups share a common ancestor. The first whales would therefore have branched off from the line of protohippos already in existence—stout, hoofed wetland-dwellers roughly the size of wild boars.

For whatever reasons, the earliest cetaceans definitely came with a mouthful of formidable teeth, perhaps used to hunt fish in the shallows. One of the first types, labeled *Pakicetus,* the Pakistan whale, was exhumed from river sediments whose other contents tell us that it lived among land dwellers, including marsupials and our own very early ancestors, squirrel-size primates. A particular mix of characteristics found in *Pakicetus*—the arrangement of cusps on its molars, middle ear bones positioned within the skull a certain way, and a subtle folding in one of those bones, the bulla—was absent in other land animals but became a signature of subsequent whales.

A million years after *Pakicetus* came *Ambulocetus natans,* Latin for the "walking-swimming whale." The beast swam like an otter, moving its spine and tail up and down, and walked on powerful, splayed-out legs. It may have been an ambush hunter, lurking with only its high-set nostrils and eyes above the water like a furry crocodile. The passage of time brought larger, still more aquatic species. Nostrils began to migrate from the top of the snout toward the top of the head. Outer ears shrank until they disappeared, while the inner ear structure continued to change so that sound vibrations reached it directly from the skull and lower jawbones via special fat pads. The neck shortened, the front legs took on more of a rudder shape, hind legs dwindled, and the pelvis anchoring them to the backbone was reduced, leaving the spine more flexible to power the developing flukes.

Picture big-headed, snaggle-toothed, web-footed sea lions or walruses five to fifteen feet long. Like modern day sea lions, cetaceans at this level probably still returned to land to breed and rear young, hauling out and schlumping along the shore partly on their bellies. Equally important shifts in physiology had been taking place as well. For instance, scientists can tell from the ratio of oxygen isotopes in fossil teeth that the animals were no longer drinking freshwater. Freed from that requirement, they roamed ever farther from river outlets, generation after generation a fraction more streamlined and that much closer to claiming the ocean vastness as home.

The makeover from landlubber to full-time seafarer happened in less than 10 million years—overnight on the geological time scale. At the start of the most recent millennium, A.D. 2000, I went wandering over a desert plain in far western India searching for more bones of bygone whales where the Indus River delta had rippled eons before. Sunil Bajpai of the University of Roorkee scouted a ridge to one side while Hans Thewissen, a scientist from Northeastern Ohio Universities College of Medicine, disappeared around the bend of a dry wash. The heat measured 115° Fahrenheit. Returning with a fossil skull in his daypack,

Thewissen paused to wipe sweat from his face. It was a small gesture, but it reminded me that the ancestors of all of us land animals originally crawled up from the salty sea. Then some turned around and went back.

"Whales underwent the most dramatic and complete trans-formation of any mammal," Thewissen reflected. "The early stages were so poorly known fifteen years ago that creationists held up whales as proof that species couldn't possibly have come about through natural selection. Now whales are one of the better ex-amples of evolution." Whaling crews of the past few centuries got a look at more whale bodies than anyone before or since. I wondered what they thought when they hauled aboard a fully grown adult with miniature legs sticking out from its flanks. Such throwbacks offer continuing evidence of the giants' ancient link to the land, though I'd bet most whalers just took them as further proof that the seas are too wide, too deep, and too full of strange things for humans to ever figure out.

Earth's first large, warm-blooded sea hunters experimented with all kinds of forms as they radiated out to invade new niches, many of which had lain empty since the plesiosaurs, dolphin-shaped ichthyosaurs, and other great marine reptiles vanished along with their dinosaur kin. The whales-in-progress ranged from *Basilosaurus,* so long and slender and toothy that scientists first took it for another prehistoric reptile, to a species dubbed the whale-rus for its squarish, walrus-shaped skull that bore two long, downward-pointing tusks. After going on a fossil dig in the Sharktooth Hills of Southern California with paleontologist Lawrence Barnes, I went back to his office at the Natural History Museum of Los Angeles County. He let me flip through his card files for all the different fossil species of whales catalogued to date. The total looked to be about a thousand. When I mentioned this to Barnes, he nodded and said, "My guess is, that represents 10 percent of what's out there waiting to be dug up."

At present, the order Cetacea contains nearly ninety living species. The exact number is unclear. For one thing, taxonomists keep changing their minds as to whether some closely related members ought to be classified as separate species or varieties of the same creature. For another thing, modern species are still being discovered. Several new whales were named during the latter part of the twentieth century and one more as recently as 2002. Partially decayed bodies of unfamiliar cetaceans found washed up on shores hint that the list for this order of mammals is by no means complete yet.

Modern members of the Cetacea fall into two major subdivisions: the odontocetes, or toothed whales, which include porpoises and dolphins; and the mysticetes, or baleen whales. The split took place during the Oligocene epoch, 34 million to 24 million years ago. Typical archaeocetes had an array of jagged teeth in various sizes. Odontocetes replaced them with uniform teeth. They also added sonar to their arsenal, and their efficiency in finding and chasing down food took a quantum leap upward. You can see the frontal bones becoming more concave in early specimens, taking on the shape of a dish antenna. They cupped a lens of fatty tissue, called the melon, in the forehead. This design focused high-frequency sounds produced in special air sacs off the main nasal passage into an outgoing beam. Together with thinned portions of the lower jaw, the dish also collected the sounds bouncing back from objects. Echolocation gave odontocetes the batlike ability to navigate and pinpoint prey even where conditions cut visibility to zero. Needless to say, this opened up opportunities ever deeper into the ocean's inky depths and into waters thick with silt.

The odontocetes became a highly successful, diverse group whose present membership includes species barely five feet long, such as the vaquita of the northern Gulf of Mexico, the black dolphin of coastal Chile, and the harbor porpoise. Obviously, the trend for cetaceans hasn't always been toward giantism. The fact that sediment-laden rivers in different parts of the world are now inhabited by four kinds of specialized dolphins—along with the tucuxi and finless porpoise, which have seagoing coastal populations as well—brings up another interesting point. The combination of sonar and smaller body size has even allowed some odontocetes to return to the kind of freshwater environment in which their hoofed ancestors waded. Were evolution to run its course without interference from a teeming human population, the cetaceans might eventually come full circle and begin reaching out from the aquatic empire they established and colonize the land.

The odontocetes we call killer whales, false killer whales, pygmy killer whales, long-finned pilot whales, short-finned pilot whales, and melon-headed whales are actually all big, brawny members of the Delphinidae, one of several dolphin families. Belugas and narwhals (whose nine-foot-long, spiral-grooved, ivory tusk, brandished by males when sparring with rivals, almost surely gave rise to legends about the unicorn's horn) are odontocetes too. As are the numerous but scarcely known beaked whales; the largest toothed whale, the sperm whale; and its distant cousins, the dwarf sperm whale and pygmy sperm whale, both barely ten feet long.

The mysticete branch of the Cetacea gradually lost the teeth on their lower jaw and replaced those of the upper jaw with baleen.

Made of keratin, the fibrous protein that also builds hair, hoofs, and claws, baleen grows as a series of food-trapping plates or strips. The result hangs from the roof of the mouth like a curtain—or like a weird, inside-the-mouth moustache; *mysticete* literally means moustache whale. Some Oligocene fossils recently brought to light represent intermediate forms that carried both teeth and a modest fringe of baleen. The length of the plates continued to increase along with the size of the head relative to the rest of the body until the mysticetes became, in effect, living seafood nets.

New Zealand paleontologist Ewan Fordyce has pointed out that a breakup of the supercontinents during that era led to greater temperature variations between the oceans at different latitudes. Those gradients in turn created stronger currents and upwellings of nutrients that fertilized explosions of plankton. The seas became swirlier, more diverse, and dappled with extremely food-rich patches. According to Fordyce, the baleen whales adapted to take advantage of this new set of circumstances. Suppose that on this near-magical planet of ours there came to be more and more places where savory little pieces of pizza filled the air, hovering in swarms so thick you could walk around swallowing bunch after bunch. Would you ignore them and move on, hoping to find, say, a pork chop, or work on your swarm-gulping technique?

The baleen of modern mysticetes takes the form of anywhere from four hundred to a thousand plates draped from the upper jaw. They range from short, simple arrays like the bristles on a broom to finely fringed strips ten feet from base to tip. The longer and more elaborate the structure, the smaller the type of prey it is designed to trap. Tough yet flexible, a sort of organic predecessor to plastic, baleen was in such demand for corset stays, umbrella reinforcements, tongue depressors, buggy whips, and switches (as in: "I'm going to whale the daylights out of you, young man") that, during the latter half of the nineteenth century, the market for it became more lucrative than for whale oil.

Whereas all the odontocetes have a single blowhole, all the mysticetes possess two. Taxonomists separate the baleen whales into four families on the basis of other characteristics. Four species—three types of right whale and the equally bulky bowhead whale—comprise the Balaenidae family. The pygmy right whale, which used to be classified with them, is now by itself in the family Neobalaenidae. Likewise, the gray whale is the lone member of the Eschrichtiidae. The eight remaining mysticetes—minke, Bryde's, humpback, sei, fin, and blue whales—make up the Balaenopteridae, and they have raised the art of the gulp to levels never before seen. This family is distinguished by grooves that extend all along the underside of the great mouth and throat, from the lower jaw nearly to the belly. These are actually pleated folds that expand in concertina fashion during feeding, allowing an animal to take in prodigious volumes of seawater, temporarily increasing its already massive tonnage by as much as a third. When the folds are fully stretched out, blood vessels in the otherwise pale throat skin show pink in the creases. The color gave this family its other name, the rorquals, Norse for "red whales."

This adds up to only fourteen modern species of mysticetes (fifteen if you consider northern and antarctic minkes separate species, as many experts now do). As commonly spoken, the name *whale* is less a technical term than an honorary title granted on the basis of size. We apply it to about half the Cetacea, including the big dolphins mentioned earlier. To distinguish the real leviathans, people have traditionally labeled them *great whales*. These are the blue, fin, sei, Bryde's, humpback, bowhead, right, gray, and

sperm whales. One of these humongous forms or some generalized version—usually plumper than the actual creature—is what
most people have in mind when they think of whales or depict
them in advertising logos and children's books. But once you
know a bit more, you have to be struck by the fact that twelve of
the thirteen great whales happen to be mysticetes.

The two largest kinds of shark in the world, whale sharks and
their northern counterparts, basking sharks, can reach lengths of
nearly fifty feet. Both types swim slowly through clouds of plankton with their mouths agape while structures called rakers filter
food out of the seawater passing through the gills. Many people
assume that great whales feed in a similar style, barging along
passively collecting food on their baleen. They don't. The sperm
whale is a toothed hunter of squid and fish. Baleen whales open
wide to take in food-laden water, usually in a single gulp preceded
by specialized, active hunting behavior, then close the mouth
and use their giant tongue as a plunger to force the liquid back
out through the baleen sieve. From an evolutionary standpoint,
straining your meals, however you do it, is certainly an effective
way to get big. Only two of the mysticetes—minkes and pygmy
right whales—are less than gargantuan.

By definition, every species in existence is a right answer to the
question of how best to live. Monkey-flower, monitor lizard, or
mountain goat, it percolates with solutions to the unrelenting
challenges of survival. While the likes of fungi, bacteria, and still
more "primitive" microbes are among the most enduring success
stories, we empathize with newer, larger species that we see as
having gained a different kind of preeminence because they rank
near the top of the who-eats-whom heap and are able to go pretty

much where they please. By those measures and many others, whales rule the seas. Since saltwater covers nearly three-quarters of the globe, you could make a splendid argument to the effect that whales are Earth's dominant species. Or were for millions of years, until an inordinately clever primate took to the oceans in ever bigger ships with ever more lethal weapons.

Getting to know whales better is like having laser surgery to clear cataracts from your eyes. Over the years, I've noticed that, as studies of the behavior and intelligence of these and other animals are published, more and more of the conclusions contain the potent phrase "a quality previously thought to be unique to humans" or words to that effect. Our view of *Homo sapiens* as being fundamentally different and disconnected from the rest of creation is about to change. The implications are as big as the biosphere and the future vitality of civilizations within it. This is a crucial stage of history, and to be a whale watcher right now is to have a front row seat.

THE SINGER
HUMPBACK WHALE

Announcing itself with the blast of a bushy double spout ten to twenty feet into the air, *Megaptera novaeangliae* usually surfaces four to six times in a row to breathe. It is at the crest of each rise—especially the last one in the sequence—that the names whalers gave the animal begin to make sense. Lifting high in preparation for a dive, the top side flexes sharply about two-thirds of the way toward the tail. At this stage, instead of the gently curving fuselage that most whales present when viewed from the side, you see a triangular mass of dark gray flesh with the short, thick dorsal fin

31

at the apex, like the cap on a roof. Behold: the broken-back whale, the humped-back whale, the humpback.

The leading edge of this arch is marine-mammal smooth. But the knobby vertebrae of the backbone stand out prominently all along the trailing edge, dragon-style. When the backs of several animals arise in a row, it is as if a single, vast form were undulating through the waves. Steve Zeff, the naturalist guide on a whale-watching boat in Hawaii, pointed this out to me years ago. The sun was weak and mist shrouded, the sea the color of pearl, its luster polished by breezes playing across its surface. These winds carried faint tropical fragrances from the slopes of volcano-forged islands where darker clouds clung to the peaks like smoke. Anything seemed possible in such a setting. When the silhouettes of seven or eight humped backs appeared simultaneously against the horizon, Zeff said I was probably looking at the source of many a sea serpent myth. That thought stayed with me. Every time I witness a distant procession of humpbacks in fog or twilight, it becomes a little easier to imagine some ancient mariner stunned by what he was sure was some bizarre colossus uncoiling from the depths. Yet humpbacks are sufficiently large— twenty-five to forty tons, stretching forty to fifty feet, sometimes longer—to qualify as monsters in their own right. And they have the virtue of being ones we can understand and relate to, more so all the time.

No matter what fantastic tales they may have spawned early on, humpbacks are now among the whales most familiar to the public. They are also the most closely studied, aside from several tightly knit communities of orcas off North America's northwestern coast. Ranging along the continental shelves, humpbacks come nearer to shore than most other great whales do. And given their penchant for multiton acrobatics—Herman Melville, the author of *Moby-Dick*, called them "the most gamesome and light-hearted of all the whales, making more gay foam and white-water generally than any other."—they are hard to miss when they are around.

Besides performing a good deal of pec slapping (also termed *flipper slapping*; it means floating on one side to repeatedly raise a pectoral fin aloft and whap it down on the water), lob-tailing (raising the flukes into the air and whomping them down), chin slapping (coming halfway out of the water with a forward tilt and bringing the lower jaw and throat down sharply to create a splash), and other surface displays, humpbacks are, among the truly great whales, by far the ones most given to breaching. Young humpbacks have been seen jumping scores of times in a row and may rocket completely out of the sea like dolphins. Fully grown adults approaching fifty feet in length sometimes clear the surface too. The effect is flabbergasting. Nature offers more thunderous spectacles, but they arise from tumults of weather or geology, not from living beings. The humpbacks leap vertically and with enough of a twist that they usually come down partly on their back or side, seldom on their soft belly. Some aerialists twist through a full revolution before reentry.

The breaches seem all the more striking because of this species's pectoral fins, easily the longest of any marine mammal. Each is ten to fifteen feet from shoulder to tip, white on the underside and often on the top side's far end. In the water, the proportions of the fins and flukes relative to the body give humpbacks the silhouette of a commercial passenger jet. And when the dark fuselage leaps from the waves and the pectoral fins are suddenly flung wide, flashing in the light, the wingspan seems even more impressive. It is as if a whale really were on the verge of taking flight. Though distributed worldwide, the species got its scientific label when it was sought mainly by Yankee whalers out of northeastern ports. *Megaptera novaeangliae* means "great-winged New Englander."

For all the humpbacks' aerial prowess, their most defining trait is invisible: the song. Whether you characterize it as a haunting aria or a pattern of bestial cries, it is the longest, most complex vocalization known in the animal kingdom. With notes forming phrases and the phrases arranged into themes, the song continues unbroken for as much as half an hour before ending with a distinct finale. After coming up for a few breaths, the whale will submerge to begin again, and it may keep repeating the cycle of surfacing and singing for hours on end. When scientists sent the space capsule *Voyager IV* hurtling out beyond our solar system bearing greetings intended to convey the essence of Earth and its cultures, they included sixty human languages and a humpback song.

Easier to find than most of their giant relatives, humpbacks are easier to stay with as well. Their usual pace is just two to four knots, though they can swim several times that fast in short bursts. (A knot is one nautical mile per hour and a nautical mile equals 1.15 standard miles.) It also helps that they are reasonably tolerant of boats. Some act positively attracted. Guides on whale-watching boats refer to such big visitors as "friendlies," though no one really knows whether those particular animals are really being congenial, as opposed to just bold or especially curious.

While traveling through Frederick Sound and nearby Chatham Strait in southeastern Alaska during a spell of unusually hot weather, several of us decided to jump overboard, despite the occasional iceberg drifting by to remind us of just how seriously we were going to cool down once we hit the water. Screaming as we leaped, we scrunched into cannonball and jackknife positions in a contest to raise the biggest, loudest splash. No sooner had the last plunger shivered back aboard than three humpbacks rose to the surface exactly where we had been jumping off the stern. They floated there facing our boat with their noses almost touching the transom for a minute or two before submerging as gradually as they had appeared. Two minutes slipped by in perfect silence. Then they and four or five other humpbacks reappeared in flight, beginning one of the most awesome displays of breaching, pec slapping, lob-tailing, and general bombast I had ever witnessed, and it went on for almost half an hour. It would be the height of arrogance to assume we inspired forty-ton behemoths to compete with us. But I saw what I saw.

Later, I met a man from the port of Petersburg who had begun using his fishing boat for whale-watching tours. He said that, as he was drifting not far from a feeding group of humpbacks one day, a mother came over with her calf and began swimming around the vessel's hull. The mother eventually made a move to leave, but her offspring appeared too intrigued to follow. After trying unsuccessfully to round up the calf and escort it away, she went off by herself to join the feeding group. When she returned to the boat much later, the calf was still right there, and they departed together. The next day, the man was out cruising again, and he came upon the same female and calf. They swam directly to his boat, whereupon the mother immediately left to join the feeding group while the young humpback stayed. "She just dropped the little one off with us," the man told me, convinced the mother had him figured for a babysitter—a humpback day care service. Her behavior could be interpreted in other ways, but maybe he was exactly right.

Before disappearing below the surface during the final stage of a dive, humpbacks typically lift their broad flukes almost vertically into the air. The patterns of black and white pigments revealed on the underside turn out to be as unique as fingerprints, allowing researchers to build up photo catalogues of known animals. Notches and other scarring make it simpler yet to tell one set of flukes from the next. Even a novice viewing the pictures will notice tails that immediately stand out. This strengthens the sense that these titans are individuals, each with a life history all its own.

There are also a lot more to identify than anyone dared hope a few decades ago. As for most cetaceans, any estimate of the humpback's prewhaling numbers is only a half step away from a wild guess. Some authorities have suggested 25,000 for the North Atlantic, a roughly equal number for the North Pacific, and another 75,000 or so for the Southern Hemisphere. Others think the degree of genetic variation found in DNA samples implies a global population that was far larger. However many there used to be, whalers took at least 100,000, mostly during the first half of the twentieth century and mainly for oil. Before the first restrictions on hunting went into effect in 1966, the worldwide total number of humpbacks may have sunk as low as 6,000. Lately, though, populations have been multiplying at an impressive rate, boosting the numbers to at least 12,000 in the North Atlantic and somewhere between 10,000 and 15,000 in the North Pacific. While no solid estimate is available for the Southern Hemisphere, the signs look encouraging there too.

Near eastern Australia, Japan's Bonin Islands, Hawaii, Alaska, New England, various Caribbean islands, and many other shores, humpback watching has turned into big business. Profits are on the rise, and the potential for expansion is excellent, both for the market and the performers themselves. At last: a whale-related industry founded upon sheer delight. By now I must have passed tens of thousands of people leaning over tour boat rails with rapt expressions and tightly gripped cameras, cheering every move these mega-acrobats make. They have become ambassadors for whales and oceans in general. Surely the most effusive sea monsters that have ever made themselves known, humpbacks even specialize in blowing bubbles. As it happens, there is a bundle of insight to be gained from the fact that they do.

The first time I looked closely at a feeding humpback, it was slipping beneath the waves off Plymouth, Massachusetts. A short while later, bursts of bubbles appeared every few feet, rising from below in a pattern that began to take the shape of a vertical tube fifteen feet in diameter. Moments later, the whale rose nose-first in the middle with its mouth open. Open may be an understatement. The lower jaw was at a ninety-degree angle to the rostrum, or upper jaw. As this maw lifted above sea level, it became an approximately fifteen-thousand-gallon pool filled with water still frothy with bursting capsules of air. Hundreds of small, slender fish called sand lance were dashing back and forth through it, taking their final swim inside a whale's mouth. Gulls swooped down between the jaws to pick fish off the pool's surface. A few of the sand lance leaped clear to make it back into the ocean. Then the mouth shut, and all that escaped was saltwater cascading out from the sides.

As the mysticete branch of evolving whales dispensed with teeth in favor of baleen and the world's biggest heads, they effectively turned themselves into sentient purse seine fishing nets. This humpback I was watching had moved one step beyond, constructing a barrier around a fish school by exhaling air while swimming in a circle below. The technique, called bubble netting, was unknown to science until 1979, when Charles Jurasz reported seeing the activity in southeastern Alaska. His interpretation was greeted with skepticism at first, if only because it described whales performing a behavior more elaborate than people were prepared to explain. Doesn't bubble netting imply some sort of assessment of a situation on the whale's part? Forethought? Planning? Is it reasonable to compare casting a net of air from below to what human fishermen do from above? Should this be construed as another example of animals using a tool?

An individual humpback fashioning a bubble net may vary the circumference according to how the prey is distributed. And the bubbles the whale chooses to release may be as small as BBs or as large as soccer balls, perhaps partly depending upon the prey's size. Some North Atlantic humpbacks forego the net roundup strategy in favor of "cloud feeding." The whale manipulates its nasal passages to produce minibubbles that envelop the prey in a plume fizzing like champagne, then follows the obscuring cloud upward, rising slowly, stealthily, and open mouthed to the surface.

While a trap made of air might seem like an illusion aimed at easily fooled little creatures, it is in reality a device with a surprising amount of substance to it. If you've ventured underwater with scuba gear, you already know how distracting and disorienting streams of bubbles can be. They form a marked visual barrier and a hissing, crackling, popping acoustic barrier at the same time. Bubbles are also much more tangible than you might imagine until you have felt columns of them bumping against your skin at depth. Although no one has documented other whales using bubbles as an aid in capturing prey, marine scientists did recently record bottlenose dolphins purposefully stirring up mud as they circled schools of mullet in shallow water, trapping the fish within an opaque pen of sediment. In Shark Bay, Australia, some of the resident bottlenose dolphins carry soft sea sponges on the ends of their beaks, apparently to protect their sensitive snouts while foraging on sea-bottom sites. As far as researchers can determine, the behavior does not occur in any pattern dependent upon genes. Rather, it is a cultural inheritance, passed along as young learn this type of tool use directly from their mothers.

It doesn't seem likely that we will ever be sure whether bubble netting is a somewhat recent invention by humpbacks or a time-honored technique. Not all populations are known to practice it, but most are enthusiastic bubblers in other aspects of their life. A male escorting a female during the mating season will discharge long ribbons of bubbles like jet contrails. The action typically occurs in the presence of competing males and might be an aggressive display—a humpback warning shot across a rival's bow. Photographer Flip Nicklin has also seen a courting male blowing bubbles that bathed a female's body, possibly serving as a stimulant. Other observers told me of mothers emitting bubble bursts underneath their calves. It seemed that the sole purpose was to produce tingling clouds for them to frolic in.

The practice of blowing bubbles to help capture fish takes a staggering leap upward in complexity when an entire group participates. After watching a number of humpbacks dive at the same time, onlookers would soon see a wide ring of bubbles come fulminating up from the depths followed by all the whales, which would simultaneously converge in the center with open mouths. This was obviously a highly cooperative hunt. Trying to discover how the whales were coordinating their actions, more than one researcher placed his or her vessel as near as possible to the rising bubble corral. I wasn't surprised to hear stories from some who had been dutifully recording details when it dawned on them that they were in the middle of the forming ring, where hundreds of tons of gaping-mouthed titans were about to join them.

Close as they ventured, scientists still couldn't quite figure out how group bubble netting operated, mainly because they couldn't see far enough into the water. Choice summer feeding areas are usually soupy with the plankton proliferating at the base of the food chain. Silt from coastal runoff often lowers the visibility further. But Fred Sharpe of the Alaska Whale Foundation persisted. He and I rendezvoused in Frederick Sound, a few hours by boat from Petersburg. It was pouring rain. Clouds smothered the forests and peaks and marched across the water on spindly tendrils of mist. Sharpe was standing in an inflatable runabout wearing a fuzzy pink hat of some sort and holding an umbrella over his head as our boat drew alongside. For him, this wasn't foul weather; it was simply a normal day on the coast. He had been working in the area for years, dangling hydrophones in the water by day and anchoring his skiff in coves to pass the nights under a tarp. That evening over a driftwood beach fire that kept the drizzle at bay, he told me that members of certain cooperative humpback groups were old acquaintances. Though not necessarily related, they met each year on summer feeding grounds and associated for weeks at a time. They were fishing buddies. It stood to reason,

Sharpe said, that individuals familiar with one another would be able to work together more efficiently than strangers could.

A tremendous call carried through the night air from somewhere out in a channel as we were speaking. I asked if it was one of the feeding noises humpbacks make. Sharpe's associate, Lisa Walker, replied, "Trumpeting like that [through the blowhole] is associated with a high level of excitement. We hear it when killer whales are around and the humpbacks are alarmed. But we also hear it when the feeding is especially good, which makes us wonder if they are sending a message for companions to come join them. Underwater [where humpback calls are made internally by squeezing air through sinuses and connecting passageways; cetaceans lack vocal cords] they can blast out at 170 decibels—louder than a jet's roar. They also make all kinds of lower intensity social sounds. I wish I knew what they were talking about. What I like about humpback research is the way it lets your imagination roam free."

Assembling data from the hydrophones, sonar, and a video camera that he and a *National Geographic* "crittercam" team temporarily attached to whales with suction cups, Sharpe worked out much of the choreography of cooperative group feeding over the next several seasons. He envisions it this way: Suppose a school of herring is traveling at a depth of 80 to 120 feet. Circling partway down, a single humpback will start creating the bubble ring above the fish. It may be the same individual making the corral each time, at least in some groups. Compared to a lone whale blowing a bubble net, the group's corral maker stays fairly shallow, descending perhaps no more than 20 to 30 feet. Meanwhile, the other whales are spreading out deeper to physically surround the fish, forcing them into a tighter school.

The amount of light penetrating murky water falls off rapidly with increasing depth. Down there in the gloom, nothing catches your attention as reliably as a glimpse of white. Researchers had speculated that humpbacks might flash the white undersides of their extralong flippers to help herd fish, like cowboys waving their arms to haze cattle into a pen. That was what appeared to be going on when Sharpe reviewed images taken by the critter cam. He then subjected herring in a laboratory aquarium to a paddle abruptly flipped from a dark side to a white side and confirmed that the fish had a strong reaction.

While most of the whales in the cooperative group are busy containing the fish, another whale dives down beneath the school. And then that animal emits an incredibly loud noise variously described as a scream, a cry, or a feeding call. Able to pick out different humpback voices by analyzing the sound patterns, Sharpe concluded that feeding calls are made by the same individual in the group each time, a sort of designated deep-diver and shouter. The huge bursts of sound probably act as an assembly cue for the whales. At the same time, the noise may further discombobulate the trapped and panicky fish school. Sharpe found his laboratory herring definitely reacting to some of the frequencies, though these probably aren't picked up by the fishes' inner ears so much as felt as vibrations in their swim bladder, the gas-filled internal structure that regulates buoyancy. The screamer rises, still wailing like an overgrown banshee, and the group surrounding the school closes in. Trying to escape upward, many of the herring are forced into the confines of the shining, blinding, concatenating cylinder of bubbles. At that stage, the whales converge toward the middle and surface en masse within a matter of seconds, mouths fully open and fast becoming fish ponds.

If this were a food-gathering technique practiced by indigenous humans, it would give an anthropologist enough material for publications on toolmaking traditions, communication techniques, and social divisions of labor. But since it is whales doing the fishing, whoever tries to categorize the behavior and deduce the cognitive abilities involved has to like pushing beyond the edge of familiar scientific territory. Sometimes I think of this as X biology: *X* for *extreme*.

Alone or in a cooperative group, feeding humpbacks don't automatically repeat the same routine. They can adjust it to suit different situations and types of prey. Such behavioral flexibility is closely allied with intelligence and learning. All creatures have ways of adapting to changes in their environment. Being smart multiplies an animal's options.

I went on a survey in Glacier Bay National Park, Alaska, with Chris Gabriele, a park service scientist who has studied humpbacks in that area for years. About fifty feet off the sheer rock face of an island, we noticed four wide, humped backs floating more or less parallel to one another, a couple of pectoral fin lengths apart. All four animals were facing the wall, and from time to time one would lift its head slightly to take in a mouthful of food. We couldn't prove that this wasn't a case of four animals feeding independently on a common bounty, but it certainly appeared to be a group working in concert to keep their prey penned against the rocks. Flip Nicklin watched humpbacks in Antarctica drive surface-swarming krill against the massive body of one whale facing crossways to the others.

According to Fred Sharpe, whales that work in cooperative groups to round up herring on the eastern side of southeastern Alaska's Admiralty Island switch to individual bubble netting to feed on smaller prey, krill, along the western side. In between, they may hunt both fish and krill without either buddies or bubbles. North Atlantic humpbacks will concentrate fish schools by circling around them lob-tailing—creating a pen of agitated water and shock waves. Southern Hemisphere humpbacks have been seen performing the same sort of roundups using slaps of their flippers.

Up and down the North Pacific coast, observers find individuals flick feeding, which is yet another method of harvesting a meal, generally krill. One I watched positioned itself almost vertically, with its head slightly above the surface, and lashed its tail forward one or more times, creating a whirlpool-like vortex. Rolling forward, the humpback then dived into the prey trapped and concentrated by the spinning coils of current.

Bumps give a scalloped shape to the forward edge of the humpback's long pectoral fins. After using models to compare this unusual design to a smooth-edged fin, Frank Fish and engineers at the U.S. Naval Academy and Duke University announced in 2004 that the scalloped edge increased lift—the upward force on a wing—by 8 percent and reduced drag by 32 percent. The bumps create vortices in the water flowing over the upper side of the fin. This directed turbulence is what adds the lift. At the same time, it prevents more chaotic turbulence, the source of drag, from developing. It's a life-changing boost in efficiency. The net effect allows the humpback to make an extremely tight turn while herding prey, setting a bubble net around it, or maneuvering within the net to feed, just as a good wing design allows pilots to maintain a sharp angle of attack relative to the air without slipping off course or stalling out. Naturally, engineers are already considering ways to apply the humpback's invention to planes and boats.

When you slip into the ocean with bright sun overhead and look below, an optical effect makes it seem as if javelins of light are penetrating the water and converging toward a target somewhere underneath you. When you move to one side, this cone of light beams moves with you, constantly flickering as the sun strikes the waves at different angles. When you free-dive downward, the point of convergence goes deeper too, always ahead of you, beckoning. If you are in Hawaiian waters, your descent takes place through vivid blue. And if you are out in the Au'au Channel between Maui and Lanai, far from the sediments that flow off the land or are stirred up by waves, this blue becomes so pure and luminous that you feel suspended within a jewel.

People often compare probing the ocean to probing space. They usually mean to convey the idea of exploring the canyon sides and plains of a still largely unknown world. But blue-water diving is like being in space itself—in that void between stars and planets. Weightless and adrift without a frame of reference in any direction, you have a glimpse of infinity. It is at once beautiful, liberating, and frighteningly impersonal. And, by the way, you are about to run out of breath. You rise from whatever level you have been hovering at, part the opalescent membrane of the surface, and gasp in air. Get your bearings. Glimpse a noddy tern in flight veering toward you, perhaps drawn by the splash you made. Make sure you can still find your boat. Then you roll and kick downward, drawn to do it all again. You have found a way to slip the bonds of Earth and enter a new state of existence for a minute or two at a time—more if you can hold your breath any longer.

I'm sure one reason I found in-water encounters with humpbacks in Hawaii so transcendent is that I was already half intoxicated by my immersion in boundless blue. I would have been happy just to keep free-diving. But when the whales did come, what a marvel they were in that warm, liquid light! And what an opportunity for research. With North Pacific humpbacks believed to be increasing at the rate of 7 percent yearly, the current estimate is that five thousand to seven thousand now gather around Hawaii, where scientists counted barely a third as many two decades ago. The shallow Au'au Channel—no more than six hundred feet deep, whereas the seafloor elsewhere off the Hawaiian chain lies three miles down—appears to be one of their favorite hangouts. Teeming with humpbacks and protected from open ocean swells by surrounding islands, it is without a doubt one of the premier places on the planet for seeing what whales do after they drop below the surface. It may be the best of all. This is one reason Flip, Jim, and their scientist colleague Meagan Jones chose Maui as the base for Whale Trust, a nonprofit organization they founded to combine research with education and conservation.

Standing on a boat's bow, you spy blows everywhere, dark backs rising into view, and uplifted tails sliding down. There are days when you can't turn a complete circle without catching a breach somewhere on the horizon. Underwater, your vision stays sharp enough that, when a humpback enters the scene, you find it is a mobile reef. Hard-shelled barnacles encrust various edges of the giant. Soft, stalked barnacles dangle from the dorsal fin and flukes. Rainbow runners, a type of jack, orbit the body in passing, flashing electric blue and yellow stripes, while hundreds of smaller fish called opelo school along the whale's back to feed on dead, flaking skin.

The humpbacks themselves have rarely been seen feeding in this winter range. Living off fat stored beneath the skin as blubber, they are in Hawaii to court, mate, give birth, and rear young. Here, the extralong pectoral fins so effective in maneuvering after prey are put to use in a variety of social behaviors. You'll see a flipper raised into the air and waved back and forth or whapped down onto the surface over and over, perhaps to make a humpback exclamation. Or both flippers raised parallel as an animal lolls on its back. But until I was able to watch through the transparent water, I didn't know these wings were flexible enough that a humpback could curl just the outermost part to softly touch a companion or stroke its side. Nor did I have any idea that a wave of one tip would be enough to start the immense body spiraling. Or that a tilt of the flippers and a slight lowering of the tail could turn a glide into an effortless loop-de-loop.

More visions of outer space came to mind, because the patterns of movement reminded me of films showing astronauts in zero gravity. Upside down, right side up: it looked to be all the same to the humpbacks. I was already aware that they were nothing like the ungainly underwater blimps many folks imagine great whales to be, but I could never have imagined their suppleness until I witnessed weightless ballets down in the blue. And for every humpback engaged in the sort of pounding, whitewater surface activity that draws a chorus of cries from whale-watching boats, we found many others drifting along in the Au'au Channel's modest current at a depth of forty to eighty feet, scarcely moving a muscle. Some were singing. Many were just resting, listening, quietly conserving energy for the next event in their lives.

Jim, Flip, Meagan Jones, and Jason Sturgis, who documents behavior on video, usually work from two boats operating separately but in the same general area. They track the animals at a comfortable distance, timing their activity patterns and taking identification photos. Once the whales are down, the observers will slowly guide the boat closer, disengaging the propeller so there is no danger of a humpback suddenly coming up and getting sliced.

An ideal position is directly over the "footprint" a whale leaves where it dives. This is the large circle of smooth water created by currents that well up in a column to replace the volume pushed aside by the descending animal. Spooling eddies keep the waves at bay for a minute or two, creating a window into the depths. In good light, it is possible to see well enough through this temporary pane to locate the animal below, even when it is sixty feet down or more. Jim and Flip have watched humpbacks come over to a boat and create a window with a blast of large bubbles or by bobbing up and down, then position themselves vertically just below the surface to look up. It is tempting to conclude that these animals intended to fashion a better view for themselves. Whether the scenario is a whale scrutinizing the passengers in a boat this way or a captive dolphin purposefully failing a test because it is bored with it and wants something more challenging, the question of just who is studying whom keeps arising fairly regularly in work with cetaceans.

Humpbacks that spend the warm months feeding in Alaska and the Pacific Northwest begin arriving around the Hawaiian Islands as early as November. How they navigate from the North American coast to a handful of relatively small islands out toward the middle of the Pacific is one more of the mysteries surrounding whales. Are they guided by Earth's geomagnetic field? Angles of sunlight? The position of stars? Currents? Sound? Someone proposed that the whales home in on submarine rumblings from

Hawaii's active volcanoes. Could be, but how do the animals find their way back to the shores of British Columbia and Alaska?

A woman I met in Maui went out whale watching in a small boat for a number of days in a row. Though intrigued by the animals, she wasn't the type seeking a special personal connection with them. She was a medical specialist who simply wanted to learn more about whales while on vacation. However, she happened to be six months pregnant, and on several occasions when the boat passed close to a singing humpback, her baby woke up and started kicking. Once you consider how the powerful pulses of a whale's voice rising from the ocean would resonate in a human womb—the sea of amniotic fluid in which each of us experiences the first months of awareness—what happened becomes readily explainable. It was still a wondrous connection.

A rhythmic, structured melody fifteen minutes to half an hour long, the song is a phenomenon in itself. But what is its role in the humpbacks' lives? Since the animals are noisiest on their winter ranges, the song is thought to be part of the social behavior tied to competition and mating. Only males sing, yet, as Jim was discovering, only other males seem drawn to investigate or join the singer, undermining the bird model of performing tunes to attract mates. If the call is to proclaim territory or status instead, an incoming male ought to act like a challenger, yet some of the most graceful interactions Jim and Flip have witnessed involved singers and joiners spiraling around each other and then moving on together. This bolsters the alternative theory of the song as a recruiting tool, helping spark the formation of male groups that cooperate to find females, control their movements, challenge their escorts, or all of the above. Maybe a gang of bachelors doesn't have to drive off a big, dominant male attending a female; they just need to distract him long enough for one to move in and have a chance of breeding.

Others have put forward the chorus frog model, in which males assemble and their combined calls serve to attract females to the area. The more voices, the greater the volume, and the more widely the advertisement is heeded. It isn't likely that the humpback chorus is what brings females to Hawaii in the first place, but it could influence where among the islands arriving females choose to spend time. Thus, a male drawn to the vicinity of a singing male would ultimately increase its chances of meeting a mate.

The truth is, you can invent just about any role you like for the song and still have a shot at being proved right one day. A majority of singers are solitary, stationary, and in a characteristic crooning pose: hanging head-down in the blue with pectoral fins partly outstretched. Yet others continue to sing while escorting a female or while in the company of some other adult. Moreover, as researchers begin to listen in other places at other times of year, they are picking up humpbacks singing outside of the breeding season and beyond known breeding ranges. Jan Straley, a biologist with the University of Alaska who has studied humpbacks since 1979, noticed some whales singing near Sitka through late autumn. In December, she even witnessed the kind of aggression associated with courtship.

After biologist Chris Gabriele of the National Park Service deployed a hydrophone in Glacier Bay, Alaska, she started hearing humpback songs during spring and early summer. Similarly, Chris Clark of Cornell University and other observers recently reported North Atlantic humpbacks singing on their feeding range during late fall and again in early spring. Then humpbacks near Alaska's Aleutian Islands were recorded singing in late summer. I'm not sure that there is still a month during which northern humpbacks have *not* been heard giving voice to what was once considered a mating song reserved for their sojourn in the tropics.

The other fascinating aspect of this subject is that each population's song is constantly evolving from one year to the next and, at times, even from month to month. Handing me the earphones to listen to what his hydrophone was picking up, Jim explained that a series of grumbles might be added or a lengthy squeal shortened, some notes shifted slightly higher in pitch, a theme dropped altogether, and so on, with the change spreading across a population. For a song this long and intricate, the number of possible permutations is nearly unlimited.

What sparks a change? Do individuals experiment with different takes on the tune? Why? And what would make one particular innovation a hit soon adopted by others? Or is it more appropriate to compare the song's constant revision to human language, which changes at a rate that forces dictionary publishers to issue new editions every few years? Few modern English speakers could still converse easily with someone from Shakespeare's era, much less from medieval times. It makes you wonder what a humpback tune sounded like in the Stone Age—or a million years before that. I keep coming back to Lisa Walker's comment over a beach campfire by Frederick Sound: "What I like about humpback research is the way it lets your imagination roam free."

Looking at the song's function in relation to breeding might be too narrow a focus. Perhaps this highly structured vocalization encodes crucial information about the singer's identity and group relationships. Along those lines, I wouldn't discount even the wildest theories, including the notion that these troubadours are reciting an epic ballad about the history of their kind—who they are and where they come from and how fate shapes their voyages through the seas.

Hawaiian numbers of humpbacks peak between late January and early March, and most of the animals have departed by mid-April. Once in these tropical waters, females impregnated the previous winter give birth. Newborns are about twelve feet long, pale, and slender, weighing around three thousand pounds. Lingering creases on one side show how they were folded to fit within the womb. Their lungs aren't inflated when they emerge from the birth canal, and the babies would sink if their mothers didn't nudge and lift them to the surface for their first taste of air. It is the start of a life that can span at least five decades, going by whaling records, and probably more, judging from known ages of other great whales. The humpback's biggest rorqual relatives, fin and blue whales, may live as long as a century. There is a record of a bowhead judged to be 125 years old by an analysis of its eye lens, and some believe that bowheads might reach an age of 200-plus.

In its early weeks, the humpback infant can't go more than a few minutes before popping up to breathe. If the huge, watchful mother waits below instead of accompanying her newborn to the surface, this is about the only time you will find the pair more than a fin's length apart. The favorite places for the baby to rest underwater are beneath Mom's chin or one of her "wings." When active, the infant will rub and slide and roll around the mother's body, and if she rises to float on the surface, look for a miniature humpback squirming across her top side in play. With luck, you might watch a mother take a baby for a ride on her nose or her upper jaw, which is a fairly flat platform. Dolphins and porpoises sometimes swim with great whales, usually in advance like heralds. Now and then, the smaller cetaceans position themselves right in front of the nose and ride the giants' bow waves. This trait, coupled with the whales' habit of giving babies a lift, might account for the photograph someone snapped of a humpback with its rostrum raised high above the water and a big dolphin perched on top.

Like many kinds of young mammals, baby humpbacks are naturally curious about their environment. The mother is the only thing close and safe enough for it to explore. If a boat enters the scene, a percentage of the young—perhaps one in four—may make a move to investigate. But before the small whale can get far, the mother is suddenly on the move to cut off the infant and shepherd it away, keeping her bulk between the baby and the subject of its interest. Her protective impulse is linked to the fact that 25 percent or more of the humpbacks surveyed in some North Pacific subpopulations bear tooth rake marks, generally on the tail, or deformations where bites mangled the flesh. The majority of the scars match the tooth pattern of killer whales, which share the humpbacks' summer range and are sometimes seen around Hawaii as well. An array of other big biters shares the tropical waters, including tiger, hammerhead, great white, and mako sharks. It is not the sort of thing to ponder too hard when you're bobbing with a snorkel out there in the blue like big-eyed bait, peering into the depths as you scout for a humpback that just swam out of view.

Other than sick and weakened individuals, young humpbacks are naturally the most vulnerable to predation. Their best defense is their mothers. A mouth full of baleen rather than fangs may not be much of a weapon, but a sideways chop from an adult's immensely powerful tail can whack the largest shark into tomorrow. Ironically, almost every whale in Hawaii bears a pattern of small, circular bite marks left by cookie cutter sharks, which are less than two feet long. By day, these little hunters keep to the depths, where they sometimes give off a phosphorescent green glow. Come nightfall, they rise in search of large fish and marine mammals, grab on with round mouths that grip flesh like a suction cup, and nip out a chunk with a quick twist of their bodies.

A humpback calf can reach a length of sixteen feet within three months, putting on five pounds per hour on a diet of milk that is about 50 percent fat. The older and stronger it grows, the farther it strays. Now, while Mom rests below, the young whale often lingers by itself on the surface, rolling and sloshing around, acting slaphappy with its fins or flukes, and sometimes going on a breaching jag. People have seen calves carry on leaping for hours, as if practicing to become flying fish. If her offspring swims over to a boat, the mother may not intervene nearly as soon as she would have when the baby was younger.

Debbie Glockner-Ferrari first went into the water with a humpback mother and calf in Hawaii during the 1970s. When she came out, she knew what she wanted to do with the rest of her life. She has not missed a winter season of research in the thirty-one years since. "These are highly individualistic animals," she said, recalling humpbacks with personalities like Mary Poppins and others more like the boat-rushing male they were currently calling Charlie Manson. One of her favorites was Daisy, "a wonderful, friendly female and a very important whale scientifically," to Debbie's eyes. At the time, scientists believed humpback females gave birth only every second or third year, since the eleven-month pregnancy was followed by at least one year of nursing and caring for the youngster. But Daisy appeared with a brand new calf every year for four years.

Altogether, 16 percent of the females recognized by Debbie and her husband, Mark Ferrari, were coming into heat again shortly after giving birth—a condition known as postpartum estrus—and producing offspring annually. This helps explain the impressive rate of increase for the North Pacific humpback population. It also explains why almost every mature female around Hawaii, with or without a calf, is attended by an interested male, sometimes referred to as the principal escort or primary escort. People used to assume that an adult accompanying a cow and calf was a female, perhaps a relative, there to assist with young-rearing duties. Then Debbie learned to tell the sexes apart by differences in the lobes around the genitalia. After she had examined enough cow-calf-companion trios closely underwater, she surfaced with the news that good old helpful "auntie" was a guy. Females almost never associate on the winter range. If anything, they appear to keep themselves spaced widely apart.

A standard scene viewed from the surface is that of a female coming up to begin a sequence of blows and a second adult emerging not far behind. This second animal is usually noticeably darker and more scratched and scarred, but not necessarily larger, because female rorquals tend to be heavier than males. The escort may speed up and angle in toward the female as if to force her in one direction or another, or he may move in front to block her advance. At other times, he circles outward, perhaps on the lookout for potential rivals. Underwater, you will find the escort continuing the same pattern: following, herding, checking the periphery. When the female rests in one place, he hovers nearby, disappearing from time to time on patrols. When you are approaching a female by boat or by swimming, an escort may suddenly appear out of nowhere, making a pass to intercept you, as if saying, "That's close enough." If she is moving and the boat tags along behind, he may get in line between her and the bow and bang his tail down hard on the water. Escorts perform the same tail thwack in front of the noses of male humpbacks pursuing the female. Consider yourself warned.

Yet active solicitations of the female by the hardworking suitor are surprisingly few or else subtle and hard to interpret. Courtship seems to be more of a waiting game for a male, until the object of his desire gives off some sort of chemical or behavioral clue that signals her readiness to take the next step. No researcher yet knows exactly what that is. Actual coupling itself has not been recorded, though some casual observers claim to have witnessed it.

Often, the female and suitor are visited by other males, either lone bulls or several traveling in a group. How they locate a pair floating quietly out in the blue is another thing researchers haven't figured out. Since the nostrils of cetaceans serve as blowholes, these animals lack a sense of smell as such. The distinctive knobs, or tubercles, that ornament a humpback's head each contain clusters of nerves surrounding a single modified mammalian whisker. This sensory packet probably responds to subtle changes in water pressure such as the movements that a nearby body would cause, but the organ may also be able to detect ingredients of the whales' environment that we are barely aware of.

Maybe the answer to how humpbacks find others at a distance even when they appear to be silent is that they really aren't. A variety of social sounds passes between mothers and calves at times, and between females and escorts as well. The humpbacks may also be emitting noises in frequencies too low for the human ear to detect. Infrasound, as it is known, is the chief component of the broadcast calls of larger rorquals such as blues and fins. It turns out to be an important means of communication for some land giants too, namely, elephants and, according to recent studies, rhinos.

In any case, once other males discover a female and suitor, it is up to the escort to discourage the drop-ins. If he doesn't, he may find himself replaced. The means by which rival males judge one another's relative strength or dominance when they first meet underwater is yet another question mark. What the scientists do know is that the participants in the encounter occasionally become a surface-active group whose members go plunging along together through the waves, jockeying for position around the female. Mark Ferrari told me that he and Debbie followed one bunch that raced for half the day at speeds of up to ten knots.

The males in such groups blow long bubble trails. They jerk their tails up and perform flip-turns in front of others to cut them off. They breach. They give off excited trumpet blasts. They circle, swimming on their sides with a flipper and one fluke cutting through the waves like the back of some great sailfish. They swim so close to rivals that their pectoral fins wrap around the other animal. When they break above the surface, some raise their heads while surging forward and fill their mouths with water and air. This may be an attempt to increase their apparent size, the equivalent of a land mammal puffing up and erecting a mane to create a more imposing profile. The males could also be gulping air for release from the mouth underwater to add to their bubble display. Dan Salden, former chairman of the department of speech communication at Southern Illinois University and currently head of the Maui-based Hawaii Whale Research Foundation, offers a third possibility. He told me that he wouldn't be surprised if, instead of putting on a display, the males are collecting water near the female to taste for pheromones that will tell them about her estrous condition. Years earlier, Debbie Glockner-Ferrari had found that females secrete streams or threads of mucus containing estrogen from the genital area.

The whitewater action and accompanying sounds—an amazing cacophony of mews, groans, chirps, and snargles—attract other humpbacks in the area. You may count, say, ten animals in a snapshot of the throng. However, if you were keeping track of those joining in and departing at different times or simply falling farther and farther behind as they struggle to keep up, the total number involved might be double or triple this amount. Observers are rarely able to identify each of the participants. But the chances are that—except for the cow and her calf, if she has an offspring—they are all males. Their ranks often include some smallish young ones joining in with little hope of ever displacing the primary escort, much less being accepted by the female. For them, taking part must be more like a learning experience, for they don't even reach sexual maturity until about age five and won't attain maximum size for many years after that.

Out in the Au'au Channel, Jim, Flip, Meagan Jones, and I were fending off an advanced state of afternoon stupefaction under the sun's heat and glare as we drifted along near Lanai. The island's unmarked slopes shone green and inviting with carpets of shade

spread beneath the palms along its shore. Our boat's awning offered only a stingy square of shade that rotated from port to starboard as the *Never Satisfied* slowly spun on the currents, and
the four of us practiced a sort of polite dance around the deck,
trying to squeeze into the little patch of darkness as often as possible without hogging anyone else's space. I would have sworn
I could feel the sun pushing against my skin. The exposed parts
of the boat's floor had grown too hot to touch with bare feet any
longer. Quiet in every direction, the sea itself looked heat dazed.
We hadn't seen a whale for what seemed an awfully long time
when at least twenty-three of them abruptly appeared between
Lanai and Kaho'olawe. Jim drove the boat into a good position to
observe the humpbacks as they passed. Unlike a typical surface-
active group, they mainly swam straight ahead with few major
swerves, cutoff moves, or sudden accelerations, which made my
companions wonder if there was even a female in the group.
Intrigued, Flip decided to duck into the water for a still better look
and asked if I would join him as a safety diver.

I had never seen so many big whales together before. Trusting
that Flip's years of experience made him good judge of reasonable risk, I followed him overboard. At least I could cool down.
But when I looked through the blue water in the direction the jug-
gernaut would be coming from, it had already arrived. I felt like I
had just parachuted into the flight path of a whole fleet of jumbo
jets. By the time I glanced over to see how my mentor planned
to handle this, he was curled up in a ball, spinning in the after-
wash of the giant set of flukes passing right over his head. Bodies
were shooting by on all sides. Onrushing noses dipped slightly,
replaced by backs the size of living rooms. They passed just under my flippers. Outstretched pectoral fins lifted a fraction and

arced over my head. Such power and yet such finesse! Reassured that I wasn't going to get bumped aside like so much flotsam, I was kicking hard to buy a few more seconds of time with the group before the last jumbo jet had gone by. It was long enough for me to see one whale veer into the side of another with an audible Whumph!

In the postwhaling era, more and more writers took to describing humpbacks with the catchphrase "gentle giants of the sea." I wouldn't argue that they don't deserve the title; at times, they seem to embody the word *serene*. But as we're learning, they can also be typical, aggressive, dominance-fixated mammals putting it all on the line for an opportunity to mate. Granted, a good deal of what someone might take to be furious clashing amid an explosion of foam is merely what it looks like when forty-ton beasts make threat displays—postures and moves designed to avoid actual fighting and the risk of injury. These are part of the behavior of a wide array of animals. On the other hand, so are direct attacks on competitors. Male humpbacks in surface-active groups do appear to use their flukes and flippers as striking weapons, and they will definitely bang their noses into rivals' sides. In addition to the sheer force of impact, the barnacles that encrust portions of the flippers and head can scrape and cut a foe's flesh. Many of the scratch marks on males and the scars whitening their dorsal fins are lingering testimony to contests with their own kind.

In a way, a surface-active group is like a total fitness exam for competitors—an all-out test of endurance as well as brute strength. The female seems to set the pace. If she slows or stops, so does the hubbub. But whenever she goes faster, the others rev their engines alongside. The primary escort must not only keep up with her the whole time but also fend off one or two main challengers and perhaps a suite of secondary males that may be cooperating with one another. A male powerful enough to continue doing this without tiring is offering abundant proof that he carries good genes. Does the female become more responsive to him as a result? Well, nobody really knows the answer to that one either.

Whenever I asked experts about aspects of humpback natural history, at least 90 percent of the replies I got were variations of "Beats me." It was frustrating at first, given that this is the best studied of the great whales. The scientists were just being honest, letting me know that whale research is a terrific frontier in which to go looking for answers but a tough place to find any. When scientists spend countless hours among the waves, burning fuel and breaking equipment, getting sunburned, windblown, tossed around, beat up, and every so often scared to death, they really feel like they ought to be coming away with some new conclusions. But the best they get most of the time is the ability to speculate more intelligently about what they saw. The trick is not to confuse the two, succumbing to what I call the tour guide syndrome.

Some of the folks employed as naturalists on whale-watching boats have a terrible time saying, "I don't know." After all, they're supposed to be informative. So when someone asks what's going on with the whales in view, you can count on some guides to assemble their best guesses into a story line and present it as fact. For example: "That male probably got run off by the bigger male over by the cow and calf we passed, so he's pretty wound up right now, and that's why he's sitting there lob-tailing." It sounds plausible. It satisfies the customers. It might well be true. But if the teller of the tale has proof of a connection between frustration and lob-tailing, he or she ought to publish it, because no scientist has. We all contend daily with the difference between what we know and what we think we know. Whale researchers have to stay extra vigilant.

Mark Ferrari and Debbie Glockner-Ferrari would agree, but they have witnessed behavior that science is prepared to deal with only up to a point. "One day we saw a female mugging boats, and there was an odd pattern to it," Mark recalled. "She would curve her tail in front of the bow to hold this ship in place and bring her head around so that her eye was close to the propeller. Then we noticed that her calf had a series of deep, healing gashes along its back. You could tell it had been badly cut up by prop blades. Now, maybe it only looked like this mother was inspecting propellers, searching for the guilty boat. But I kept thinking: Man, I don't want to be around when she finds it."

Another time, observers near an active group noticed that one member, a male, was no longer surfacing. They realized after a while that it had died. When the group eventually left, a single male stayed on, using its flippers to stroke the corpse, occasionally trying to lift it above the water as if to give it air. The companion remained all through the afternoon and drove Mark away when he approached by swimming. Both whales were still there when darkness fell.

Mark told this story after a morning spent with an unusually light-colored young male that he and Debbie identified as Moby. The animal was about two years old, stout, and in a mood to frolic. He spun and looped around our boat for the better part of two hours, periodically breaking off to rush over to a nearby vessel and nose around the stern, sometimes bumping the hull or even slapping it with a fluke when he turned. None of his actions seemed ill intentioned, but we were dealing with a thirty-ton beast that was perhaps slightly aggressive by dint of being a juvenile male and that might or might not know his own strength.

During one period when I was in the waves with him, he kept zooming straight toward me, peeling off at the last instant the way sea lions often will when you're submerged. Then he bolted so fast that I completely lost track of him. Surfacing, I saw brown boobies and an albatross sail overhead. I took in our boat bobbing in the distance. But I couldn't locate Moby. When I had almost finished treading water in a circle, I found him. Moby was airborne in a breach and coming down fast in my direction. I dived and kicked for deep water as fast as I could because I was convinced I was about to get landed on. That's my story, though part of my mind knows very well that Moby was nowhere as close in reality as he seemed just then.

At the very opposite end of the spectrum from the tour guide syndrome, Jim Darling is reluctant to state what he is virtually convinced of, reasoning that there may be one more possible explanation, some additional factor not yet evident. Where others leap to conclusions, he tiptoes toward maybe's. Jim deals with scientific uncertainty by having made it his friend. This is probably the result of studying humpback song for much of his life.

Hawaii's waters are by no means the only winter range for North Pacific humpbacks. Those found in the summer between Washington State and northern Mexico migrate to southern Mexican waters to breed, while humpbacks summering off Siberia in the Sea of Okhotsk and the western Bering Sea reappear near southern Japan and the Philippines over winter. These groups are thought to represent separate subpopulations. However, since individuals sighted off Hawaii have also been recorded either near Japan or by California and Mexico, we now know that the subpopulations exchange members at times. This may account for why they all sing the same song. Although the melody has local variations, it is shared across the entire North Pacific ocean basin and yet remains distinct from the songs sung by humpbacks in other parts of the world.

Jim has lately been investigating humpbacks discovered off Africa's western coast near Gabon. Since they appear during the Southern Hemisphere winters, they are probably coming from Antarctic feeding ranges. They share their song with humpbacks wintering on the opposite side of the South Atlantic, near the coast of Brazil.

It's hard for scientists to puzzle out something as multidimensional as humpback song when they still face major gaps in their knowledge of the species's basic natural history. Data about the animals' movement patterns are in especially short supply. The subpopulation that summers along the coasts of British Columbia and Alaska makes a round-trip to Hawaii of roughly five thousand miles annually. But the questions of when they depart, which routes they travel to reach warmer waters, and how long they linger once there remain open.

The standard notion about humpbacks, as for most great whales, has been that the shift to the tropics takes up nearly half the year, counting travel time. Cruising in her boat near Sitka while snapping fluke photos of two humpbacks she had first identified at least fifteen years earlier, Jan Straley said, "I'm starting to see offspring of the offspring of whales I first knew as calves." In her surveys, she was finding enough animals present during

Alaska's long winter that she was beginning to wonder if some of them, particularly females, might not be zipping over to Hawaii, breeding, and then rushing back north to the dinner table.

The sort of radio transmitters used to track the movements of wildlife on land are of limited use for following whales across long distances. The animals can too easily move beyond the receiving range of a chase boat, especially during a spell of foul weather. By contrast, radio beacons that can be picked up by satellite hold tremendous promise. The trick is to develop a reliable, saltwater-proof combination of transmitter, power source, and antenna, along with some way to get the package onto a whale and keep it there. It's not as though you can go knock humpbacks down with tranquilizer darts and then strap radio collars around their necks.

Bruce Mate of Oregon State University's Hatfield Marine Science Center has studied great whales of almost every kind in various corners of the world. He also attends far-flung scientific symposia, advises committees on ocean resources, publishes frequently, and teaches. In between, he fixes up old houses and sells them. His own house has an oversize garage in which he restores classic sports cars, and he goes so far as to machine complicated engine parts if the originals are no longer available. The man is a dynamo, and he surely ranks as the world's foremost practitioner of the esoteric art of affixing satellite radios to whales.

During a foray to stick the latest technology on some humpbacks in Hawaii, Bruce filled in details about the project's history. It was not a tale of overnight success. The first satellite-radio package he concocted, from electronic components still more macro than micro at the time, was the size of a cantaloupe. His plan was to lower it onto the broad back of a humpback entangled in a fishing net, using a boom that extended from one side of an inflatable skiff. Small explosive charges around the bulky radio's base would then be detonated, forcing small, hooked prongs into the whale's hide, after which the animal would be freed of the net. Everything went more or less as hoped, except the part where the detonations were also supposed to break two nylon screws that connected the radio to the boom. The screws held. Bruce and his wife, Mary Lou, had hooked a whale and now couldn't let go. Had there been a length of rope between the side boom and the increasingly agitated giant, they might have headed off on a Nantucket sleigh ride, a New England whalers' term for getting towed through the waves by a harpooned target. But since the boom was now essentially stuck to the whale, the little boat was more likely to be tipped over and swamped. Luckily, the hump-back didn't dive. Bruce stretched hand over hand along the boom pole, gripping a pocket knife in his teeth, until he was able to cut and hack the nylon screws loose. The radio canister worked for only five days. Yet even in that short period before the signal quit, the whale traveled several hundred miles offshore.

Next, Bruce tried using a remote-controlled model helicopter to deliver a slightly smaller satellite-radio package onto a whale. Launched from a rolling boat, the helicopter caught on a line and crashed back onto the deck, attaching the tag to the floor. The aircraft's rotor blade had meanwhile broken loose and gone whistling between Bruce's legs. In his own estimation, he came far closer to castrating himself than to solving the problem of how to relay data from huge seafaring mammals to vehicles orbiting in space.

Before our Hawaiian outing, Bruce had settled on using a dart crammed with advanced circuitry. It was attached to the head of an arrow to be fired from a crossbow. The design was such that the projectile would punch through the skin and outer blubber layer, but only to a depth of a few inches. A protruding gasket stopped further penetration, leaving a stub bearing the antenna exposed. As long as the whale was submerged, the electrical conductivity of saltwater created a closed circuit that kept the radio silent. But when the whale surfaced to breathe, the radio would transmit the whale's exact position from anywhere on the globe. With continually more miniaturized electronics to choose from, Bruce had been refining the dart's cigar shape from that of a fat stogy to something more like a slender cheroot. And whereas earlier models had often quit working after several weeks, if not sooner, advances in battery technology gave Bruce hope that the beacon would continue transmitting for several months.

One problem he had not solved was how to add floatability to the dart without interfering with its aerodynamics or its insertion into the whale. His target was the upper part of the back in front of the dorsal fin. If he undershot and the dart hit too low on the side, it might stay submerged throughout many of the whale's rises and be unable to send out a signal. If he overshot, the thing was just going to plunk into the ocean and sink. "That would be about a four-thousand-dollar miss," he said. The crossbow string broke during one chase on the first day we went out. Bruce quickly replaced it with a spare. Later on, the fiberglass bow itself delaminated from prolonged exposure to heat and saltwater. The fact that he carried a spare of that part too told me that he hadn't even come close to recounting all the days of trial and error that went into developing his current system. In the end, his aim was true, and he put several humpbacks on the air, where their signals joined those of other whale species around the globe that he had tagged.

"Almost every [kind of whale] I study is capable of swimming through the waters of at least three countries a month," he told me, emphasizing how sorely something with the reach of satellite-radio technology has been needed. A female humpback he darted off Maui proceeded to visit the waters around all the major Hawaiian islands within roughly a week, answering with one tour the long-standing question of whether or not the females keep to a special locale or territory during the breeding season. Another of Bruce's radio-tagged humpbacks made a direct twenty-six-hundred-mile trip from Hawaii to Alaska in only thirty days, arguing against suggestions that the animals pass a good portion of the winter season just moseying to and from the breeding range.

"One swam directly [from Hawaii] to the Queen Charlotte Islands off British Columbia," he said, "then headed north up the buffet line, hitting feeding sites along the outer coast until it reached Baranof Island. Then it quickly returned to the Queen Charlottes, four hundred miles in four days, including stops at all its previous feeding sites." A different humpback radio-tagged in Hawaii swam due north to the Aleutian Islands. Instead of moving southeast from there along the Alaskan coast as expected, the whale cut west and settled down along Russia's Kamchatka Peninsula before the beacon went dead. "Almost every time we radio-tag a whale, we find it traveling far more than people suspected," Bruce told me. His hunch is that, if researchers ever find the money to place satellite beacons on more than a handful of subjects at a time, the results will transform our view of how these animals use the seas. Like the information emerging about cooperative bubble netting or humpback song, they will reveal the grandest of lives being lived on an even greater scale than we have been able to imagine before.

THE DIVER
NORTHERN BOTTLENOSE WHALE

E arly in August I arrived in Halifax, Nova Scotia, and began looking for a water taxi. I needed a lift from shore out to a forty-foot sailboat. The catch was that this sailboat wasn't lying at anchor in the harbor. It was 230 miles away through the open Atlantic Ocean in the general direction of Europe, cruising over a submarine trench called The Gully. I made a deal with the captain of a vessel previously used to ferry crews and equipment for the bridge being built to link New Brunswick with Prince Edward Island. The craft's name was the *J.V. Runner,* and it was a rigid-hull inflatable boat, essentially a heavy-duty rubber raft with a hard, V-shaped bottom. Typically, such boats are small, open craft powered by an outboard motor. The *J.V. Runner* was an eclectic-looking seventy-five-footer with a deck and cabin of welded aluminum atop twin inboard jet engines.

We cleared the harbor late, the captain, a mate, and I, gunning one of the world's biggest blow-up speedboats into night seas rolling under a twenty-five-knot wind. Stripped down for construction-work day trips, the *J.V. Runner* made no concession whatsoever to comfort. I spread my flotation jacket on the deck and tried to sleep while the metal housing amplified the engines' roar to rock concert levels. By morning, we were sipping coffee boiled over a portable camping stove set on the same throbbing floor when wild horses appeared through the window.

Sable Island, 185 miles east of Halifax, is merely the visible part of a much larger deposit of sandy sediments called the Scotian Shelf. The ground emerges as a series of low dunes strung out in a crescent less than 2 miles wide but 26 miles long. The dimensions vary over time, as does their exact location. With storms and currents continuously sluicing away one side while adding deposits to another, Sable slowly wanders the ocean like a lost beach. Yet the dunes support grasses and hold two freshwater ponds. They in turn sustain horses descended from livestock turned loose long ago. We saw several shaggy members of a herd grazing just up from the shore while some of the gray seals and harbor seals that come to give birth here bellied around on the beaches. The Greenland sharks that patrol just beyond to catch inexperienced pups making their first forays out from the rookeries stayed out of view.

Situated between the busy ports of eastern North America and what used to be the world's richest fishing grounds, the Grand Banks, Sable Island also lies near major shipping lanes between the New World and Europe. Many a colonial-era captain ran afoul of this wisp of dry ground rising so unexpectedly far from the mainland. Even after the area was better charted, gales and blindfolding fogbanks continued to drive vessels onto the shifting shoals until the wreckage of wood, iron, flesh, and bone from more than five hundred ships and ten thousand passengers lay mixed with Sable's sands. Graveyard of the Atlantic, people took to calling the place. The mists that so often stream over the dunes, draining their colors, have become reminders of the legions of ghosts marooned here.

I was already dealing with a vague sense of foreboding, because I had never boated so far beyond sight of the mainland before. Most of us who regularly go adventuring develop an approach with a certain level of mental comfort built in—a feeling that we can remain in control of the inherent risks through sufficient knowledge, preparation, backup safety measures, experience, steady nerves, and so forth. We have to believe that making the right choices is going to keep us alive. My problem was that, once the choice becomes to head to sea, the game changes. If a tempest brews full force offshore, the most experienced captain in the best-equipped boat is going to be at the mercy of the elements. The only way to prepare for that possibility is to learn to accept it. Oceans are the biggest, trickiest, strongest, and most relentless surfaces on earth. Journeying on them requires a giving-over of the self in some measure to fate or luck or however you want to address the insurmountable forces at play out there. You can hope for good weather. You can pray that you will at least be able to outrun the worst. And then you take what comes.

Before I left for The Gully, people kept informing me that this is the part of the North Atlantic where late-summer hurricanes or their remnants sometimes spin up from the south. On occasion, one will mix with another massive weather system coming east out of the Great Lakes, plus a third front blowing down from the arctic latitudes of Labrador. The result was chronicled in a riveting book, *The Perfect Storm*. Among its highlights are descriptions of hundred-foot waves building in the vicinity of The Gully, and a clinically detailed, second-by-second evocation of what it is like to drown. I was amazed at the number of acquaintances who said, "You're going out past Sable Island? Oh, you've got to take this book along to read," as if I had told them, "I really crave a clearer picture of the most desperate, terrifying, and helpless of all possible situations at sea where I'll be. Is there anything you could recommend?"

Petroleum had recently been discovered beneath the Scotian Shelf. One of the drilling platforms anchored in the shallows also served as a lifeguard station, the modern-day version of a special outpost once set up on Sable Island to help haul survivors in through the waves. As we stopped at the platform to refuel, fog blotted out the horizon. A flame of natural gas being flared off high overhead roared like dragon's breath. Its orange glow suffused the mist and glistened along the steel pillars and pipes and the smooth hulls of the rescue pods moored beside them. Debarking, I felt as if I were visiting a colony on a planet with a different sun and atmosphere. We made our way to an operations center seventy feet up in the tower. There, a man at the control console informed me that he had once watched waves cresting ten feet below the floor we were standing on. Well hell, I thought, I might as well have brought the book.

We motored on through the morning and eventually drew near enough to The Gully to raise the sailboat on the ship's radio.

"*Balaena, Balaena*. This is the *J.V. Runner*."

"Hello, *J.V. Runner*. This is the *Balaena*."

I took over the microphone: "Yeah, I'm with Speedy's pizza delivery service. We had an order for one with anchovies?"

Photographer Flip Nicklin and I had always joked about calling out for a pizza when we found ourselves following whales in remote settings. I knew that he was aboard the *Balaena* with Hal Whitehead, an authority on whales who teaches at Dalhousie University in Halifax. Standing beside them when the sailboat appeared about half an hour later were Whitehead's wife, Lindy Weilgart; their three young children, Benjiman, Stefanie, and Sonja; and a couple of research assistants. The seas were too choppy to risk drawing the ships together, so I loaded my gear into a rubber dinghy and rowed the final yards of the voyage to join the small crowd lining the deck.

Flip, who had sailed with the Whitehead family on whale expeditions before, told me that the crew had been out for three weeks during this trip. He was able to make pictures on three days. Every other day brought rain, dense fog, or a full-blown storm. As he finished filling me in, Flip gave a light shrug that I understood to mean weather is weather, and whales are whales. He had once spent three and a half months poised with cameras ready on the edge of the arctic ice pack without being able to snap a single decent image of narwhals. The next day, he got all the photos he needed in seven hours. As whale photography goes, having opportunities three days out of twenty-one wasn't a bad ratio, especially taking into account the kind of whales we were after.

Balaena is the genus name for the bowhead whale, *Balaena mysticetus*. But at the moment, Whitehead wasn't searching for the giant bowheads or even for the species he knew best, the sperm whale. He and his colleagues were carrying out a study of *Hyperoodon ampullatus,* the northern bottlenose whale. It is found only in the North Atlantic. A more widely distributed counterpart, the southern bottlenose, *Hyperoodon planifrons,* has been observed throughout the Southern Ocean, which circles the globe between the Tropic of Capricorn and Antarctica. Both are classified in the family Ziphiidae, commonly known as beaked whales. So are at least twenty other species (not all taxonomists agree on the distinctions between some similar-looking types). Twenty-two different ziphiids add up to approximately one-quarter of all known cetaceans and fully half of the species considered to be whales. Yet the average person has never even heard rumors of beaked whales and wouldn't recognize one if it surged through the living room.

Ziphiids range from less than twelve feet long in the form of the pygmy beaked whale to more than forty-two feet in the form of Baird's beaked whale. Unlike other cetaceans, they have no central notch in the trailing edge of their flukes to separate the two halves. They come in colors ranging from steely gray and soft blue to brown with white splotches and streaks. Most keep to deep waters beyond the continental shelves, and they don't appear to spend much time traveling along or near the surface. As a result, they can be difficult for even an experienced observer to find, much less tell apart. The existence of some came to light only after people stumbled upon carcasses rotting on shore. Longman's beaked whale was defined on the basis of two weather-beaten skulls. Other species are known solely from a meager number of sightings. It's too soon to say whether the scarcity of observations means that the animals themselves are quite rare or restricted in range. Three new ziphiids have been added to the list just since 1990. One, temporarily assigned the scientific name of *Mesoplodon* species A, for years had no common name other than "unidentified beaked whale," and science may have several ziphiids left to discover. If not more; it's a big ocean out there.

The characteristic beak is much the same sort of extension of the jaws and mouth as seen in familiar dolphins. Beaked whales are a type of odontocete but generally carry just one or two pairs of teeth, all on the lower jaw. While these may aid in feeding, they probably play a more important role in social interactions. They typically appear only in males, which more often bear scratch marks and scars suggestive of rivalries than females do. The ginko-toothed beaked whale is so named because its teeth happen to be squat cones with crenulations that reminded someone of a ginko leaf, ginko trees being native to Japan, where the first specimens of this whale were recorded. By contrast, the strap-toothed whale produces a pair of tusks that curl up and eventually cross over the upper jaw, preventing the mouth from opening wide enough to take a bite of anything. Scientists assume that such animals have to feed by suctioning in their food. This wouldn't be difficult if the prey is soft bodied, and according to the stomach contents of stranded ziphiids, most dine primarily on squid. Some add a greater or lesser variety of deep-sea fish to the menu. Alone among the ziphiids, Shepherd's beaked whale has a full, dolphin-like set of teeth in both the lower and upper jaws. This points to a diet heavier on fish, and limited evidence confirms it. The odd sea star and sea cucumber also found in ziphiid stomachs indicates that the animals occasionally feed directly off the bottom.

There. You now know more than 99.9 percent of humanity does about the world's least familiar, least studied group of large mammals. The Dalhousie University team's research on the northern bottlenose was the first thorough field study of the species undertaken. It also represented the only systematic investigation of ecology, behavior, or population dynamics for any ziphiid anywhere. I'd never seen a beaked whale myself outside of a book. Half an hour after boarding the *Balaena,* I had three bottlenoses in view—two adults twenty to thirty feet long and a smaller juvenile, blowing and rolling amid the waves while storm petrels and shearwaters skimmed the surface around them.

Considering the mystery associated with beaked whales' lives, I suppose I was subconsciously expecting these creatures to be exotic looking. They did have bulging foreheads much like narwhals and belugas possess. *Hyperoodon,* meaning "above the tooth," refers to that forehead, particularly prominent in male bottlenoses; *ampullatus,* from the Latin for "flask," describes the beak, which is longer and narrower—more bottle shaped—than for most ziphiids. Two small teeth project from the males' lower lips. For the most part, however, the northern bottlenose whales just resembled seriously overgrown dolphins.

Sperm whales, the deep divers and squid hunters best known to the public, have deeply wrinkled skin that conjures visions of a zucchini gone bad or of the fingertips of a person who lingered too long in the bath. This puckered texture is thought to help the animals cope with shrinkage and expansion of body volume during their vertical travels. By comparison, the bottlenoses appeared normally smooth and rounded. Their skin was gray with brownish tones that I was told may be emphasized by a coating of the golden brown, single-celled algae known as diatoms. The animals' undersides, mouths, and foreheads were pale to creamy white with a yellowish-to-tan tinge, perhaps also due to diatoms. The last thing I noticed was the flippers, which seemed rather small relative to the whales' size. Then the trio dove out of sight, and Hal warned me not to expect them again for a while.

Most whales stay under for anywhere from ten minutes to half an hour at a time. Sperm whales will dive for as long as an hour, commonly descending to between one thousand and fifteen hundred feet. Over the years, Hal recorded bottlenoses remaining down longer still, and he wondered if they weren't diving deeper as well. A scientist named P. F. Scholander, writing in 1940, was convinced that bottlenoses do dive deeper and longer than any other whale. He based this in part on old whaling records that described harpooned northern bottlenoses taking out five hundred fathoms (three thousand feet) of line in under two minutes straight toward the bottom. One took out six thousand feet. Such wounded animals were reported to stay down an hour or even two.

The year before I visited, the Dalhousie team used a rubber suction cup to attach a time-depth recorder, or TDR, to a bottlenose, but the circuitry had failed. Earlier this season, they managed to stick a TDR on another whale. After about two and a half hours, the suction cup worked loose, and the instrument package, roughly the size of a human hand, floated to the surface. The researchers located it by its radio beacon and downloaded the data, the first ever obtained for a ziphiid in its submarine realm. The data told them that the whale had gone to a depth of 850 meters, or twenty-eight hundred feet.

As a scuba diver recalling how hard my skull and tissues felt squeezed at depths below one hundred feet, I was completely unable to envision a warm-blooded, air-breathing animal operating more than half a mile down. The pressure at that level is close to a hundred atmospheres. It would collapse most metal structures and transform a human body into a wad of goo within seconds. Yet the bottlenoses are apparently cruising around down there in the cold and total darkness picking off squid, dive after dive.

As we sat on the deck by the stern, hoping to sight a spout, Hal raised the possibility that deepwater squid live where they do in order to avoid most whales. In that case, the northern bottlenose thrives by having become an exception—a whale adapted to exploit those very squid that have carved out a niche toward the basement of the sea.

"Beaked whales are in many ways some of the most extreme and advanced animals on the entire planet, and we hardly know anything about them," Hal continued. "They have a reasonably complex social system. Roger Payne [a longtime cetacean researcher] thinks they might be some of the most intelligent of all whales, which means they are among the very brightest animals on the planet. They certainly appear to be the deepest divers on the planet." He paused to adjust the sailboat's heading and appeared lost in thought for a while. Then he added, "It's like if you found a whole bunch of apes that . . . seemed as complex as gorillas and chimps but lived deep in the forest and remained a mystery. The beaked whales are a whole new frontier."

Despite its generalized appearance, a bottlenose requires a whole suite of remarkable specializations to make its living plundering the abyss. An indispensable one, shared by other deepdiving whales, is the ability to store an adequate oxygen supply in special blood and muscle proteins rather than the lungs, since the body becomes so compressed during a descent that the heart can scarcely pump and the lungs are virtually flattened. Owning the densest skull bones of any known mammal is another key bottlenose asset: a crush-proof case for the brain. The bulbous head is laden with oils as well, including spermaceti—the same light, waxy substance whalers sought from sperm whales and sold to the makers of ointments, perfumes, fine candles, and cosmetics. Like cooking grease, the fatty compounds may shift between a liquid and semisolid, congealed state, depending upon the amount of heat delivered by the blood. This may act to further resist and redistribute pressures.

In a black universe broken only by the phosphorescent lures and semaphores of other life-forms scattered like stars, sonar is ideal for navigation and pinpointing targets. Ask any submariner. The bottlenose's stout skull is shaped like a dish in front, the better to send and receive the signals it uses for echolocation. A touch of asymmetry makes it still more sophisticated. Through the course of evolution, the paired frontal bones took on a twist so that one projects farther forward than the other. This makes it easier to detect variations in the way an incoming signal strikes the two sides. By comparing these differences, the bottlenose can gauge which direction the sound came from, just as other mammals do with two external ears.

From river dolphins to pygmy sperm whales, toothed whales in general possess this organic sonar technology. On the water's surface, many make burblings and ripe-sounding "raspberry" noises, snorting air from their blowholes. But no one is certain of exactly how they vocalize underwater. The assumption is that the sound vibrations arise from the rapid movement of air through various chambers and sinus cavities in the head. To humans, the recorded calls of northern bottlenose whales are a loud, staccato ticking, as if someone were dragging a stick along a picket fence. Played at full volume, they sound more like a two-cycle chain saw engine starting up. Called "click trains," the sounds are actually rapid-fire bursts of high frequencies that are mostly beyond our range of hearing. The Dalhousie team searches for the animals not only by looking for spouts but also by tossing a hydrophone into the water from time to time and running the results through a bat sonar detector. Much like putting an old 78 rpm record on a turntable and playing it at a slower speed, the device shifts the frequencies into a lower range so people can listen in and recognize patterns.

With the hydrophone's help, we came upon four more bottle-noses. When they surfaced, Hal began scrutinizing dorsal fin shapes, skin pigment patterns, nicks, and scars. In short order, he identified an adult female as one that his crew had previously named Patches. She was accompanied by her calf and two older juveniles. A baby bottlenose comes out of the womb measuring nine to eleven and a half feet long. The nursing young, which is to say animals up to one year of age, remain distinctly light colored, especially on the head. The juveniles grow slowly, adding only a couple of feet in length by the end of their second year.

Social units such as the female-calf-juvenile group we came upon looked like families, but it was too early to say that all the whales present were in fact related. In addition to more detailed observations, the researchers needed DNA samples to resolve questions of kinship within groups. Thus far, the most consistent long-term bonds Hal and his team had been able to recognize were between males. Larger social groups with as many as a dozen animals may form when these bachelor bands join females and young. This seems to occur most often toward late summer. While the males' great domed foreheads may make them look like aquatic geniuses, their motivation for socializing in mixed groups is assumed to be ordinary lust—courtship and breeding.

All hands were mustered to document everything possible as long as Patches's group lingered on the surface. Binoculars and camera lenses zoomed in on individual physical characteristics. Video footage recorded distances between animals and their orientation relative to one another. Sketches were drawn and notes scribbled to describe behavior, including reactions to the boat. I was fascinated to see that the whales' chief response to the presence of the *Balaena* was to linger by it. My shipmates took this for granted. The northern bottlenose acts exceptionally curious around boats, they explained. It doesn't come to bow-ride the waves, dolphin style. Nor does it come to make a few exploratory passes and then depart, as some of the great whales do. It arrives, and it hangs out—not always, but often enough for this to be a general characteristic.

At the same time, Hal had the impression that some of the bottlenoses he knew had grown so used to the *Balaena* that they no longer showed up to visit as dependably as during the early years of the study, and when they did swim over, they no longer stuck around quite as long. That made sense to me, the more so if bottlenoses were as smart as some suspected. On an expedition into part of the most remote headwaters of the Congo River, the small party I was in met chimpanzees that had almost certainly never seen humans before. During our initial encounter, the chimps put on a hugely excited display. Edging as close as they dared, they lingered for hours, staring intently much of the time, with expressions flickering between apparent wonder and fear. The next encounter was shorter but still full of shrieking, branch shaking, and rapt gazes. By the third and fourth meetings, the animals seemed to have taken our measure. They bustled around us with cursory glances and soon moved on to other affairs.

Young mammals are often the most curious members of their kind. Being naturally exploratory, and lacking the experience of their elders, makes them the most likely of all to approach a novel or otherwise intriguing object. This is true of several types of whales I know, humpbacks included, and Patches's calf was no exception. While the other bottlenoses in the group kept thirty to fifty feet distant, the calf swam over toward the hull several times. On each occasion, Patches spurted forward to herd the youngster aside. Then the group would resume floating in place like swollen logs—in fact, the behavior is called logging—a comfortable distance away, facing our direction as if taking mental notes. The older animals may have been watching an object by now somewhat familiar to them, just as the scientists were, but as far as I could tell, this didn't stop either species from making additional observations.

The following day, the feeling that we were the ones being examined only grew stronger as three big adults rested side by side next to the *Balaena*. Each kept itself oriented toward the boat, its tail slightly down and its head correspondingly tilted up, dark eyes lifted clear of the water much of the time. Every so often, one would spy-hop, raising its head straight up high above the sea as though interested in evaluating the situation from a different angle. Then the whale would settle back to resume monitoring us, and not just by sight. The hydrophone confirmed that we were being "pinged." Scanned with click trains, rat-a-tat-tat. Bright fog patches came and went as though the ocean were exhaling into the cold air and then drawing its sodden breath in again. When mist blotted out the world except for a clear patch enclosing us and the whales, the sense of a parley intensified. I'd felt this before with humpbacks: the impression of two intelligent, communicative life-forms met in a vast, silent setting, locking onto each other with their minds.

People have a knack for unknowingly telling themselves a story, making animals actors in it, and convincing themselves that this tale is what they are truly seeing. Call it self-fulfilling wild-life observation. My friend Ken Balcomb, a cetacean researcher based on San Juan Island, Washington, has another name for this: woo-woo science. You find an extraordinary amount of it around whales. Superstars even among big, charismatic animals, they readily lend themselves to anthropomorphism and more. They attract groupies and telepathy fans and spiritual seekers and hold them in thrall for a lifetime. Maybe I was headed that way. As far as my imagination was concerned at the moment, I was beyond woo-woo. I was on the bridge of the Starship *Enterprise* experiencing first contact with the Bottlenosians.

Click-click-click-click.

My background is in wildlife biology, and I try to stay objective. But it's a struggle and a constant source of confusion. Being objective means hewing to what you know to be factual, and I no longer think the facts we allow ourselves to work with are up to the job of explaining what some of our fellow creatures are capable of. Who among us has enough facts at hand to define the line between a simple curious approach and a sentient overture? Which animal communication specialist can tell when a whale is, in effect, saying, "That's interesting; let's watch for a while," from when it is saying, "Hello"?

For me, our time with the three bottlenoses represented interspecies engagement, a mutual probing by two types of brains with a great deal in common—a provocative, midocean tête-à-tête that traditional biology has no categories for. I don't mean to suggest that there was anything mystical about the encounter. The experience was transcendent but also as real as life gets, and I wish science had a format for discussing what it is like to be studied by whales. Even if it is found that most of the animals' interest is actually sparked by the whale-shaped boat hull or perhaps by some noise the vessel makes, this wouldn't account for the time they spend raising their great heads or rolling onto one side to look up at the people on deck. No matter how much of what we think passes back and forth during such meetings turns out to be yet another example of humans' boundless capacity for fooling themselves, the chance to visit whales that go out of their way to visit you is still a tremendous privilege. To me, it feels more like an honor.

We were floating over an area where the bottom suddenly falls out of the seafloor as the continental shelf is incised by the biggest ravine off Canada's east coast. Mariners took to calling it The Gully, but it is more like a drowned Grand Canyon, a dozen miles wide and a mile deep in places. While studying sperm whales around its edges, Hal had become intrigued by reports of bottlenoses toward the center. The first time he went out looking specifically for them, he got skunked. On the next trip, he was fogbound, finding nothing again, when the whales found him and came over for a visit next to the boat. "They stayed close a long time, rather like today," he told me, "and I felt a special connection. That was ten years ago."

Hal Whitehead definitely doesn't do woo-woo science. He is a rigorous investigator with a penchant for statistics. First and foremost, though, he is a sailor truly in love with the sea. The man looks like he carries Viking genes, with his ruddy complexion and unruly red hair and beard. He started handling his own sailboat at the age of eight in his native England, then moved to Maine, where he sailed some more before going on to major in mathematics in college. Hal turned to ecology for his graduate research and has specialized in whales ever since, but the mathematician in him never receded. Nor did the sailor. His publications are dense with calculus equations and numerical matrices. Yet in between fulfilling his responsibilities at the university, he has piloted the *Balaena* thousands of miles on the open Atlantic and twice across the Pacific.

It is a proven vessel and a home with a more-than-lived-in feel, the cabin a cramped cottage and the deck its tiny yard. Apples, oranges, and potatoes rolled along an upper shelf that ran nearly the length of the interior, while cabbages swayed overhead in a light hammock strung from the ceiling. A medley of books and gear was crammed into the woodwork through a clever arrangement of cupboards. Like all the boat's shelves, our bunks were narrow and edged with a high wooden lip to keep their cargo—in this case, snoozing humans—from spilling onto the floor. The swells ran six to eight feet high many days, and tacking into the wind often kept the *Balaena* heeled over with one edge of its deck skimming the surface. At any given time, the only object in the boat likely to have a horizontal surface was the stove, which swung on gimbals. You might have to brace yourself at a steep angle to keep from crashing into or away from the thing while cooking, but by God the pots on the burners stayed more or less level.

Moving around was an orangutan exercise requiring both hands as well as the feet. Naturally, the Whiteheads' three children took to the challenge with relish. Sonja, however, had to work harder than the others, for she was afflicted with a neuromuscular condition that made parts of her body go rigid. Mom

and Dad spent hours every day reading with the children, practicing foreign languages, and massaging Sonja's little limbs. This
was the child's first long trip at sea. Happily, Lindy found that it
helped relieve Sonja's spasticity to some extent; it seemed the
constant need to counterbalance the boat's rocking was a massage
in itself. Sonja liked to make whooshing sounds to imitate the
bottlenoses. Even when she was below deck, if someone cried out,
"Sonja, look! Whales!" she would puff out her cheeks and reply
with a wide-eyed "Poohf!" followed by a broad smile.

Traveling on wind power kept research costs down, but the
real reason Hal Whitehead chased bottlenoses by sail was because
. . . well, because that's how a sailor travels. Sometimes when the
wind backed off and we were barely doing two or three knots,
the crew would beg him to start up the diesel engine and make
some time. Hal usually pleaded a need to conserve fuel or to avoid
a sudden disturbance that could throw off the natural patterns
of whale activity we hoped to record. An intuitive sailor, he was
taking in the whistling of air currents in the rigging and the way
the fulmars and gulls set their wings to slip across the wind and
how the waves thrummed the hull depending on the direction
the seas were running, and I think he would rather have been
keelhauled than switch on a damn motor and chug along like
some tugboat skipper.

The voyage back to Halifax to make minor repairs, resupply, and
swap crews for the next outing was a leisurely one, as the wind
all but died inshore of Sable Island. With the sails luffing on
the last gasps of a breeze, I took advantage of the slack time to
read through various publications on board about bottlenoses.
Although they made a thin stack relative to what was available for

other kinds of whales, more historical information could be had for this species than for any of its close kin, because bottlenoses and, to a lesser extent, Baird's beaked whales had been the only ziphiids commercially hunted. A large male bottlenose carries as much as four hundred pounds of prized spermaceti-like oil in its forehead. The lower jaw yielded a different type of oil, used for lubricating precision instruments, and two to three tons of lower quality oil might be rendered from the animal's blubber and flesh.

The first account of a whaling boat taking a bottlenose dates back to 1852. It was a Scottish vessel. Norwegians joined in later, followed by Icelanders and eventually Canadians. All took full advantage of two strong bottlenose behavioral traits. The first is their tendency to approach boats. An unwillingness to leave an injured or dying companion is the second. As with every other commercially sought whale, the use of cannon-fired lances with grenade tips to kill highly intelligent mammals was spoken of as a "fishery" and said to be based upon the "sustainable harvest" of "stocks," when the reality was unchecked strip-mining of rich fat and flesh from one locale after another in the absence of any worthwhile data about populations.

A reasonable rule of thumb for calculating the true impact of whaling is to take the official tally and add 25 to 35 percent to account for animals that were struck by a harpoon but who tore loose and escaped only to die later from their wounds, or were never put down on the books. The records show about fifty thousand northern bottlenose whales taken between 1882 and 1914. Thousands more were added to the toll by 1927, but per-haps fewer than a thousand from 1938 through 1954. The rapidly falling figures reflected a dampened market due to the spread of cheap, petroleum-derived substitutes for whale oil. It was also obvious that bottlenoses had become harder and harder to find.

Toward the end, the whalers shifted to hunting them for meat sold to fur farms in various northern countries and to pet food companies located mainly in the British Isles. "I had no idea," Hal told me, "that the dogs and cats of my childhood were eating these strange, endearing animals." The demand was such that 5,000 were killed from 1955 through 1972. That included 87 taken by Nova Scotia–based boats that stalked The Gully for five years during the 1960s and killed 129 off Labrador as late as 1971. The Gully ceased to be bottlenose hunting grounds in 1973, after the British government banned the import of whale products for pet food.

Although scientists knew next to nothing about bottlenose life at sea, whaling provided them with literal tons of raw material for measurements and autopsy data. Thus, it has been known for decades that adult male bottlenoses average about 27.5 feet long, adult females 22, and they weigh between five and seven and a half tons, on a par with African elephants. Males live to be at least thirty-seven years old (based on counts of annual layers in teeth) and females twenty-seven. The onset of female sexual maturity occurs between the ages of seven and eleven. Pregnancy lasts twelve months. Mothers nurse their offspring for a year and are capable of producing young every other year. And this ziphiid's favorite food is indeed squid; the multichambered stomachs of some corpses contained in excess of ten thousand tough, slow-to-digest squid beaks.

Working from the totals of northern bottlenoses known to have been killed annually, and accounting for reproduction by dwindling groups of survivors, experts have come up with a prewhaling population of approximately 130,000. Exploitation knocked it down by at least 70 percent and possibly by more than 90 percent. In the *Red Data Book,* the list of species at risk compiled by the UN-sponsored International Union for the Conservation of Nature, the northern bottlenose is currently classed as "vulnerable." It means not yet threatened or endangered by extinction but liable to be unless its numbers improve.

Milelong drift nets that destroy sea life indiscriminately are still used by commercial fishing fleets from Far Eastern nations despite worldwide criticism. They intercept ziphiids along with everything else and drown them. Other northern bottlenoses get wrapped in trawl nets and entangled in ropes and other loose fishing debris. Some may get caught on the hooks of long-liners such as the swordfishing industry. The Dalhousie team has witnessed a bottlenose wrapped in a longline in The Gully and probably dying. There are similar observations from Labrador waters. Faeroe Islanders continue to harpoon bottlenoses today, claiming that it is a cultural tradition extant since at least medieval times. Hal didn't think they called it hunting, though, or even whaling. "They use the term *assisted strandings* or some such semantic nicety," he said.

Nobody has very accurate figures for the present-day population. Not that there haven't been official guesses. Iceland, for example, came up with a precise total of 4,925 northern bottlenoses within its territorial waters as of 1987. How? By counting a tiny fraction of that number and conjuring the rest through statistics. It sounds grossly inadequate and, by some standards, would be considered disingenuous. But in an environment as wide and borderless as a section of ocean, the best any agency can usually do is send out observers to concentrate on a few sample areas or travel an invisible grid of survey lines. The results must then be multiplied by whatever someone decides will compensate for periods of limited visibility due to weather, and multiplied again to start filling in the immense spaces not covered at all.

On maps, the range of northern bottlenose whales may be depicted by a uniform color that sweeps across the North Atlantic from northern New England to northern Europe and up into the Arctic. In actuality, the distribution of animals is extremely patchy. Populations in the western Atlantic appear to be limited to areas around The Gully and portions of Davis Strait between Greenland and Labrador. In the eastern Atlantic, the whales are found in a few spots off Iceland, Norway, and the high Arctic islands to the north called Jan Mayen Land. If other strongholds for the species exist, they remain undiscovered. There are, however, hints of far-flung travels. The northernmost sighting was off Baffin Island, and reports of groups of northern bottlenose whales following leads for miles inside the arctic ice pack are not uncommon. Carcasses or direct observations have also come from as far south as the Carolinas and the Mediterranean Sea. Sightings at even lower latitudes in the Atlantic may have been of southern bottlenose whales. A surprising report of *Hyperoodon* from the tropical Pacific had experts wondering if there might be a third, as-yet unclassified species of bottlenose whale, before detective work revealed that this was Longman's beaked whale, itself scarcely known to science.

Whitehead was not being boastful when he told me that the only meaningful bottlenose count anywhere was for The Gully. Applying a technique based on individual identification and the ratio of repeat sightings of known animals to sightings of previously unknown ones during subsequent surveys, the Dalhousie researchers could be fairly sure that at least 180 of these whales were using the area year-round. What the team couldn't be certain of was whether the numbers in The Gully represented a robust, normally distributed population or one still recovering from the effects of whaling. Their core range, where they were most often sighted, was tiny by the sprawling standards of oceangoing creatures. It covered just sixty square miles toward the center and throat—the deepest parts—of this steep-sided fissure in the continental shelf. The next-closest known northern bottlenose population was nine hundred miles north, in the Davis Strait.

Three major currents meet over The Gully: the warm, north-flowing Gulf Stream; the icy, south-flowing waters of the Labrador Current out of Davis Strait; and the Belle Island Current flowing offshore from the continent. They mix and swirl and churn up nutrients from the seafloor, nourishing enough plankton to form the foundation of an extraordinarily rich food pyramid. Some speculate that a reversing current, known as a seiche, creates a sort of bulge, or standing wave, where the currents meet, and that this, together with a surface gyre, helps keep the upwelling minerals and organic elements suspended up in the sunlit zone, further boosting the rate of plankton production.

However such forces operate, they have made The Gully one of the most important localized marine mammal habitats in the world. Almost fifteen kinds of cetaceans have been recorded in and around this site, a dozen of them regularly. In addition to northern bottlenoses, they include sperm whales, long-finned pilot whales, humpbacks, blues, fins, seis, minkes, common dolphins, and, most abundant of all, Atlantic white-sided dolphins. White-beaked dolphins arrive in the cold months. During late summer, when the water is warmest, striped dolphins, more typical of the tropics, swarm through.

The Gully is so abrupt and deep that it bends storm currents, causing much of the sediment load they carry to settle out along the Scotian Shelf. Ironically, because of its underlying wealth of hydrocarbons, this massive sandpile now threatens to pose problems for the undersea trench that helped form it. New drilling operations were planned for six natural gas fields near The Gully, in some cases within three miles of its walls. Busier traffic through the area would increase the risk of injury and death to whales from ship strikes. Drilling fluids and other industrial chemicals could contaminate the food chain. And of course, the potential for a major oil spill on the brink of this biological hot spot loomed in environmentalists' imaginations like one of those hundred-foot waves in a perfect storm.

Conservationists had been holding public meetings, directing letter-writing campaigns, and arranging talks with the oil and gas companies in an effort to negotiate a compromise plan that would keep future drilling farther from the trench. Canada was contemplating establishing a series of marine protected areas in its territorial waters partially modeled on the U.S. National Marine Sanctuary System. Among the organizations pushing to make The Gully number one on the government's list of possibilities, the Canadian branch of the World Wildlife Fund had taken a leading role.

When the *Balaena* headed out from port for another two- to three-week research cruise, I found myself part of an entirely new crew that included a marine sanctuary specialist helping to manage the World Wildlife Fund's campaign. Her name was Cherry Recchia. Annie Gorgone, a whale-watching guide, was along as well. The first mate was Brad Carter, a wiry, ponytailed young salt who took whatever jobs would keep him under sail at sea. His dream was to acquire his own boat one day and single-hand it to the far corners of the world.

Robin Baird, who had worked extensively with killer whales off the continent's west coast, came to lend his expertise in collecting data. The chief researcher was Sascha Hooker. A slender woman in her twenties studying for her doctoral degree under Hal Whitehead's guidance, she happened to be a descendant of the biologist for whom Hooker's sea lion (*Phocarctos hookeri,* now more often called the New Zealand sea lion) was named. Since Sascha was also the captain, I found it reassuring that she combined years of sailing experience with a calm, confident style. Each of us was to share in the cooking and washing, in roaming the deck to scout for bottlenoses, and in sailing, taking the *Balaena*'s helm for two two-hour watches each day. While Sascha plotted the course on her charts, all of us were to take turns entering weather and sea conditions in the ship's log every three hours and noting sightings of marine mammals other than bottlenoses in a separate journal whenever we came upon them.

My first watch began at 4 A.M. The night sky is nowhere more encompassing than above the perfectly uncluttered, unbounded surface of an ocean. When conditions are right, you can even make out the earth curving along the horizon, its opacity bending down and away toward the far edges to let in more stars. Every direction glittered with constellations as I first stepped out onto the deck, and meteors burned arcs between them. As we neared The Gully, though, dense fog closed over the heavens. With the stars winking out in one quadrant after another, I felt as though I were bearing witness to a cosmic dust cloud marking the end of space and time. My world was transformed into the hermetic one that all aboard would come to know only too well: a boat, a mast reaching up into the mist, the billowing geometry of the mainsail, and a circle of dark water into which an endless succession of waves pulsed to lift and tilt the *Balaena* and then pass on.

During my second watch, in midafternoon, the sea quieted and the sun burned through. I climbed the mast to perch in the crow's nest and look out over 360 degrees of saltwater, with the curvature of the planet once again visible under the sky. I was supposed to find whale spouts somewhere within it. Eventually, we did spy a group of three bottlenoses and sailed over toward them. The goal was to observe them, of course, but at some point we were also going to try to shoot them. We were nonlethal whalers equipped with a crossbow. Each arrow shaft was encased in foam toward the forward end, from which protruded a sharp-edged, hollow cylinder roughly the size of the eraser on a pencil. It was designed to punch out a half-inch-long plug of skin and blubber from the multiton target, fall off under its own weight, and float, awaiting retrieval with a scoop net.

The skin would yield DNA for identifying individuals and determining degrees of relatedness—within groups, between different groups encountered in The Gully, and between the whales inhabiting The Gully and other populations. The blubber could be analyzed for contaminants and for fatty acids that would reveal the various types of food being eaten. Biopsies were also useful in determining the sex of subadults that had not yet developed the physical characteristics of mature animals, such as the adult male's conspicuous forehead. As a rule, animals struck with the arrow reacted with a shudder quickly followed by a dive. But the dive was usually brief, and after resurfacing, the whale would still stay around the boat and would resume approaching it closely at times. Even so, the team placed groups with calves off-limits to sampling in order to avoid any risk of separating mothers and nursing young.

We biopsied two of the three whales in that first group, sailed on, and found another cluster of five. Later, we located four more bottlenoses and got close enough to them for two more biopsies. The afternoon turned out to be quite productive, increasing the number of tissue samples the Dalhousie team had ever taken from six to ten. It was also a rewarding afternoon in terms of noting behavior. To begin with, each of the first two groups was loosely keeping company with pilot whales and Atlantic white-sided dolphins, or vice versa. Part of the interspecies relationship could probably be defined as neutral affiliation—similar creatures finding themselves in the same spot and staying together a while. How much play, aggression, or curiosity might be involved was anything but clear. Brad Carter once saw a bottlenose calf leaping along the surface with white-sided dolphins. Robin Baird had watched both dolphins and pilot whales pursuing bottlenoses, yet he had also seen a bottlenose chase a seventy-foot fin whale.

All three bottlenose groups spent almost as much time swimming toward, next to, or under the boat as we spent chasing them. A juvenile that bolted from one group to have a closer encounter with the *Balaena* got cut off by an older animal. I also noticed some instances of one adult bumping another aside. They had a few head-on interactions as well. Scars on the head of a different juvenile resembled rake marks from teeth, though not necessarily those of a male bottlenose. The apparent gouges could have been inflicted by a dolphin or pilot whale, my companions pointed out. Bottlenoses may also incur deep scratches from navigating through pack ice.

Toward evening, Captain Sascha was cooking potatoes, keeping track of garlic bread in the oven, and setting chili out on the dining table. On a second table, she was simultaneously trying to divide each of the biopsy samples into six equal parts to be stored in vials of preservative and properly labeled. And in between, she was dashing up the steps and onto the deck to confirm where whale spouts were last seen, check the trim of the sails, and make adjustments to our course. While we finished the meal, the fog closed in. Once again, we became six warm bodies on a narrow strip of hard footing forty feet long surrounded by liquid and mist, following beaked whales by the sounds of their breath toward destinations unknown.

We added four more biopsies the next day. It was how I pictured the rhythms of old-time whaling: long, vigilant hours of waiting followed by frantic flurries of action. Our arrangement was to have at least two lookouts posted on deck facing opposite directions as long as the weather permitted any visibility at all. If we were in the core of the whales' range or expecting animals seen earlier to resurface, four sets of eyes were called for, each sweeping a quarter of the encircling horizon. Robin took it upon himself to enforce the rule when people inevitably succumbed to daydreams or distractions or the lure of the cabin's dry warmth. He usually managed this with humor but was not averse to sterner reminders of why we had left shore to test our mettle against the Atlantic.

So it was Aye-Aye, sir, and back out on deck in the wind and spray, and I would pass the time trying to distinguish between sooty, greater, Cory's, and Manx shearwaters sailing low over the waves with set wings, using the air currents reflected off the water's surface for lift. Or identify differences between the shearwaters and the northern fulmar. Or tell Leach's from Wilson's storm petrels. Both danced light as butterflies just above the surface with dangling legs, seeming to tiptoe upon the sea. (The name petrel comes from Peter and refers to the story of this disciple walking on water with Jesus' help.) No larger than American robins, storm petrels seemed too delicate to endure these gale-swept expanses, and yet they had mastered them, becoming some of the most abundant seabirds in the world.

The silhouettes of great skuas and great black-backed gulls looked similar at a distance, and I practiced telling them apart as well. Then there was the south polar skua, which breeds in the Antarctic, and the greater shearwater, from breeding grounds in the South Atlantic, and I would reflect on what it might be like to ride so many winds across so many thousands of miles twice annually, tacking through ice storms and running before steamy tropical squalls and on and on, setting down on land for only a few weeks out of the year.

A red-breasted nuthatch, a tiny forest inhabitant blown off course or plagued by a faulty inner compass, paused to rest on the boat, alighting on a spar, on the cabin's roof, then on my hand with a whirr of narrow brown wings. When it finally ventured on, my thoughts were drawn out behind it over the endless, quivering gray-and-blue-and-silver brine, up onto reefs of clouds spread low in the sky, farther up to the feathery cirrus cloud streaks known as mares' tails, back down over the waves, noting the way the sun glinted to make lanes of pure light . . . and then the shout went up:

Whales! Twenty degrees to port! Three hundred meters, maybe 350!

As often as not that day, they were pilot whales rather than bottlenoses. We came upon a number of great whales as well, including four of the very biggest: blues. As with identifying sea-birds, I needed practice to distinguish the thirty-foot-tall column of a blue-whale spout from the lower, bushier spout a hump-back makes, and then to tell those from the spouts of other great whales. And on the open sea, with no fixed reference point for perspective, even dolphin spouts can be mistaken by an inexperi-enced eye for the spout of a much larger but more distant whale. I once alerted the crew to what I thought were faraway blows that turned out to be splashes from the big birds called gannets plummeting into the swells after fish.

Through early afternoon, the wind swung around from south-west to northeast, but it stayed steady at four to five knots. The flatter the seas, the farther away spouts can be detected, and the lighter the wind, the longer the blows hang in the air before dis-sipating. Intermittent sightings continued at an encouraging pace. During the sudden scramble from quarters, someone usually mon-keyed up the mast to get the best angle for looking down into the water and calling out directions: Whales forty degrees starboard, a hundred meters! Turning! One still to starboard, the others are circling around behind us. Fifty meters! Forty meters! Two big ones coming straight toward the stern! Beside us now. Fire!

All the effects of biopsy darting that I saw were minor, and yet each strike and shudder made me aware of how many bottle-noses we could readily have killed if we were firing harpoons instead. Once a whaling boat made its way into the heart of The Gully, the only real defense left for creatures so big, curious, and benign would be foul weather.

There was plenty of that in due course. The breeze had picked up by late afternoon when we came upon a titanic sperm whale logging on the surface. Only mature males seem to travel to this region; females and juveniles keep to warmer latitudes, where the males will rejoin them to breed. The head of a male constitutes 35 percent of its body and is deemed the largest in the animal kingdom. It is so steep and square in front that the whale appears to be shoving a boxcar through the waves. Floating high on the water with its spout spewing laterally from a single blowhole set to one side of that head, and its angular backbone ridges sticking up behind the dorsal fin amid yards and yards of wrinkled-prune skin, this particular male seemed as if he must be resting from the sheer labor of bulling his way from place to place, for he was surely the most ungainly looking marine mammal I had ever seen.

During my watch at the helm, I browsed a book on weather. It described the low sky coming our way as perlucidus, a lovely name for a pearly mixture of ice crystals and water vapor. Technically, the clouds were a type of altocumulus. The book said that they herald precipitation.

It rained through the night and into the morning. The wind rose to twenty knots, and I sat on the deck keeping watch over the spume blown off the crests of each oncoming wave. Would that roller be the one that would tip the *Balaena* over too far? What of those rogue waves I'd always heard about that come out of nowhere at twice the height of the others? It was strictly a landlubber's frame of mind, sitting there viewing each big wave as another assault on normality. A seafarer understands that a world of big waves in the Atlantic *is* normality, and that worrying about them only wears you down, for the ocean never, ever tires. A sailboat like the *Balaena* could probably take three times the seas that were coming at us and still ride them like a well-behaved cork, balanced by the weight of the keel, but I didn't know that in my gut. As usual, I would give in to the chill after a while and go

below, and although the cabin was like the funhouse in an amuse-
ment park, all tilted planes and objects that appeared to roll uphill
at times, the walls created one reassuring illusion, and that was of
protection from whatever lay outside.

The storm subsided enough for me to relax a bit and rub the
soreness from bruised shoulders and hips, but conditions were
still too choppy for us to find whales or to work with them if we
happened upon any. Captain Sascha decided to salvage the situation by declaring this a transect day, which meant we would sail
back and forth across The Gully along a grid, taking readings of
water temperature, salinity, clarity (an indirect measure of plankton production), and other environmental factors. By the following day, we were chasing bottlenoses again. I saw them breaching
for the first time, and a juvenile engaged in a vigorous bout of
lob-tailing close to the boat. It was only 9:30 A.M., and we were
already in the thick of whales unknown to most of the world.
I even recognized a male in one group by a notch behind his dorsal fin, which had caught my attention on a previous day.

As of 9:47, the whales had all sounded, and I was up in the
crow's nest. It was my new favorite place in the world to be, given
the limited options. I don't know how high up the mast this small
platform actually was; probably less than thirty feet, but it was
as private a spot as one could find other than the head, as ship-
board bathrooms are called. In payment for a 360-degree view,
I was subjected to a nonstop tilt-a-whirl ride at the fair, because
the pitch and yaw of the hull was magnified by the length of the
tower I was on. If the hull heels over thirty degrees, a person
standing on the deck amidships might be moved two or three
feet that direction. A body three stories up in the crow's nest
goes whipping several times as far, several times as fast. It's the

catapult effect, and you're the missile, except that you really don't want to be released. If you keep your eyes fixed in one direction, facing a world evenly divided between water and sky, you go arcing through every angle relative to the rows of waves and past every shade of blue between clouds shaped like every imaginable object. Then you do it again in reverse.

Many leagues away, a group of bottlenoses appeared, swimming with white-sided dolphins. Before the day was out, we had watched a solitary bottlenose keep a blue whale company for half an hour. We had also fulfilled one of the research goals for the trip, for we now had a total of twenty biopsy samples. It was time to try shooting bottlenoses with a suction-tipped arrow holding a detachable time-depth recorder instead.

Although the animals' core range covered only sixty square miles on the surface, their actual range would be more like sixty cubic miles if it extended nearly to the seafloor—a tremendous difference and one that might well define their way of life. The bottlenoses plainly had a close connection with the canyon yawning beneath the waves, but the only data in regard to their vertical travels came from a single previous attachment of a TDR. I wondered why the effort to put on another hadn't taken precedence during the trip. A couple of hours, several long chases, and perhaps a dozen opportunities later, I understood. Getting one of these packages stuck on a bottlenose was going to take an ocean of luck. First, the boat had to draw almost exactly parallel to a whale so the arrow from the crossbow would strike at an angle perpendicular to the body, giving the suction cup the best chance of making full contact and forming an even seal. Second, unless the whale was almost close enough to run over, the archer needed to aim substantially higher than the target to account for the drop during the arrow's flight due to the weight of the instrument package. Third, I learned that, of three TDRs carried on board, one had somehow frazzled its innards and another was showing symptoms of serious battery problems. The remaining one, brought along as a last resort, was a bulky prototype. When attached to an arrow, it made for a package even more lopsided than an ordinary TDR, which was unwieldy enough with its electronic component plus enough flotation material to keep it from sinking after a miss. Even in the unlikely event that the shooter did everything else just right—taking aim in a way that constantly adjusted for the roll of the boat on a swell, timing the release to match the emergence of a whale's side through the water as it surfaced to breathe, and judging how far the arrow would drop en route—this missile seemed determined to turn sideways before it hit or else to go pinwheeling entirely off course.

Whssst . . . splash. Whssst . . . bump, splash. Utter, clumsy, dismal, repeated, ridiculous failure was our lot, and I couldn't foretell any other. At the same time, the enterprise called up a flood of fond memories from childhood, when my pals and I—slingshot artists and would-be warriors with homemade bows—came up with similar types of contraptions. The folks responsible for putting this one together happened to have university degrees, and the fact that theirs worked just about as well as ours did back in the old neighborhood—splat into the drink—was kind of delightful. And none of us was able to dream up a more effective means of attaching the last functional TDR to a bottlenose. The scientists had tried attaching a TDR suction cup with a long pole during earlier outings, but they could ne-e-e-e-ver quite reach far enough. Consequently, we carried on, and on, with a Whssst . . . splash . . . *%$#! across the briny deep.

We had splendid chances with easygoing whales and a window of weather so fair that we took a break and jumped off the *Balaena* for a combination swim and much-needed bath. As soon as the next morning dawned, we knew we would never get a shot away that day. The sea looked like iron and surged at us in heavy swells before a thirty-knot wind. It was a minor gale. All we could do was sit hove-to with the sails reefed, leaving just enough canvas to keep our nose into the waves, and tough it out—wait and rock and fly around in the cabin and listen to the rigging moan and the water hiss along the hull. The wind made loose clothing snap like a whip and practically tear loose from your body. I wondered how it could be strong enough to push me around the deck like a howling bully and still not blow away the fog.

Another day, another flip-flop in the weather. Under partially open skies, we met four large male bottlenoses, and one of them had a dorsal fin curled over to one side. Each time they emerged from a dive, they approached the *Balaena* as though they definitely had something in mind. They logged on the surface, eyeing us at close range, spy-hopped, and scanned us with click trains. When covered by only a few feet of water, their bodies shone light blue within the dark blue of the sea. Scars, scratches, and missing chunks of skin stood out as white streaks and cross-hatching. One broad, pale patch looked like a healed-over gouge. Besides the lopsided fin, the group's members collectively owned a partially bent fin, a fin with a hole in it, and another with a notch, reminding us of how little we understood of the dramas that mark bottlenose lives. Had some run into killer whales? What prey and what enemies waited in the awesome black depths to which they descended? Did bottlenoses know monsters that science has no inkling of? For all the luck we had taking potshots at the whales

with our TDR-on-an-arrow gizmo, we would never even know
how deep they really go.

Day number . . . ? I was beginning to lose track. Rousing for
a two-hour watch in the middle of the night wasn't helping to
sharpen my wits. What counted was that the day was a workable
one, and we watched a bottlenose bow-riding on the pressure
waves of a fast-moving, seventy-foot-long fin whale. That was
the high point. Whssst . . . bump, splash! The count of failed attempts to attach a TDR must have been approaching forty. As we
cruised endlessly back and forth two-hundred-some miles from
shore, loosing one wildly tumbling arrow after another into the
water near creatures that hardly anyone back on land knew of or
cared about, I sometimes felt that I had joined, if not a ship of
fools, then one of the oddest enterprises ever undertaken by a half
dozen adults. It was absurd to be out here doing this. And it was
wonderful that someone would try, regardless.

Toward evening, the sunset horizon was broken by the leaping of a kind of dolphin we had not yet seen on this trip. It was
called by the same name: bottlenose. Heavyweights among their
kind, some bottlenose dolphins reach nearly fifteen hundred
pounds and lengths of more than twelve feet. They were nevertheless able to put seven or eight feet of air beneath them when
they jumped near the boat, and captives in aquariums have been
trained to soar almost twice as high for a food reward.

With the forecast of a serious gale being repeated on the
marine weather channel, Sascha made the decision to run for
the nearest port. That was Canso, halfway up the outer coast of
Nova Scotia on a course straight west from us. Sailing for land,
we unexpectedly passed into a balmy stretch of flat water and
hot sun. There were great whales everywhere: humpbacks with

angel-wing pectoral fins, far whiter than the pectorals of North Pacific populations; fin whales; and minkes. The place was alive with dolphins as well. Our charts showed that the bottom here was just three hundred to six hundred feet deep, a kiddie pool compared to where we had been. Currents or a localized upwelling had temporarily filled the place with a concentration of krill and small, schooling fish such as herring, sand lance, or capelin. Countless seabirds worked among the whales. When one humpback surfaced, its spout literally blew a swimming shearwater up into the sky.

Four fin whales swam in a great sweeping arc and came toward the sailboat like a submarine squadron, diving beneath our prow with only a few feet to spare. Brad decided that if these huge rorquals were going to show an interest in us, which they don't often do, he would slip in with a mask and snorkel and see what he could learn. We dragged him on a line behind the boat, partly because some whales respond well to a figure moving along that way and partly so we could keep track of him. Raising his head as best he could while plowing through the water at four knots, Brad shouted to ask where the giants were. We yelled back that one was coming straight toward him. He put his face back underwater to look.

Fin whales have a unique asymmetrical color pattern. The thin, white chevron flaring out from behind the eye is always more pronounced on the right side. Moreover, the lower jaw, part of the upper lip, and some of the baleen plates in the mouth are all white on the right side but dark brownish gray on the left. As a fin whale angled in and passed just below, I felt sure that no matter how badly the water was clouded with plankton, Brad would be able to make out some of the white glimmering on the animal's side. Nothing. His head stayed down, searching back and forth in vain.

A second whale closed in behind and slid directly underneath Brad. Again, nothing. No reaction on the snorkeler's part. The whale's head was visible in front of him and its tail visible behind, and we were shouting over the hiss and splash of the water to get Brad's attention. It looked as if he were about to be lifted by the whale's back at any moment. When Brad finally looked up, every one of us was hollering and pointing straight underneath him. Clambering back aboard later, he told us that he thought he could see a big brown shape, and that was about all. It had been terrific entertainment for the rest of us, though, and it made for way better morale than getting banged around out in The Gully while waiting for the worst of the gale to hit.

When I awakened from sleep after midnight, about twenty-two hours after we first set our course for Canso, the world felt different somehow. Shuffling up onto the deck, I restrained my-self from shouting "Land ho," just as I had resisted crying, "Thar she blows!" from the crow's nest out in The Gully. I figured that every novice on a whale research boat yelled those things, and my status as the least experienced sailor on deck was already evident enough. But I did want to shout with joy when I first noticed lights that didn't bob up and down and first smelled earthen scents in the air and then made out a dark, massive outline—land! real land!—looming above the lights. And as morning dawned, every tree and every flowerbed, every leaf, and every patch of lawn and each picket fence and wooden house in Canso, all the fixtures of ordinary existence I had taken for granted—ice cream! a sidewalk to stroll!—became splendors to refresh the spirit as I wandered on shore renewing my acquaintance with the continent.

Having been around many wretched degrees of seasickness, I know how lucky I am not to suffer from it. But I get hit by a disorienting reaction that sailors recognize and describe as being landsick. On a scuba diving trip that once kept me roaming the Coral Sea for several weeks straight, I took a break to visit a remote island, and I couldn't stand upright when I hit the sand. I tried to walk down a road that must have been forty feet across. That wasn't wide enough. Like the proverbial drunken sailor on shore leave, I kept staggering off into thickets to one side or the other, my internal balance next to useless because it was still compensating for the roll of the sea that was no longer there.

As I was weaving along beside the crew during our first full night in Canso, we were drawn to a blaze of revolving neon lights. And after all the days when the *Balaena*'s cabin had become a funhouse you couldn't pay to leave and the crow's nest a tilt-a-whirl, there before us stood the real thing. We had picked the week the carnival was in town, complete with rides guaranteed to rearrange your innards under centrifugal force. Maybe those machines would have snapped me out of my landsickness, but paying to get on one was the least attractive idea imaginable to me. Not to the others, though. Cherry Recchia and Annie Gorgone led the way laughing and hooting onto the Octopus and the Hammer and I don't know what else, because I went off by myself and sat still as a statue while the world continued to sway back and forth around me.

We only had about four days left on the entire expedition. The idea of spending a day and a half sailing back to The Gully to fire a few arrows into the ocean, then sailing another two days to reach Halifax, did not excite everyone. The gale had not yet fully blown itself out. It was raining hard, and the seas were still running big. We could spend another day in Canso instead and then scoot home down the coast. For Brad, the sooner we went to sea, the better. Land held little allure. It was too hot. The air felt stuffy, and it came with biting insects. But almost everyone else was at least tempted by the prospect of having more hours to walk on solid ground, not to mention the chance at another restaurant meal. To be honest, there was not one inspired cook among the crew, unless you consider mashed turnips on rice inspirational.

Hearing the scuttlebutt, Sascha let it be known that she would brook no mutinous clinging to shore. We loaded gear, and the captain nosed the *Balaena* back out onto the ocean. As if viewing the change through Brad's eyes, I found it a relief in a way to slip loose from the muddy hubbub and sensory overload of land existence to inhabit once more the circumscribed boundaries of a ship with everything aboard serving a purpose and close at hand, sufficient unto ourselves. But we were right back on a carnival ride in the cabin, whose floor kept turning onto one side while the walls tilted overhead. The *Balaena* was wallowing through agitated waters between two areas of low pressure—the gale behind us, now dissipating its force on land, and a new one building out at sea. We could only hope conditions in The Gully wouldn't break down completely for a day or two.

Upon rising from our bunks back in bottlenose range, we found the ocean alive with tremendous waves. But rather than rushing at us steep-sided and cresting, they took the form of broad swells. They rose and fell so smoothly that you never grasped how big they were until you went on deck to see a terrain that looked like prairie hills. It was early afternoon before we spied bottlenose blows, but when we came upon the group it proved to be the largest we had encountered, with eleven animals. Sascha and Robin were bothered by the fact that we still hadn't counted any new calves during the voyage. Two members of the group were big males. One bore the most remarkable series of long scars I had yet witnessed, and each mark caused me to reflect anew on how much of these animals' existence remained hidden.

Whssst . . . splash. Whssst . . . splash. Then all at once, on Brad's third shot—attempt number fifty-plus for the trip—we heard, "Whssst . . . thok. . . . Yes! YES! Alllriiiiight!" I'd have bet money that we would see a fabled giant squid wrestle a sperm whale before we got a suction cup to stick on. I was wrong. The bottlenoses, which had so often paid little heed to a biopsy dart, roared off almost at once, but we could make out the bright red TDR clinging to the side of one animal like a lamprey as the group plunged away through the swells.

Sascha flipped on the sonar to scan what oceanographers call the deep-scattering layer, formed by concentrations of living organisms, most of them quite small. This gave her an electronic picture of the depth and thickness of the band where food was most abundant at that particular time of day. It was where sperm whales usually hunted, and the bottlenoses might focus on the same locale. Then again, they might plunge down through it to feed deeper. All we could do was to sail around on top of the water column and be ready for them when they came up. The recorder package included a radio that would signal when not submerged: that is, it would be activated only when the tagged whale broke the surface and exposed a circuit to the air or else when the device came off and floated up. Since the previous recorder had stayed on little more than two hours, expectations for a quick recovery were high. And it wasn't long before our normally self-contained skipper was racing around the deck hollering, "Beep! Beep! There it is! Beep!" raising a finger aloft with each announcement.

She did hear a signal, but intermittently. The whale must have risen for just a few breaths before beginning another descent. We settled back into a state of enforced idleness. The close of this day—the day of the bull's-eye hit with the world's clunkiest suction cup arrow—brought a second miracle, at least for me. I had heard for most of my life about the green flash that was supposed to be visible, mainly in the tropics, at the instant the sun disappears completely into the sea. And like many people, I had looked and waited for it countless times in equatorial settings without success, until I began to think of the green flash as being akin to giant squid. Yet that evening in the stormy North Atlantic, the sun dropped free of a cloudbank to cast red and orange light over the waters, and dolphins came leaping through the last rays, and when all that was left of the sinking sun was a dot burning exactly on the horizon line, neon green suddenly exploded out from it to encompass the world. Dazzled, I felt that I was beholding the sun for exactly what it is: a colossal thermonuclear phenomenon. And then, just as quickly, it was gone.

Heavy, sodden darkness closed in, and as soon as it did, the question became whether our precious instrument package would still be within radio range when it floated free, and whether we could track it down in the night if that was the case. The seas were growing unpleasant, to say the least. We spent the dark hours hove-to in strong gusts, only too aware that another full gale was supposed to be bearing down on The Gully. If it didn't slam us there, it might catch the boat on its return to Halifax unless we got under way soon.

An assortment of scientists, conservationists, and vagabonds, my shipmates were good-hearted people all. We had worked well together under trying conditions, avoiding the kind of personality conflicts that can debilitate a group forced to live at close quarters, and we had gotten better by the day at our appointed tasks (except cooking). Our common bond was an open-minded enthusiasm for a very esoteric subject. With the prospect of a gale ahead, no one spoke up to say, "How much is this information we're waiting for worth?" But all members of the expedition were starting to ask themselves the question. Perhaps. Maybe it was just me.

During my watch at the helm from 2 to 4 A.M., I could see the lights of great cargo ships passing in the distance. That was a good sign; the atmosphere still offered fair visibility. Sometime during those hours, I heard a *beep*. I awakened Sascha to confirm the signal, and we detected a few more. They weren't strong, and they vanished before long, but that was encouraging in a way. Rather than having popped to the surface and drifted off to parts unknown, the recorder was still close enough to be in radio range, and it had to still be attached to the bottlenose, which was continuing to dive, or the transmitter would have kept broadcasting. More dives, more TDR data.

The average time that suction cups remained attached to whales of all kinds in various studies was around five hours. Robin thought the maximum was something like seventy-two hours on a fin whale. We had no interest in going for a record, because once the gale struck, our chances of homing in on the recorder by its radio signal and picking it up before surface currents carried it away were negligible. We would be too busy merely surviving. Throughout the day, we ran through streaks of fog to find one bottlenose group after another until they added up to more whales than we had encountered on any other day. But while we sailed hopefully toward whichever bunch we had just spied across miles of waves, the signal always came from somewhere else when we finally heard beeps. Concern that the tagged animal's group would eventually move off without our knowing it and cause us to lose track of the recorder nagged at us even as we netted a bounty of details about population structure and social behavior from watching the others.

The worry ebbed when the beeps began coming in more clearly. Waving the directional antennae about, we fixed a general direction and sailed on that compass heading until we noticed a bunch of bottlenoses numbering nine or ten. Closing in, we could see the red instrument package still attached to our target animal. The group replenished its oxygen and commenced another dive, but the weather was still workable, and unless the whales made a strong lateral move while down in the abyss, we could expect to be reasonably close at the time they resurfaced. When was the suction cup going to work loose, though? Before dark? Before the gale? A betting pool was formed with everyone chipping in a loonie (the Canadian one-dollar coin with a loon gracing one side; the two-dollar coin is called a toonie).

In midafternoon, minutes after the last bet was placed, the least frivolous person on the ship once again abruptly bolted for the bow with the radio receiver in hand, wearing the earphones and a goofy grin and lifting her free finger each time she squealed, "Beep! Beep! Beep! Beep!" Sascha kept at this long enough that we realized the radio was sending a continuous signal. The TDR was floating free, and close by. It had been on the whale for twenty-eight hours. On top of all that luck, the captain won the betting pool.

We tracked down the signal. I raced up the port side with a net and scooped the TDR from the ocean. No sooner had the last cheers for the captain faded than we were busy rearranging gear and setting a course straight for Halifax. We passed Sable Island at sunset. No green flash detonated that evening. The final rays were an astonishing crimson that turned the low cloud ceiling and streamers of fog incandescent. This color from the west flared so brightly and transformed the most ordinary objects—birds, waves, the sail—so thoroughly that I stood with my face uplifted and gave a silent, pagan prayer of thanks to the heavenly ball that imparts its fire to all life, and I meant every word.

Upon docking in Halifax, we had traveled sixteen hundred miles under Sascha's command. It was the last of four bottlenose research trips, covering a total of more than six thousand miles that summer. When I visited Hal Whitehead at his office, he said that The Gully's bottlenose population probably produces no more than a dozen or so calves per year. This year, the researchers had seen just one, and calf sightings had been rare the previous year as well. Meanwhile, observations of groups with big males in them had increased. He needed to know whether this meant that production of young was falling off or the female segment of the population was shifting its core area of use to another locale. If for no other reason than to answer that question, the years would bring more adventures out there beyond Sable Island.

Hal viewed the bottlenoses' noteworthy curiosity as a function of having an unusually small range for a large animal, especially since, being nonmigratory, they used the range twelve months of the year. "If you live in a very limited area," he said, "it is to your advantage to check everything out. It pays to know what's going on in your home." Along those lines, he wanted to find out what lay in store for The Gully relative to petroleum development. Because the bottlenoses were restricted to such a limited area and remained year-round, they were obviously the most vulnerable of the many cetaceans concentrated there.

It was a while before the time-depth data could be extracted, double-checked for accuracy, and used to chart the tagged animal's dive profile, so I had no idea of what had come from the most intense part of our trip until I reached Sascha by telephone weeks later. She told me that the bottlenose had made nineteen dives deeper than half a mile, often resting less than twenty minutes on the surface in between. The dives included one of seventy minutes to 4,767 feet and three others nearly as far down. The pressure at that level, beneath the weight of almost a full mile of water, surpassed a ton per square inch. Far exceeding the usual levels reached by the two deepest divers known among air breathers, sperm whales and elephant seals, our suction-cup-wearing male bottlenose had made a strong bid to establish his species as the deepest divers of all—at least until someone sticks some time-depth recorders on other kinds of ziphiids. Either way, being part of an investigation at the stage where information from a single specimen can illuminate so much about a fellow mammal's mode of life was like a green flash that stays with you a good, long while.

As the scientists turned to analyzing the DNA obtained from biopsy darts, they were taken aback by a surprisingly low degree of genetic diversity within The Gully's northern bottlenose population. They couldn't say whether this was the result of some bottleneck blocking interchange between groups under Ice Age conditions or reflected a more recent decline and isolation, possibly related to losses from whaling. But they were determined to gather more samples and find out how vulnerable The Gully's small population might be to the effects of inbreeding.

Not all the publications coming out of the Dalhousie scientists' offices were technical. Before departing Halifax, I read an opinion piece by Hal in the daily newspaper. His subject was the proposed extension of the Sable Offshore Energy Project. Hal raised the issue of disturbed sediments possibly flowing into The Gully and collecting there in the current gyre along with solvents, lubricants, and other drilling wastes. Developing half a dozen new gas fields near the trench would place one of Canada's most dynamic, productive, and fascinating marine ecosystems in harm's way. Mobil Canada's refusal to agree to a proposed exclusionary zone intended to keep petroleum-related ship traffic out of The Gully was equally disappointing.

Over the months that followed, Hal continued laying out the scientific justification for protecting Canada's submerged Grand Canyon and its living resources. Cherry Recchia and her colleagues in the conservation community pursued their public campaign to have The Gully declared a marine sanctuary. *National Geographic* published the article that Flip and I prepared on the bottlenoses there. We'll never know if it helped change anyone's mind, but The Gully did become one of Canada's first official marine protected areas. And Hal Whitehead and his colleagues are still out sailing across that great drowned canyon as the weather permits—and sometimes when it doesn't—gathering information about whales, especially those strange, friendly divers almost nobody else knows who search the bottom a mile below the nearest air.

THE KILLER
ORCA

A lthough fireweed still brightened the late summer shores of Alaska's Prince William Sound, the forests behind were dark and tangled in mist. The sky stayed a cloudy mess, held aloft along its edges by snowy peaks and sagging in the center, pouring its heaviest rain straight into the sea. As residents of the port of Homer, on the Kenai Peninsula farther north, Craig Matkin and his partner, Eva Saulitis, were used to conditions like these. They sat out part of a storm in the cabin of Craig's thirty-four-foot boat, the *Natoa,* in a sheltering bay. When it looked like the deluge wasn't going to let up, they decided they might as well kayak to shore and pick currants. The other thing Eva would do while waiting at anchor was paddle to the base of the nearest waterfall or other cascade coming off the mountainsides, dip a container into the stream's mouth, and drink from it. She liked to savor as many freshets as she could during her coastal travels. It was a North Country version of touring the vineyards of California or France.

Eva had conducted killer whale research for a decade and a half. She was also a teacher, writer, and poet who collected words such as *goosh daiheen,* the Tlingit Indian name for the swirl left behind a killer whale's dorsal fin as it vanishes under the water. Craig, director of the North Gulf Oceanic Society, had been studying the orcas for more than two decades, using his boat for commercial fishing to support himself in between. But expertise isn't always enough. Days had passed since our last close sighting of a killer whale. If you had pulled alongside the *Natoa,* you might have found Eva, Craig, Flip Nicklin, and me gathered over the cabin table staring at a tableau composed of a toy killer whale, stuffed toy puffin, elephant figurine, miniature plastic cat, sprigs of sweet sage, and offerings of Craig and Eva's most valued possession on the boat—squares of imported dark chocolate—arrayed around a flaming candle, which bore the colorful image of Our Lady of Fatima. We figured it couldn't hurt to ask for a little outside help.

The following day, areas of blue showed in the sky, and sun streamed through them to dazzle the water's surface. Large groups of Dall's porpoises swam by. They may be the speediest mammals in the seas. Topping thirty-five miles per hour at times, they surface with an audible zipping sound while raising a rooster tail of spray behind their dorsal fins. The sight of them lifted our hopes, if only because, like killer whales, they come in an elegant pattern of contrasting black and white. Some tourists seeing the five- to seven-foot-long Dall's for the first time think they are baby orcas, especially when the porpoises are buzzing around a pod, as groups of killer whales are traditionally called. Dall's love to do this, for reasons so far known only to the porpoises. Another researcher, Volker Deecke, described Dall's to me as "nature's personal watercraft"—organic versions of hot-rodding Jet Ski boats. Craig kept track of one that actually joined a pod of killer whales for several months as they ranged between Prince William Sound and the Kenai Peninsula. The porpoise even altered the timing of its surfacings to better match the breathing pattern of its huge companions, he said.

Sea otters floating on their backs watched us pass in their bemused and bewhiskered way, like grizzled Alaskan sourdoughs out for their annual bath. Sea lions came by to give us a look as well. Finally, after lowering a hydrophone overboard for the hundredth time in the hope of picking up orca voices, Eva came running into the cabin shouting, "I hear them!" When she turned up the speaker, we all did: high-pitched squeals and typical calls that sounded like a lilting "Eeeeeer" with a whistle at the end. They were very faint; we would have to motor closer to find the whales. But which way? Craig got out his directional receiver: a wok, or Chinese cooking bowl, with sound-baffling neoprene foam pasted to the backside, mounted on a pole. Placing the hydrophone in its center, he plunged the metal wok underwater, rotating it through 360 degrees. The strongest reception came when the apparatus faced north. Craig spun the *Natoa*'s wheel to aim us at a different set of mountains rising from the sun-patched sea.

Found worldwide, killer whales, *Orcinus orca,* are technically dolphins—the brawniest of all of them, brawnier even than many other cetaceans commonly labeled whales. The bulk of what is known about orcas comes from studies of populations on this edge of the Gulf of Alaska and farther south in the Pacific Northwest. These investigations didn't really begin until the early 1970s, when a visionary Canadian named Michael Bigg overcame skeptics to prove that the animals could be individually recognized. Working principally in the Johnstone Strait area between Vancouver Island and mainland British Columbia, Bigg focused on their dorsal fin, as tall as three feet in adult females and six feet—the height of a standing human—in males. The overall size and shape, irregularities such as nicks, tears, or a tilt to one side, plus the pattern of the light-colored saddle patch below the fin's trailing edge, add up to a unique, lifelong marker.

With photo-ID catalogues in hand, a small cadre of researchers was soon charting births, deaths, and social changes in family-based groups—the various pods, which they labeled with a letter or combination of letters. Pod members were then assigned numbers, so that, for example, a new calf that is the forty-fourth animal to be recorded in G pod becomes G44. On a given day, observers could not only pick out G44 but also record the activities of its mother, grandmother, aunts, uncles, cousins, brothers, and sisters as well, because, with some exceptions, a killer whale's entire life is spent in the constant company of its family. Led by the oldest female, the matriarch, the group swims, rests, romps, and feeds together, often cooperating to capture prey. Not even the large males—which may weigh nine or ten tons and reach a length of thirty-three feet to the average female's four or five tons and fifteen to twenty feet—become independent as adults. Long taken for harem bulls, they turn out to be more on the order of what Craig likes to describe as "big momma's boys."

The scientists were on their way to learning that, like humans, orcas may nurse for several years as infants, become sexually mature in their teens, experience menopause in their forties, and reach an age of eighty years or more. A family—or *matriline,* to use the scientists' term—may split if the matriarch dies or the group grows too large, but the new matriline often continues to join the first in its activities. Thus, the typical killer whale pod may consist either of several generations in a single matriline or of closely related matrilines traveling together. Pods with common ancestors are considered a clan, and clans that regularly associate and share the same range form a distinct population, known as a community.

The whales we eventually caught up to that day proved to be the AJ pod. In addition to being the largest group in the Gulf of Alaska region, with nearly forty members, it was often joined in its travels by a subgroup from a different pod, the ABs. We cruised along with the AJs for the next five hours, trying to identify all the different members as they hunted salmon. They acted at ease with the presence of our boat and spent a fair amount of time swimming beneath it, lolling beside it, and dining on salmon sushi just in front of the bow. At one point, I noticed that our course was taking us toward a rainbow. It had an unusual look, more like a thick, low bridge over the water than a typical arch. I had thought the effect of water droplets breaking light into the spectrum of colors depended upon the beholder being at a distance, which was why you could never quite get close enough to find that fabled pot of gold at a rainbow's end. But something different was happening with atmospheric conditions that day.

As the whales' spouts all turned into multihued geysers, they led us straight into one end of the low rainbow bridge.

No gold lay in sight. On the other hand, we found two whales we had somehow missed on earlier passes through the spread-out pod. One was AJ29, an adult female also known as Cloud, born in 1987, and she had a calf at her side. This baby was quite small. The orange color of the oval patch above the calf's eye further identified it as an infant, for this marking turns white in older calves. "We were here two weeks ago, and Cloud didn't have a baby, so it's definitely brand new," Eva said. "This is only the second time in twenty years that we've recorded one being born in summer."

Toward evening, a squall blew in from the south as one of the matrilines within the AJ pod moved into a long, narrow channel called Fleming Passage. These were the AJ8s, named after the matriarch, born in 1953. (Researchers estimate the age of females born before the studies began by the number of offspring they have in the group and the average interval between births plus the time required to reach sexual maturity.) Pink salmon were leaping by the hundreds along the shores on either side. Here and there, coho, or silver, salmon, which the whales most often sought in Prince William Sound, were jumping as well. So were a few sockeye, or red, salmon, also called sliders for the sideways trajectory of their leaps. The rain fell in fine drops that had the effect of calming the channel, turning it into a green ribbon of silk. Its color came from reflections of the looming forest rather than from blooms of plankton. The water itself was exceptionally clear, rendering each whale perfectly visible for the length of its body as the pod proceeded slowly at the surface.

After having stayed dispersed much of the afternoon, the AJ8s now gathered into two subgroups, each so tightly knit that its members' bodies rubbed against one another. Abruptly, the lead subgroup ceased swimming. While a few made partial spy-hops, most of the whales just floated, or logged, on the surface with heads slightly elevated. The second group approached slowly with their heads raised as well, and as they did, the first group turned to face them. The groups met, not so much in two lines as in two halves of a circle, each animal's nose pointing toward the center, each body now a petal in a rosette of whales. If possible, they became even more still than before. Craig and Eva commented that it was common for a pod to bunch up after a long period of dispersed feeding, but to go dead quiet this way was . . . They wondered if the behavior had anything to do with the new baby in their midst.

Then a big male swam ahead with forceful strokes, and the rest of the AJ8s followed in a tight formation, swimming at shallow depths for about 150 feet at a time, then surfacing to breathe as a unit. We were running parallel to them in the *Natoa*, as we had been all along, when the boat suddenly became the center of their attention. For the next half hour, one of us could have reached out at any moment and patted an AJ8. It was as if they were in a contest to see which could come closest to the blue hull without actually touching it, which could spy-hop high enough to look us in the eye at deck level, and which could swim on its back to give us the fullest view of its belly.

I wouldn't suggest that they were intentionally communicating with us rather than merely amusing themselves with an odd plaything throbbing with engine vibrations. They were certainly making calls to each other the whole time. If they had paused to put their heads up together and squeal, "Hello there," I doubt that any of us would have been totally shocked, because it felt like that was what was going on anyway.

When they spread out and began moving faster near dusk, the hydrophone picked up bursts of the high-frequency sounds orcas use for echolocation. These sonar pulses, which sound to us like a rapid series of clicks varying in strength from typewriter tapping to machine-gun fire, are generally a sign of hunting. A moment later, though, the speaker on the boat registered grunts, whoops, and glubs—excited social noises—and the AJ8s boiled to the surface, milling and whapping the water. Eva and Craig quickly tallied more tall male fins than the membership of the AJ8s could account for. They had met another group. By the time Craig identified the newcomers as belonging to the AF pod, the AF and AJ8 males had formed a cluster and were rolling over each other. One was using its head to push another along by the tail. Several had their penises out, flopping around between the water, the air, and the backs of other males.

That's an afternoon with killer whales: a few hours that raise enough questions to last months or years, partial glimpses of a thousand possibilities, notes penciled onto data sheets, and, almost always, a glimmer of magic in between the lines. Still under way after three decades, the investigation of orcas along the Pacific Northwest coast has become one of the great sustained efforts on the frontiers of science. As you pore over the detailed life histories of so many individual animals and the branching kinship charts that link families and clans, you can hardly escape the sense that what has been accomplished is practically an anthropological study of long-mysterious underwater tribes. The comparison seems more apt in light of behavior such as the group circle the AJ8s formed, which had the dimensions of ceremony.

While I was preparing to leave Snug Harbor, on the north end of Washington's San Juan Island, a researcher named Richard Osborne told me about two Puget Sound pods that encountered each other fairly regularly. Sometimes all they did was calmly join up and travel together a while. At other times, they engaged in leaping, lob-tailing, and pec-slapping displays as they assembled. And once in a great while, the members of each pod might line up side by side first to form two straight lines. Then the pods would approach each other gradually on the surface, pausing a few whale-lengths apart. Within a minute or so, they would submerge and then burst to the surface together in milling subgroups. If this was a greeting ceremony, Osborne once saw what looked to be a still more formal, or ritualized, version. The two lines swam slowly toward each other and met, keeping to the surface the whole time, then they drew apart, firmed up their respective lines, and repeated the sequence. Then they did it a third time.

"That," Osborne said, "was when J15 (a five-year-old male) was sick and dying."

For a while, Osborne worked with Ken Balcomb, a former navy man who led the first studies of Puget Sound orcas in the mid-1970s and who has kept the research project going ever since. Ken is the one who liked to use the phrase "woo-woo science" for the tendency to ascribe captivating qualities to whales based on anecdotal observations. At the same time, no one understood better than he how impossible it is to fit some of the things killer whales do into conventional categories. As an example, he mentioned seeing animals traveling along with freshly caught salmon

draped over their pectoral fins or on their heads. The phenomenon, or fad, or whatever it amounted to, was fairly common for
part of one season, but he never saw it again.

When I first met Ken on San Juan Island, Astrid van Ginneken
had arrived to join his team as she does nearly every summer. The
rest of the year, she puts her Ph.D. and M.D. to work developing
computer-based medical information systems in the Netherlands.
One autumn, she went to watch killer whales above the Arctic
Circle off the coast of Norway. There, she found an adult male
and female swimming side by side in the weak November light.
One had a baby draped over its head. Van Ginneken had seen this
activity before as a form of play, with the mother lifting the infant
from below or the baby swimming onto her head as if to hitch
a ride. But there were only two spouts rising from this group of
three. The baby, she realized, was dead.

Next, van Ginneken saw the male rise with its head high
above the water as in a spy-hop. It was carrying the baby on its
pectoral fins, held forward the way we would carry a child in
our arms. A larger group came into view nearby. The male and
female left. As they did, the group formed a straight line and
began swimming forward. Van Ginneken couldn't see the baby
any longer, so when the group changed their pattern from a line
to a ring, she thought they might be readying themselves to hunt
herring. Orcas in Norwegian waters often go about corralling the
fish within a moving circle of whale bodies while individuals take
turns lashing the balled-up school with their flukes, a cooperative
technique called carousel feeding. Yet the whales were staying in
place, and van Ginneken saw that they had arranged themselves
with their heads partly raised and facing inward toward the center of the ring. There in the middle floated the baby's corpse. Time

and again, the whales broke off, reformed their line at a distance, approached the infant, and spread out to face it in a circle. A storm gathered, sucking what little brightness remained from the sky. As van Ginneken's boat left for shore, the ceremony was still being repeated.

At the time that Michael Bigg was pioneering identification techniques, the prevailing view of killer whales was basically the same as for every top predator—and most native peoples—that Western culture had encountered in the past thousand years. They were held to be savage brutes. A 1973 U.S. Navy diving manual flatly stated that killer whales "will attack human beings at every opportunity." Where this piece of military intelligence came from is hard to fathom, for the only documented assault on humans in the wild—ever—is the case of an orca that once grabbed a surfer and just as quickly let him go. To declare that "humans will attack killer whales at every opportunity" would have been closer to the truth. Japan and Russia were hunting them for meat at the time. Norway had a bounty on orcas because they competed with the fishing industry for herring. North American commercial fishermen had been shooting at orcas for decades. Sportfishing interests even talked the Canadian government into mounting a machine gun at the narrow head of Johnstone Strait to strafe the killer whales that frequent this passage.

The machine gun's trigger was never pulled. However, from the 1960s through the mid-1970s, the orca populations of Johnstone Strait and Puget Sound were seriously depleted by commercial live-capture operations as scores of orcas were rounded up with nets and transported to theme parks and aquariums for display. (About a quarter of them carried new and old gunshot wounds.) To counter objections from the growing environmental and antiwhaling movements of the time, the business interests claimed that, since people saw tall black dorsal fins in just about every part of the region, it had to be loaded with killer whales, perhaps as many as three thousand. After Michael Bigg and his coworkers completed their first surveys, they came up with a total closer to three hundred; those telltale fins surfacing all over belonged to the same few pods roaming a hundred miles a day or more.

Whether or not you can personally countenance the idea of imprisoning killer whales, those performing in captivity did give the general public its first look at beautiful, agile, inquisitive social mammals that face no natural enemies at sea. Careening around pools, they seemed to have the strength of tides and yet were as attentive as sheep dogs to commands made with the wave of a trainer's arm. Bright and responsive, they could fine-tune their motions delicately enough to rise and take a single small fish from the fingers of a person leaning over their tank and then, after a turn toward the bottom, explode high into the air like some plump, panda-patterned missile fired from a submarine. They were, in sum, magnificent. And their public image quickly began changing: they went from shadowy bite-you's lurking in the depths to one of the most popular icons of the ocean realm.

The animals' common name likely came from mariners who saw pods attacking great whales. Descriptions of whale killers or killers of whales got modified into *killer whales*. Admirers started casting around for a less judgmental name; most animals take lives in order to eat, after all, yet we don't call sandpipers killer shorebirds or lions killer felines. The term *orca* came into fashion, borrowed from the species's Latin label, *Orcinus orca*. As long as you don't know that this translates as "whale from the underworld of the dead," it counts as an upgrade.

The lives of the killer whales that reside in Johnstone Strait and Puget Sound from summer through fall have been chronicled more closely and for a longer time than those of other populations or, for that matter, of any other whales in the world. Each year, though, as winter's cold comes on, the animals depart the region. And none of the experts can yet report where these animals go, except for rare sightings off Oregon and California, or what they do for fully half the year.

The Kwakwaka'wakw (formerly called Kwakiutl) people native to the Pacific Northwest have said the whales swim far out to sea until they reach the shores of an island. There, they assume human form and walk up onto the beach, donning wonderful robes. They also put on hats with prominent crests. Like the dorsal fins they carry when in animal form, the height of the headdress signifies their age and social position. On this island, the whales/people/spirits pass the winter in a great lodge, perhaps holding council, exchanging information, and performing ceremonies. Then, when the weather begins to warm, they walk back out of the lodge and down onto the beach, casting off their apparel. Resuming killer whale form, they return toward the Pacific Northwest. When they arrive, they are welcomed with joy, for they bring the abundance of the sea with them: the little fish, the silver shoals of herring, and above all the salmon.

Tom Sewitt, a Kwakwaka'wakw from a village near northern Vancouver Island, British Columbia, explained this, partly in time-honored song. He told me he shares the traditional belief that, when he dies, his spirit will enter a baby killer whale, and he will finally get to see what the world looks like under the rich waters he has fished in and traveled upon all his life. Like many First Nations people (as Native Americans are called in Canada), Sewitt finds it normal to view populations of orcas as other tribes; they just happen to be tribes with extraordinary powers. This seems to me as accurate a view of the species as any I have heard.

Years ago, when he was a graduate student in anthropology, Richard Osborne proposed an analysis of killer whale society around the San Juan Islands for his doctoral thesis. He wanted to delve into kinship patterns, cultural traditions, and the transmission of learned knowledge, all from the perspective of his chosen field. You don't have to be a Kwakwaka'wakw to appreciate the parallels between orca and human social organization. The anthropology department nevertheless turned Osborne down. He had to pick another project. Yet after graduating with his advanced degree in anthropology, he went off to study killer whales and today is the research director of the Whale Museum in Friday Harbor on San Juan Island. Meanwhile the exploration of culture in social animals has become an exciting academic trend, one increasingly valued not only for illuminating the workings of nature but also for the perspective it brings to the study of human nature—that is, to anthropology.

Humans think they are special creatures, and we are. But trying to hoard certain valued qualities for *Homo sapiens* just by defining them as exclusively human is becoming a lost cause. It's bad science because it's driven by dogma, and it holds us back from learning exactly what it is that does make us unique. It can't be culture, language abilities, complex emotions, abstract thought, foresight, moral judgment, or a sense of self, because all those traits appear to have been demonstrated by at least one other species. And it can't be the vaunted size of our brains. Neanderthal brains were bigger than those of modern humans. Those of killer whales are four times the weight of ours.

"They have the biggest brains on Earth," Osborne told me. "Blue whales have really large brains as well, but the brains of some male killer whales are larger." As in humans, the cerebral cortex, held to be the seat of advanced mental activity, constitutes a major portion of the killer whale's brain. And just as with humans, the overlying neocortex is highly convoluted. This is a way of increasing the total surface area of the organ without having to expand the heavy skull, like building more powerful computing abilities into a laptop machine while keeping it easily portable.

A commonly held opinion is that the best gauge of intelligence is not absolute brain size but the brain-size-to-body-weight ratio. Of course, we're fond of this standard because it puts *Homo sapiens* back on top. Interestingly, the next four species in rank are dolphins, killer whales being one of them, followed by great apes. Killer whales also beat out our ancestor *Australopithecus.* I wonder: if an enclave of australopithecines were found surviving in some forgotten corner of the world and Richard Osborne asked to study them, how would the anthropology department respond, having turned down a study of orcas that are clearly brighter, according to the brain-size-to-body-weight ratio?

When odontocetes sleep, they do so with only half their brain at a time. The other half remains alert to make sure the whale continues surfacing to breathe and perhaps to detect danger. Still, scientists were surprised when studies of captive killer whales and other dolphins published in 2005 reported that mothers and newborns remain completely awake and active for nearly a month after birth, apparently without any negative effects on their abilities. Maybe this pattern will be uncovered in additional cetaceans, but for now it is unknown among any other mammals, and it brings into question our understanding of the role of sleep in brain development and learning—in fact, of the whole nature of brain function. Can the orcas do it because they have brainpower to spare?

Along with the high-frequency sonar pulses that killer whales produce to orient themselves and locate prey, each population has a characteristic number of distinct calls that members rely on to make contact and convey information over long distances. During the 1970s, John Ford, a researcher who is now chief marine mammal scientist for the Pacific Station of Canada's Department of Fisheries and Oceans, realized that every pod has its own version of the plaintive calls, which vary in pitch, pattern, and the number typically used. He labeled this their dialect. On the basis of still more refined analyses since then, it appears that each separate matriline has one.

We can tell a lot by the patterns and tenor of another person's speech. Yet being such a visual species, we have trouble truly grasping how much of the orcas' social context is acoustic. We are what others' eyes see us to be. Killer whales are much more what they are heard to be. The dialect is their badge of identity. Youngsters learn the appropriate style of calls from their mothers and older siblings. They also learn to recognize the dialects of other pods. Since killer whales want to fraternize with their nearest kin but must pick mates from among the most distantly related pods within the community in order to avoid inbreeding, they need an easy way to tell which is which in the often dim waters they ply. The calls do the job, for the more similar one pod's dialect is to that of another, the closer the bloodlines.

As it turns out, a killer whale can do more than recognize other dialects. One morning in early June, I found Candice Emmons, an acoustic specialist working with Ken Balcomb, wearing an odd expression as she listened to orca voices recorded the night before. They were from the local J pod, recently returned to Puget Sound from their winter travels. Their frequent warm-season companions, the K and L pods, had not yet arrived. They were getting close, though. People had reported seeing killer whales in the Strait of Juan de Fuca, which leads from the open Pacific into Puget Sound. J pod would almost surely have heard them. "It's the Js' regular call," Emmons said, "but it's like they're trying to make an L call or calling with an L-pod accent." Were the Js offering greetings or an invitation? Expressing anticipation? Maybe the inflection was a way of giving voice to memories welling up. An animal being studied in a display tank years ago suddenly switched from its characteristic calls, which it had been making over and over, to the dialect of a neighboring matriline back in its home range. Then it proceeded to imitate the dialects of the other matrilines there, running through a series of them as if desperate to make contact in its isolation.

One of the people studying the capabilities of captive orcas was a psychologist, Paul Spong. Unable to bear watching beings so intelligent live out their days in confinement any longer, he decided that he needed to be with free-roaming pods. Moving to the Johnstone Strait area, he won a reputation for going out alone in a kayak to float among the killer whales. That people considered this unbelievably risky was a measure of the legacy of fear and misunderstanding still lingering around the animals. It was only a matter of time, many muttered, before one of the whales smashed Spong's little boat to pieces along with his romantic illusions. The Kwakwaka'wakw must have found this amusing, their ancestors having canoed among orcas for countless generations. Still, every day that Spong interacted with the animals or just hung out nearby sped up the revision of public opinion about them.

We now know that killer whales are remarkably unaggressive toward their own kind too. Nobody has ever seen behavior that could be interpreted as fighting within families. If there are rivalries over status or breeding privileges between the different matrilines within a community, no one has reported those either, and different communities largely ignore each other when their travels overlap. That such powerful, predatory mammals have found ways to live together in seeming harmony never ceases to amaze us scrappy primates keeping watch.

Of all the facts learned about killer whales over the years, perhaps the most startling is that there is not a single type out there but several. At least three coexist in the North Pacific. They may be different subspecies, and possibly different species, and the same holds for an array of other types ranging through other seas.

During the days of commercial roundups, a pod of five orcas was caught near Victoria, British Columbia, at the southern end of Vancouver Island. Two were sent off for display. The other three were kept in a net pen at Pedder Bay, where keepers threw them fish every day. None of the whales would eat any, not after a week, a month, or even seventy-five days, when one died of starvation. Four days later, the last two survivors finally started to accept fish as food, and they continued to do so through several more months of captivity before someone sank part of the net barrier to free them, and they escaped back into the wild.

People had seen killer whales dining on fish throughout the region for generations. They also saw killer whales attack an assortment of animals, from little harbor porpoises to great whales. Because our mental image was of instinct-driven predators huge and strong enough to kill and eat whatever they came upon, we just assumed that this is what they were doing. As ever, the truth is more fascinating.

The most familiar pods along the coast, the residents, generally live in groups of ten to forty and follow regular travel patterns within a seasonal range. They make calls about half the time they are submerged and broadcast sonar bursts freely to pick out food. At the surface, they are noisy and conspicuous, often floating like logs in plain view while resting, when not making another big splash on the social scene. Their diet is salmon and more salmon, with the occasional lingcod, halibut, or other flavor of fish thrown in.

Mike Bigg and other early observers had noticed small gangs of two to six killer whales that moved more randomly and across a far greater area than residents usually did. Though they even looked a little different, it was the 1980s before scientists realized that these were killer whales whose meals were exclusively warm blooded: seals, sea lions, sea otters, dolphins, porpoises, and whales. They swallow a few seabirds—targeted mostly to teach young whales to develop hunting skills—and sometimes help themselves to a swimming moose or deer. But fish? No way, as the captives in Pedder Bay demonstrated for seventy-eight days in a row while the keepers scratched their heads. These different orcas also make longer dives than residents do, probe more closely along shorelines, and call less than 5 percent of the time. To orient themselves, they send out sonar clicks in brief patterns that blend in with noises like stones knocking together in the surf. Otherwise, they run silent, listening—stalking. Researchers continued to label resident pods alphabetically but reserved the letter T for these smaller, less predictable groups. *T* stands for *transients,* the hunters of mammals.

Compared with residents, transients have stouter jaws, possibly to deal with bigger, tougher prey, whose defensive abilities might also explain transients' more tattered-looking dorsal fins. The fins are also slightly more upright and sharper-tipped, and the saddle patch of transients sits farther forward than that of residents. Nor do the two types share any of the calls in their repertoires.

As in resident pods, transient males remain at their mothers' sides past maturity. However, Craig Matkin and other researchers are finding that some strike out on their own beginning around age twenty, and other family members may split off to travel apart or with another transient group for a while. There are only about 250 transient killer whales known along the Pacific coast of North America from California to Glacier Bay, Alaska. With minor exceptions, they are considered a single, wide-ranging population. A different, genetically distinct, less numerous transient population ranges across the Gulf of Alaska as far west as Kodiak Island. Then there are the transients of the eastern Aleutian Islands, whose range extends into the Bering Sea. Although genetic analysis of this group is not yet complete, Matkin feels that they, too, are a distinct population, since they don't associate with other groups or share the particular pattern of calls they make. Resident, or fish-eating, killer whales along the continent's Pacific coast are somewhat more common, numbering closer to a thousand, and that total is comprised of four largely separate populations. They use different traditional ranges and don't mix socially with each other, much less with transients. After analyzing the DNA in skin samples, Lance Barrett-Lennard of the Vancouver Aquarium Marine Science Centre concluded that residents and transients have probably not interbred for at least ten thousand years.

From time to time, as many as 60 killer whales traveling together appear near the continent's Pacific coast. The animals are smaller than either residents or transients, their dorsal fins are more often ripped and nicked, and they seldom stick around long. By the 1990s, observers finally had enough photographs and sound recordings to convince themselves that they were dealing with a third major type of killer whale. The researchers labeled them *offshores,* on the theory that they spend most of their time well out at sea. They appear to range even more widely than transients, for a few of the same individuals sighted as far south as California have also been observed in the Gulf of Alaska or the Bering Sea. Little else is known about their lifestyle, but since they are highly vocal compared to stealthy hunting transients, the offshores probably don't dine on mammals. Whatever they do eat seems to wear down their teeth. Guesses include sharks, which have sandpaper-tough skin.

Pods in the tropics have been documented killing shark species up to and including great whites. Some orcas around New Zealand seem to specialize in entering very shallow bays to nose skates and rays up out of the bottom sediments. The suite of killer whale types in antarctic waters somewhat parallels that in North America's Pacific Northwest, for there are small groups that specialize in hunting mammals and then fish-eaters that number as many as 200 in a pod. These fish-eaters have a unique cape of dark gray on their backs and smaller eye patches slanted at a different angle, and they are three to five feet shorter than most killer whales. Russian scientists have proposed declaring them a separate species, *Orcinus glacialis*. However, recent observers have discovered more than one type: the first works the outer edges of the ice pack well offshore, and the other, which looks different, hunts Antarctic toothfish (sold as Chilean sea bass) in leads inside the ice pack.

The North Atlantic supports both mammal-hunting killer whales and fish-eaters, but some members of one particular fish-eating pod near Norway have been seen chasing seals. (And just recently, Balcomb and others have found some individuals within one of Puget Sound's resident pods starting to hunt and kill harbor porpoises.) Since such residents don't generally eat their mammal victims, it is hard to interpret whether such hunting behavior represents unusually rambunctious play, practice, or something more akin to hooliganism on the part of a few juveniles or subadults. Fish-eating orcas held captive at Marineland, a display in Niagara Falls, Canada, were known to occasionally nab one of the gulls that visited the outdoor tank. Then in 2001, a young male orca learned a new trick on its own. The animal would partially chew a fish and spit the remains out onto the water's surface. When a gull was attracted to the floating bits of meat, the whale, waiting quietly now within lunging distance, struck. Within three months, the gull-hunter's younger half brother had taken up this bait-and-lunge technique, which later spread to two adult female orcas sharing the tank. On the shores of Patagonia at Argentina's southern tip, male killer whales purposefully beach themselves to grab the young of southern sea lions and southern elephant seals at rookeries. Among the subantarctic Crozet Islands, females also beach themselves to take southern elephant seal pups. However, it appears that the orcas around the Crozet

Islands turn to hunting fish once the seals leave. Elsewhere, various killer whales have been found eating tuna, squid, sea turtles, and penguins.

On a rare calm afternoon of fine weather in Prince William Sound, a group of about twenty killer whales known as the AE pod came swimming through Knight Island Passage. Tour boat operators had taken to calling this the circus pod. With the days of fishermen shooting at them becoming a memory of decades past, the AEs had grown notably friendly around vessels and seemed especially given to leaping and other surface displays. They were all business at the moment, chasing coho. Eva Saulitis and Craig Matkin were following along as usual, trying to get close enough to photo-ID all the pod's members and make general observations. But the AEs kept spreading out in subgroups across the channel, which was miles wide. Craig cut the engine and drifted in the center while he and Eva discussed what to do next. Flip Nicklin and I continued to search the horizon.

Fork-tailed shearwaters swooped and arced past the ship, and a pair of long-tailed jaegers, which sometimes pirate fish from other seabirds, settled down onto the water. That was about all we saw moving nearby, until two dorsal fins started cutting closer from the west. It was a mother and calf. They were soon near enough to identify as AE11, born in 1970, and AE 23, born in 2000 and now a dozen feet long and approaching the time when it would be weaned. Nearer still was a solitary salmon. Plainly visible just below the surface, the coho had kept ahead of the whales until it saw the *Natoa* and dashed toward the boat's side. The smooth hull made a poor refuge, but it was the only break out here in deep, open water. In no time, we had two killer whales chasing the coho round and around the boat while we lurched fore and aft and from port to starboard, trying to keep track.

After the pursuit had gone on for several minutes, it became evident that the mother was making broader circles than her youngster and diving deeper when the fish headed downward. She wasn't trying very hard to catch this quarry. Rather, she appeared to be herding it, keeping the salmon within her orbit, while the big calf tried to close in on the fish. The nearer the calf got, the more enthusiastic it seemed to become about the whole endeavor, and the chase kept speeding up. But the fish would juke, and the calf would overshoot and have to reverse course. Then it would speed up again and draw five, four, three feet behind . . . While the mother guarded the escape routes and the salmon zigged and zagged, the calf twisted and spun through submarine somersaults. And we kept on scrambling about the deck, cheering now, mostly for the young whale, but with growing respect for this badly vexed fish stuck in the middle of the channel with two killer whales and one boat hull. In the end, it was borne off in the calf's jaws.

Craig and Eva followed and collected a leftover fish scale, a standard practice to confirm the type of prey taken. Some minutes later, the two whales were back, pursuing another salmon around the boat. They may have driven the fish in our direction. In any case, the mother caught it. Roughly an hour after that, the pair came chasing a third coho around the *Natoa*. Mom grabbed that one too. Yet as the whales were swimming away side by side, she passed it to her offspring. Then the calf gave it back. This calf didn't need the fish, not quite yet. What it needed was to become more skilled at hunting. Along with rich milk, the mother was providing lessons and opportunities for practice.

Ingrid Visser is a biologist who regularly jumps in the water with the groups of killer whales she follows around New Zealand. She told me that the young seem reluctant to enter the shallow bays where pods go in search of the skates and rays they favor, and she felt that juveniles had to learn this behavior at the urging of older animals. She has had older orcas swim over, bearing rays in their mouths to show her, much as they would display food to encourage young in their pod. The killer whales that beach themselves to hunt marine mammals in Patagonia and the Crozet Islands learn to overcome a natural fear of stranding and perform this risky behavior by imitating older, more experienced animals. Mothers in the Crozet area have been seen apparently practicing with their offspring on nearby beaches where no prey is present, nudging the young whales ashore and helping to dislodge them afterward.

Visser observed New Zealand pods that had figured out an easy way to catch sharks: simply bite them off the ends of hooks dangling from commercial fishermen's longlines, which stretch for thousands of yards across the ocean. She thinks the juveniles learn this hunting technique too by watching their elders. It doesn't seem to be a difficult trick to get the hang of. As the burgeoning market for black cod, or sablefish, sent more long-liners out in Alaskan waters, more killer whales in Prince William Sound and the Bering Sea began filching the catch off hooks. Even gigantic male sperm whales have taken to nabbing sablefish from longlines off Sitka, Alaska. Curiosity being the key to improving ways of getting at a resource, it's probably a good thing killer whales don't favor lobster as well. Visser knows of several New Zealand lobster divers who were poking in crannies on the bottom when they felt a nudge and turned to find a huge black-and-white creature looking on as if to say, "Whatcha got there, little fella?"

We're still learning what killer whales are. Clearly, there is not *a* killer whale but an assortment of ways to be a killer whale. This is a highly successful, dominant life-form that has developed a variety of lifestyles and techniques, adapting to a broad range of niches and exploiting the resources in them. Each killer whale is what it is born to be, as well as what it learns to be during a long lifetime. It is the sum of its physical traits and of what it knows, and the two categories continually influence one another.

As a group of orcas colonizes a new region, the most readily available prey may be something other than what they previously targeted. This could have been what happened when groups first began to specialize in hunting superabundant salmon populations near spawning rivers in the Pacific Northwest, for instance. As predation habits change, so does the information passed from one generation to the next, and this further reinforces trends of behavior. We can't say to what extent transients refusing to eat fish is a trait that has become hardwired into their brains over time or is a very strong cultural tradition, something like a taboo. Meanwhile, natural selection favors changes both in body characteristics and in social organization that make the animals more effective at catching their primary targets. The result is different cultures—populations of killer whales that no longer look the same, act the same, or even speak the same language.

I'm using words like *language, talk,* and *vocabulary* in the broadest sense here. To imply that orcas are actually carrying on elaborate conversations that we simply don't know yet how to decipher might be misleading. Linguists, code breakers, and mathematicians have developed some very potent methods for analyzing speech, and none indicate that the call repertoire of killer whales generates enough information to truly qualify.

Communication? Absolutely. Call and countercall? Yes, so it would appear. Actual dialogue? Not the way we think about it. That doesn't rule out the possibility that new revelations will change our opinion one day.

The waters of Johnstone Strait are full of killer whale voices most days from summer through fall. If you like, you can even tune in to local radio ORCA-FM, sponsored by the Vancouver Aquarium. The station plays nothing but wild killer whale voices picked up live by hydrophones in Robson Bight, where pods come almost daily to rub on the pebbly shallows. (Some experts think the whales do this to remove itchy skin and parasites, while others say the behavior may have started for the purpose of hygiene but developed into an excuse for regular gathering and socializing.)

Paul Spong and his wife, Helena Symonds, who live at OrcaLab, a research station they operate on Hanson Island, have hydrophones of their own at strategic points along channels where the pods travel. The whales' voices can be heard live on the OrcaLab website (www.orca-live.net). They also play through speakers inside the living quarters of the Spongs and a small tribe of assistants and visiting researchers. Even if killer whales pass by in the dead of night, people in the household are so attuned to the lilting calls that they wake up from a sound sleep and start shuffling toward the laboratory, where elaborate sound equipment and computer screens are activated to identify the matrilines making the calls and analyze the particular sequence the whales have chosen to use.

Building on the acoustic work of the Spongs, John Ford, and others, Volker Deecke began comparing the vocalizations of residents and transients while a doctoral candidate at Scotland's

University of St. Andrews. When he played recordings of resident killer whale pods to the harbor seals common in the Johnstone Strait area, they paid little attention. Calls of unfamiliar fish-eaters from an Alaskan population caused an avoidance reaction, and the calls of transients provoked immediate flight.

This means that, where the eternal race for advantage between predator and prey takes place among marine mammals, both sides are arming themselves through their learning abilities as well as with physical skills. It isn't sufficient to learn something once and then retain it, either. The Spongs, Ford, and Deecke jointly analyzed two types of resident calls recorded over a period of a dozen years and found one of the calls gradually changing, like the song of the humpback whales does. Other matrilines in the population had to learn the new variation, and so did other marine mammals in order to save themselves from reacting to a call they didn't recognize.

As I boated by a busy sea lion colony in Prince William Sound with Craig and Eva, Craig mentioned that a group of transients that favored the area, the AT1s, ignored sea lions and focused on harbor seals, harbor porpoises, and Dall's porpoises. The sea lions seemed to know this. He and Eva would see them immediately flee from other transient pods but linger in the water when the AT1s cruised through. The sea lions even went so far as to nip whales in resident pods. Like Dall's porpoises, Pacific white-sided dolphins often swim and hunt with resident killer whales. Several times, I noticed that they, too, nip residents, perhaps from a sense of competition for fish but also because these dolphins are bold, aggressive, and playful—and they know they can get away with it. Yet in the presence of transients, some have been known to hurl themselves up onto beach rocks in a suicidal effort to escape. A minke whale did the same near Johnstone Strait in 2004, but I have watched minkes swimming almost side by side with resident orca pods as both species chased fish concentrated in a turbulent meeting of tidal currents. From examples like these, it becomes easier to picture how natural selection pressures can lead not only to keener senses and stronger muscles but also to improved learning and communication abilities—more smarts, and for more than one species at a time.

When I first went out on the water with Volker Deecke, we were beating through chop in a light aluminum boat, catching air at times, while gas leaked out of a bouncing metal jerry can at my feet and spread across the deck. I pointed out to Volker that we were starting to resemble a floating bomb complete with metal-on-metal sparking devices. He stopped long enough to cover the crack in the can with a few layers of duct tape so that the leak slowed a bit, swabbed up some of the gas with a rag, and then gunned the boat on out into the heart of a channel toward the northern end of Johnstone Strait. That was my first clue. Volker, the son of Austrian physicians who were also musicians, developed a keen ear at an early age; mastered English, Spanish, Latin, and Russian in addition to his native German; went on to become absorbed by the theoretical aspects of animal communication; and never, ever slowed down. Tall, fit, and buzz cut, as if to reduce the wind resistance caused by hair, he even walked fast. I was heading out into the big blue unknown with a guy nicknamed Moby Deecke.

Rhinoceros auklets were diving for herring in rip currents at the entrance to a side channel as we approached. A series of islets lay beyond, and the water in the lee was like cellophane. Six fins jutted from it. Sharp, upright fins. The tallest had a notch near the top. Flipping through a photo catalogue, Volker identified this male as T142. It and two companions must be the T143 family, he said, and the others looked like T18s.

These transients were moving in typical stealthy style, cruising near the rocks and poking into crannies, surfacing only briefly in between. All at once, by Duncan Island, they boiled into plain view, breaching, rolling over each other like thick braids of rope, whapping flippers on the water, and generally frolicking like a resident pod. The time was 2:45 P.M. "Transients don't usually socialize like this except after a kill," Volker muttered. "How the heck did we manage to miss it?"

Later, we rendezvoused out in midchannel with Graeme Ellis, a Canadian orca expert who started working with Mike Bigg in the 1970s. By one means or another, in borrowed boats and with gas money out of his own pocket at times, he had kept following orcas ever since. Now employed alongside John Ford at the federal Department of Fisheries and Oceans, Ellis was the man to whom everyone on the Pacific Coast sent their identification photographs so that he could piece together the full summary of annual changes in the various populations. We tied our boats together and shared a snack while we drifted. Ellis by now possessed the most experienced eyes in the orca-sighting business, and, unlike us, he had witnessed a kill that day. Some whales in the T59 group had nailed a Dall's porpoise, he said.

"Where?"

"About seventeen miles south of where your group was cavorting."

"When?"

Ellis checked his notebook: "Looks like two forty-five."

The meaning hit like a breaking wave. As Ellis's group made its kill, their calls, traveling five times faster in water than in air, were funneled along submarine canyons and picked up by the animals Volker was watching, apparently stimulating them to start festivities of their own. Discovering that such excitement can be contagious for transient killer whales over long distances put Volker, the sound specialist, in a mood to frolic too. Throwing his arms wide, he proclaimed to passing gulls, "Behold the power of acoustics."

Volker and his various mentors thought that it was important to find out not just what killer whales were saying but where they were saying it. Both residents and transients seemed to know and make use of natural sound corridors when they sent out contact calls. If residents were coming through a side channel toward the main passage of Johnstone Strait, you could almost count on them to issue some sort of "We're here; who else is around?" message once they hit the intersection. The transients might call there as well—if they weren't hunting. As for the types of calls and social sounds meant mainly for communication within the pod, residents tended to make them as they went along. Transients, Volker reasoned, would reserve such talk for after a hunt or else for when they entered a bay or cove whose contours would block the voices from alerting prey. His task was to get recordings of their sounds—and absence of sounds—in order to prove this theory.

Although a resident population will have thirty to fifty different calls, the average resident matriline uses only about a dozen. Transient matrilines have still fewer. I asked Volker how much they could really be communicating when they did pause to "talk." He wouldn't hazard a guess, but he offered a perspective: "Even if you just hear me say hello on the telephone," he began, "that one word can let you know all kinds of things: I'm male. I'm adult. I'm in a good mood, or bad mood. I'm not fully caffeinated. I'm hopeful, or despondent, glad to hear from you, not so glad . . . " And all the while, Volker was mentally mapping out the underwater area in terms of acoustic habitats, thinking more and more like an orca.

A year later, Volker, Flip, and I reassembled in southeastern Alaska. We had a good-size recreational fishing boat as our mother ship, from which Volker could launch a speedier inflatable skiff to catch up with transients and drop a hydrophone down near them. Day after day, wearing the same grease-stained, red flotation jacket, salt-stained black windbreaker pants, and muck-stained leather boots that he claimed were waterproof and better than rubber but were plainly and aromatically rotting on his feet, Volker sped up and down Stephens Passage and the long fjords on one side known as Tracy Arm and Endicott Arm. Both funneled cold rainstorms onto our open skiff more often than not. But Volker remained steadfastly hatless, hunched over the outboard's throttle, buzz-cut head lowered into the wind, while I used an oar to try to push aside some of the larger ice floes broken off from the tidewater glaciers.

Mother seals gather each year by the hundreds on the floes packed toward the heads of these fjords. They are relatively safe on the ice, and perhaps a bit safer than usual in the water between them as well, Volker thought, because the air bubbles trapped within the floes create an acoustic screen as they dissolve. He put a hydrophone overboard, and all I could hear was a loud hiss of white noise. He had a point: transient sonar wouldn't be of much service in an environment like that.

But the transients would come scouting. Judging from their movements, they kept a detailed mental map of all the haul-out, or resting, spots of seal and sea lion colonies up and down the coast, including rookeries. By midsummer, some of the mothers were starting to leave the floes for more open waters with their newly weaned, months-old pups. Big-eyed, cuddly creatures with fur like plush felt from our point of view, they would be pudgy, inexperienced, snack-size morsels to transients navigating up the fjords.

There are tens of thousands of seals spread along thousands of miles of inlets and islets on the coast of southeastern Alaska and only a couple of hundred transient killer whales. We cruised and scanned without success. This was a needle-in-a-haystack venture. But it is hard to feel that fortune has abandoned you in a landscape where mileswide glaciers calve bergs big as city blocks into the sea while white arctic terns fly across the crumbling ice faces, white mountain goats clamber along the fjords' dark, ice-scarred walls, and big brown bears track the mudflats. We motored along in a vast salty moat filled with floating sculptures. Ice so dense it shone blue as lazuli gemstones melted before our eyes into wizards' castles, swan wings, ghost ships, polar bears, pale mushrooms, crescent moons, and ten thousand other shapes. One of them, spread mostly below the surface, knocked a fin off the engine as Volker sought to get up speed in what had looked like an open stretch.

We made it back but managed to puncture the inflatable at the end of another day's outing. Roaming the deck of the mother ship while we waited for our attempt at a patch on the skiff's rubber prow to dry, Volker was doing what scientists do in their slack time: ponder. "To appreciate other people's cultures," he said, "you have to shed your prejudices—strip yourself down to where you are just human and then build up your understanding. With killer whales, I feel we are moving one step beyond. You must strip all the way down to just being a mammal, then start from scratch trying to understand how whales perceive and interpret their world. Imagine 'clicking' [focusing a sonar beam] on another member of your society."

We could see barely six feet into the water, milky with freshly ground glacial debris. Yet with sonar pulses, a killer whale can monitor family members hundreds of yards away. At closer quarters, one animal might be able to tell whether another's stomach is full and if it is pregnant. Movements of blood in the other's body could indicate its level of excitement or exertion, while its overall condition could be gauged by the thickness of blubber. Think full-body sonogram. The whales may also pick up information passively, merely by listening for heartbeats and stomach rumbles from companions. They'll pick up dolphins' and porpoises' clicking and calling, too, along with the underwater barks and grunts made by seals and sea lions. Even when the prey species aren't vocalizing, the whales can detect distant splashes and breathing noises. And then there are what Volker spoke of as acoustic shadows. These are the patches of silence caused when something blocks the ever present background noises of the sea caused by lapping waves, surf, cobblestones rolling in currents, fish grunts, the scuttling of crabs and snapping of shrimp, and so on. Although we scarcely pay attention to these sounds, marine mammals may not only detect their absence but also be able to judge the dimensions of whatever is causing it.

One of the major problems plaguing a number of great whales is entanglement in nets and other fishing gear. This is less of an issue for orcas, due to their agility and echolocation skills. The same holds for ship strikes, another problem for some of the great whales. But the killer whales' echolocation abilities and their societies' reliance on relatively elaborate vocalizations may place them much more at risk from the rising levels of boat engine noises filling submarine habitats. Finally, every odontocete in the oceans, and possibly all the other cetaceans as well, may be affected by new technology called LFA (low frequency active) sonar currently being tested by the U.S. Navy. It can blanket an undersea area with a new superloud pulse to detect submarines. The energy emitted from this is so powerful that researchers have found whales and dolphins beached on shores near testing sites with their brains and inner ears leaking blood. The likelihood that these high-intensity sonic blasts could leave many more alive but with permanently damaged hearing is an equally serious concern. With other nations developing this same sonar technology on their own, we could end up deafening marine life around the globe because we humans can't figure out how to get along with one another.

Toward midmorning another day, half a dozen orcas glided past on their way out of Endicott Arm toward the point called Wood Spit. Tight pack formation, spear-tip fins; here we go. With the tear in the skiff having proved unpatchable, we took off in the fishing boat to try and keep up. As a male approached the shallows, he lifted his head out of the water for a better view. A seal on a boulder surrounded by waves did the opposite, laying its head flat against the stone and holding very still. Any seals left in the water had likely squeezed into hiding spots among rocks and kelp beds that I had come to know while kayaking over them in the evenings, watching seabirds dive after schools of fish fry. The transients rounded the point and surged on toward Stephens

Passage. After their next dive, only the biggest male reappeared, still moving away. The minutes stretched on. We were glassing the horizon for the others when they surfaced almost on the beach. Having made what looked like a feint toward open water, the whales had executed a right-angle turn in the depths and swum a quarter mile back to Wood Spit while submerged.

"They're milling!" Volker cried, dunking his hydrophone. "I've got calls. And little squeals and mews." Social noises, more signs of a probable kill. Craig Matkin and others had described transients becoming boat-friendly after a kill, swimming close as if to display a trophy while rollicking around. But this group moved off within minutes. All that was left when we pulled into the site was an oily sheen on the surface and gulls squabbling over shreds of blubber and meat. The lack of drama was a tribute to the predators' efficiency—plus the fact that adult killer whales outweigh the average 170-pound harbor seal at least 50 to 1. If transients are the proverbial wolves of the sea, this was a pack snatching a rabbit, not hauling down an elk. Swish, swish—wham! And one of those curious seal heads that followed me in my kayak around Wood Spit was no more.

Mammal-hunting orcas around Antarctica will build up speed and veer into a sharp surface turn, generating a wave that can wash seals off an ice floe. Another technique, that of breaching onto an ice floe to break it apart and knock seals into the water, is thought by some to be a seaman's tall tale, but I would be surprised if some orcas hadn't tried it. Reliable observers have seen them bust up thin sheets of ice to get at their prey and tilt one end of thicker floes until the seals slide off. Eva and Craig charted the travels of a big female they called Matushka. Originally seen several times traveling with a pod of five other transients, she then split off with her adult son. The pair specialized in hunting maturing sea lions. But after her son died in 1998, Matushka seemed to concentrate much more on sea lion pups as they came off their rookeries. One of her strategies was to make a long underwater run toward a rookery and suddenly burst into the air just in front of the rocks. She must have learned that some animals, and especially the pups, would plunge into the water in panic or get knocked in during the mad scramble for higher ground. After several years of this, she started traveling with another female, who then had a calf, and the trio has been hunting larger juvenile sea lions for some time.

According to stories collected in a 1961 book by Tom Mead called *Killers of Eden,* a group of orcas roaming southeastern Australia during the whaling era learned to herd humpback whales toward Twofold Bay, where harpooning crews were stationed. The orcas would enter the bay and leap about to get people's attention. After rowing out to kill the big whales, the men would reward the herders with choice leftovers. This supposedly went on for several generations. In light of modern discoveries about orcas, some of the author's descriptions of orca society are far enough off base to give one second thoughts about the way he and his informants interpreted the whole situation. On the other hand, there are accounts from throughout the world of dolphins cooperating with fishermen to drive schools into nets in return for a cut of the take. Transients will herd dolphins themselves into a bay, form a line to prevent escape, and then take turns attacking the trapped animals.

Plenty of stories of orcas hunting larger cetaceans have made the rounds through the years. As I child, I had heard that they made their living ripping the lips and tongues out of living whales as big as blues. Killers of whales indeed. Such scenes may take place, but pods probably wouldn't attack healthy adults that size too often. Like most predators, orcas reduce their risk by homing in on weaker, more vulnerable individuals in a population—chiefly the young as well as the very old, injured, or sick. And rather than tear out gobbets of flesh in a sharklike frenzy, killer whales are inclined to ram a target's belly or side with their heads or batter away with tail flukes. They've been seen trying to drown the young of great whales by grabbing onto their tails and tugging them underwater, piling onto the victim's topside and forcing it down, or cooperating to do both at once.

Some experts wonder if transient-type orcas didn't hunt great whales more frequently in the past and shift to other marine mammals as commercial whaling vacuumed the largest ones from the seas. Along those lines, there has been considerable debate over a recent burst of transient predation on sea otters. The otters were traditionally bypassed because they are comparatively small and insulate themselves from the cold water with dense fur rather than the fat that the mammal-hunters seem to prefer above all else when they feed. A few scientists see a correlation between the sudden interest in sea otters and the dramatic ongoing decline of harbor seals, Steller's sea lions, fur seals, and other marine species, including fish-hunting birds, along Alaska's northern coasts. Whether the drop-off is due to natural fluctuations in the ocean food chain or, as many suspect, commercial overharvest of the fish these animals rely upon, the transients may once again have had to seek alternative prey.

On the other hand, if species such as the gray whale and humpback continue their recovery from postwhaling population lows, we might see transients shift their focus back to great whales again. Scientists have lately taken a keen interest in False Pass, a route between the Alaska Peninsula and the Aleutian Islands chain used by gray whales with calves traveling north from the Gulf of Alaska into the Bering Sea. Transients now ambush the migrants at this bottleneck often enough that the local grizzly bears come to scavenge remains on the beaches in spring.

I once made my way to Glacier Bay National Park to visit Dena Matkin, Craig Matkin's former wife and the leading observer of transient pods in that area. She was not happy with the theorizing that implicated transients in the decline of sea otters along the far northern coast. It was based upon just a handful of actual observations of predation, she argued, and those might represent little more than an experiment or temporary fashion among one or two transient pods. She made sure to point out all the sea otters bobbing in Glacier Bay exactly where transients swam by in search of seals as we watched. And she told of seeing one otter directly in a transient's path suddenly go slack in the water as if paralyzed by a serious bite but then become active again and return to its usual activities. What had actually happened, she said, was that the whale had knocked the otter aside with its massive head. "It was strictly 'Get out of my way, you stinking sea weasel,'" Dena laughed. "Nobody wants to eat those hairballs." And nobody ever accused Dena Matkin of being dispassionate about the killer whales she has spent decades following.

Toward midsummer, Flip Nicklin departed to fulfill another commitment, but I stayed on in Alaska with Volker for an expedition in a twenty-one-foot speedboat acquired for him by the University of British Columbia. Some of the money came from funds to investigate links between transients and the population crash of

Steller's sea lions, now listed as threatened along the northern coast. I had just read an account of Georg Steller, the scientist who named this sea lion along with the now extinct Steller's sea cow and other species while on a Russian voyage led by Vitus Bering to explore Alaska. After years of preparation, travel across Siberia by dogsled to the outpost from which the expedition was launched, and endless delays caused by incompetence and nastiness on the part of Bering's lieutenants, poor Steller got to spend no more than a few hours actually walking on Alaskan soil before having to turn back before winter weather hit. Bering shipwrecked on a remote island near Kamchatka en route home. Already sick, he died over the winter. Steller endured unspeakably miserable months while stuck there with the survivors, finally made his way back to the heart of Russia, and then died as well, unappreciated and unfulfilled. As I helped Volker put black letters on the boat's sides to spell out the name he had settled on—*Steller Moment*—I could only hope that the Fates wouldn't notice.

The boat had a powerful inboard engine for covering a lot of territory quickly—and for satisfying a certain Volkerish need for speed. To do that, however, the *Steller Moment* went through gas at a rate that turned half of any voyage into a dash to some remote port to refill. Then, while we were looking for some transients that had somehow vanished from sight in the wide open waters of Stephens Passage, the engine quit. Luckily, sea conditions stayed calm. We drifted along, thumbing through the repair manual and tinkering with parts, until Volker finally had to put out a late-afternoon radio call for assistance. A cabin cruiser in the area eventually arrived and towed us into a little cove, and two friends made an all-night run in their boat to tow us back to Juneau for repair before the weather turned.

But I have memories from even that ill-starred outing that I wouldn't trade for diamonds: of swimming and watching harlequin ducks on a little island all our own; of wandering long, lovely, lonely beaches with chocolate lilies and wild columbine among the grasses; of wading in shallows where our feet kicked up speckled flounders half buried in the sand; and of climbing windy cliffs in a clamor of seabirds to gain altitude, the better to search the boundless horizon for tall dorsal fins, while the vast majority of humanity, far, far away, lived out their strange lives of voluntary confinement. The rich waters and shores formed a paradise for humpback whales, little biting gnats, bald eagles, marbled murrelets, and grizzly bears, among a great many other creatures, and when Volker said he would be returning for another summer and could use some company and another set of eyes, keelhaul and flog me if I didn't volunteer.

When we left the harbor in Juneau the next year, we had so many five-gallon fuel containers packed onto the deck and tied to the rails up front that I thought we should rename the *Steller Moment* the *Flammable Flyer*. And we still had to break off a couple of lengthy sessions following killer whale pods to run for a distant fuel dock before the gauge hit empty. After the fuel gauge broke, we didn't have to watch the needle sink toward E any longer, but we did need to constantly guesstimate the number of running hours we had left. Volker very nearly managed to put the boat onto a rocky reef that unaccountably rises in the center of the vast, cold expanse where Icy Strait meets Stephens Passage. The reef was well marked, and Volker slowed some distance away before he cut the engine and climbed up onto the *Steller Moment*'s roof. It was his usual routine for scanning the horizon in search of spouts or dorsal fins. But he forgot to check the pace and direction of the current.

"Oh look, kelp," I heard him say in a strange voice. Staring downward, I saw not only waving seaweed but also the rocks it was anchored to. Volker jumped into the cabin and slammed the engine into reverse. I shouted directions and gave hand signals from the bow. Although the current was strong and worked to shove us deeper into the maze of rocks, now inches below the hull, we got lucky, picking twists and turns that finally led out to deeper water. One wrong guess, and we might—at best—have spent the night clinging to the metal scaffold that rose from the reef with a warning sign. I was mostly grateful that the engine had started at all. It hadn't that morning, when we passed hours in a bay trying to fix it while a cloud of horseflies looked on, biting at will.

You can't have misadventures unless you're out having adventures to begin with, and we always found a way to keep going. One morning after we had just sighted some transients west of Admiralty Island, we got a radio message about seven orcas killing a humpback whale back by Barlow Island, just outside Auke Bay near the outskirts of Juneau. It took us a long time to get there, and the whales were gone by then. Talking with tour boat operators, we learned that the reports of a humpback being killed were, as Volker had predicted, exaggerated. In reality, a transient pod had killed one sea lion in the confluence of channels near Barlow, gouged another, then come upon one of the humpbacks often seen feeding there throughout the summer. It was a female with a calf, and the transients ganged up on the youngster. The calf would turn on its back, keeping its soft belly out of the water and less vulnerable to attack. Then the orcas tried to sink it, swimming up onto the calf. It kept breaking free of the orca pack long enough to rise headfirst and take in air. People had different interpretations of where the mother was during these struggles, but she finally came steaming over and dived down among the transients, at which point they left. "That's how humpbacks get their rake marks from killer whale teeth," Volker said. "I doubt the transients' success rate is very high when adults are near." Flip had mentioned seeing several humpbacks in the Aleutians swim over to a smaller humpback being harassed by orcas, causing them to leave. A single adult humpback will sometimes approach transients making a sea lion kill, seemingly more curious than wary. Craig and other researchers have watched sea lions mob transients near haul-out sites and drive them away.

We caught up with the transients partway down Saginaw Channel, on Admiralty Island's north side. The pod was on a tear that day. Having chomped sea lions and tried for a meal of young humpback, they were soon chasing a pair of Dall's porpoises. It was a high-velocity spectacle. Both the Dall's and their enormous black-and-white whale counterparts were going airborne as often as possible to escape the drag of the water and build speed. I'd seen residents do this while chasing chinook salmon, and it had the same effect on me. One moment, you're looking at a group of big sociable members of the dolphin family rolling smoothly along at maybe four or five knots. The next, you're in the presence of superpredators, undisputed rulers of the oceans, and you're no longer surprised in the least that they can punch out great white sharks for breakfast. The whales surge ahead, raising ten-foot-high rooster tails from their fins as though turbo-thruster engines had just kicked on, rocket into the air at nearly twenty knots, and turn in massive swirls, creating waves that set your boat rolling.

If killer whales can surprise Dall's porpoises or otherwise get a jump on them, the pod has a chance. If they can turn the porpoises, they'll chase them in relays until they tire, or a couple of pod members can swim a different route to intercept the prey's path. But we were looking at lions and gazelles on a wide, watery plain, and the fleet Dall's had got a head start. The transients, for all their power, could never catch up. They stopped and slowly swam down Douglas Channel and on into Stephens Passage. Volker and I followed until we finally lost them to the brief nighttime darkness of the Alaskan summer.

Over the past few years, a great deal of public attention has been drawn to the sagas of two orphaned killer whale calves. Springer, a female from the Johnstone Strait–area resident population, moved south into the range of the Puget Sound population after the death of her mother, where she ended up alone with winter coming on. Luna, a male from the Puget Sound resident population, went traveling north after somehow becoming separated from his mother. He wound up in Nootka Sound on the outer coast of Vancouver Island, also alone. Both orphans took to following boats and interacting with the people in them, accepting pets and belly rubs. Both had favorite sticks they would play with. Springer would bring hers over to boaters, and if they threw it for her, she would fetch it and return for another round. Luna found a little tugboat at work pushing logs in Nootka Sound, and he sometimes joined in to push one end of a log himself. Ken Balcomb, who helped monitor Springer, put it this way: "I think people who train killer whales for shows may be giving themselves a little too much credit."

After authorities began stopping boats from going too close to either orphan, both to keep the whales safe from propellers and to prevent them from becoming totally fixated on human company, Springer made her way to a Seattle-area ferry dock and swam around below the crowds that gathered there. Luna kept going to a Nootka Sound harbor for attention, even interacting with the Labrador dog that patrolled a float-plane dock.

Nobody quite knows the right thing to do for an orphaned killer whale trying everything in its power to get people to respond to it. Orcas are utterly social, communicative creatures and very tactile, used to the touch and rub of companions. A solitary young one is an aberration in every way. For any argument one can make as to the value of trying to keep such animals wild, there is a valid argument for providing them with stimulation and companionship, maybe even designated human playmates, until a natural or assisted reunion with fellow whales becomes possible. As a long winter and spring gave way to summer, Springer, who had been captured, was successfully returned to the northern population, and she began traveling with relatives from her matriline again. Luna is still alone in Nootka Sound after several years. He is healthy and has grown so big that his habit of stopping boats and sometimes jostling them in an effort to get somebody to do something, anything, with him has become a headache for safety-minded authorities. Meanwhile, a local First Nations tribe has claimed him as the reborn spirit of a deceased chief and refused to let wildlife officials relocate him back into Puget Sound. Maybe somebody in the spirit world knows what lies in store for Luna next. Nobody in this world seems to.

Volker occasionally checks up on Luna, for he is still out following killer whales these days. So are all the other orca researchers I mentioned. As with those who study different whales, the combination of work, adventure, and discovery seems to become a lifetime attraction. Surely the public has a right to be a little whale-crazy as well. Try to find a whale-watching boat skipper who hasn't seen customers scream, babble, cry tears, or fall to their knees in silence after meeting these animals for the first time. They are awesome enough to encompass whatever people need them to be. The only certainty is that, as the seventeenth-century French physicist, mathematician, and philosopher Blaise Pascal noted of humanity in general, "we believe and understand vastly more than we know."

When I asked Craig Matkin—for about the tenth time—to give me his thoughts on the more evocative dimensions of orcas, I think he decided that a reality check was in order. He said, "Sometimes, frankly, I get sick of talking about the abstract aspects of killer whales. We get data about movements, genetics, social groupings, survival, and mortality, and all anyone wants to talk about in classes I give is the brothers from outer space. But with the data we have, you can go in and argue a case if anything comes up. Overfishing. Pollution. Management strategies. We need solid stuff people can use. That's what Mike Bigg explained to me long ago. I believed him then and have ever since. It's a side benefit almost that you get to hang out with animals so intelligent that you can wonder about those other kinds of questions, and it does keep you going when you're out here every day. That's cool. That's great. But when it comes down to it, it's important enough just to find out what's going on in a place year after year—the physical results."

Bruce Mate, the leading expert in tracking whales by satellite-radio signals, once conveyed much the same message, telling me, "Those who say they want to come back as a whale or dolphin had better do something about nets, overfishing, pollution, heavy ship traffic, underwater noise . . . I mean, let's get real here, folks."

What is the outlook for killer whales overall? For those in most of the world, no one knows enough to say. The more intensely studied resident populations along North America's Pacific coast appear to be increasing gradually in northern ranges, where salmon numbers remain strong. The Johnstone Strait area population seems to have leveled off at around 220 after rebounding from the days of shootings and live captures. In the Puget Sound area, the southern population rose from its low of 71 individuals during the mid-1970s to a high of 99 by 1995. It then declined toward the low 80s, but just lately added several new members through births.

Due to dams, overfishing, and declining water quality, chinook, the orcas' principal food in the Puget Sound region, are already listed as endangered here. Citing increasing disturbance from boat traffic, noise pollution, and alarming levels of toxic chemicals in samples of killer whale tissues as well, scientists and conservationists convinced the federal government in 2005 to declare this orca population imperiled in order to spur better protection under the Endangered Species Act from harmful influences.

Some members of the public have trouble grasping how Puget Sound orcas could be in danger of dying out. Don't other killer whales frequent the waters immediately to the north? People aren't aware that neighboring resident populations don't mingle. Besides having a separate call repertoire, the Johnstone Strait area residents regularly visit rubbing beaches, whereas the southern population, Luna's society, never rubs. While its members perform more breaches and other surface displays than the northern population, the northerners engage in formal greeting ceremonies more often. If people were to do what Volker suggests—strip down to just being a mammal and reimagine the world—they would see two different cultures with different ways of life. Each population must rise and fall on its own, for whatever breeding takes place will be within the confines of its unique culture.

The North Pacific transients, not very abundant to start with, seem to be doing well enough along the southern portion of the continent's coast but dropping in the northern latitudes, where harbor seals and Steller's sea lions have suffered declines on the order of 90 percent. Craig Matkin has shown that the AT1s, a mammal-hunting pod genetically separate from the rest of the transient population south of Glacier Bay, have been dwindling ever since the *Exxon Valdez* oil spill in Prince William Sound. They have not produced offspring in a couple of decades now. Officially listed as "depleted" under the Marine Mammal Protection Act, they and their unique, haunting calls are in reality on the very cusp of extinction.

Killer whales throughout the region have accumulated alarming levels of PCBs, dioxins, and furans (from flame retardants), among other chlorinated hydrocarbons. Binding readily to fats such as blubber reserves, these contaminants may cause birth defects, problems in early development, neurological and endocrine system disorders, and a weakening of the immune system. Peter Ross of Canada's Institute of Ocean Sciences in Sidney, British Columbia, says killer whales are now the most PCB-contaminated mammals yet recorded. Residents are loaded with the stuff, as are seals, sea lions, and dolphins.

Transients, eating the eaters of fish, are doubly loaded with PCBs. Some are so tainted with toxic brews that they exceed the legal limits for the disposal of hazardous waste at sea. The sources aren't just local, Ross explained to me. They are as far away as Asia, where factory smokestacks spew the compounds into the air to begin drifting toward North America in the atmosphere. Falling with rain into the sea, they get incorporated into single-celled organisms, move up the food chain until they are taken in by salmon, then migrate with these fish toward spawning rivers on North America's west coast. Late in 2005, Norwegian scientists reported that orcas have overtaken polar bears as the most toxified mammals in the Arctic. Their blubber contains high concentrations not only of PCBs and flame retardants but also of pesticides sprayed on lands far to the south.

If only for our own sake, we need to look toward the sea more often and more carefully, thinking about what we take from it and what we are putting in. Whales help us do that by being huge, smart, and fantastic enough to keep drawing our attention in that direction. Killer whales are exceptionally good at this. The better we get at seeing the world through other eyes, hearing it through other ears, and searching out its meanings through other minds, the fuller our existence seems, the healthier the world we inhabit may become, and the more grateful we will one day be for the company of all creatures.

THE COMMONER
MINKE WHALE

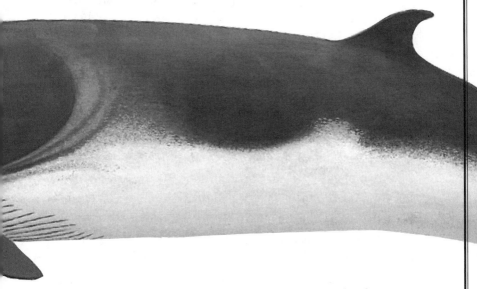

In the Outer Hebrides of northwestern Scotland, I went tramping through the heath on the Isle of Lewis to high, rugged headlands from which I could look out across the sea. At each vantage point, I would focus my telescope on tidal rips and patches of water stirred by feeding cormorants, gannets, skuas, and kittiwakes. These were the likeliest places to see the slender, dark gray back of a minke whale break the surface in a quick roll.

Minkes are probably the most common whales left around the British Isles, though nobody has a meaningful estimate of numbers. Sightings are not reported all that frequently, which was why the locals I spoke with tended to think the minkes must be thinly scattered. On the other hand, this is a whale that doesn't lend itself to being readily noticed. Just twenty-two to thirty-three feet in length and five to ten tons in weight when fully grown (females are about 5 percent larger than the males), it isn't terribly big. Nor does it make much of a spout when it rises to breathe, and the dorsal fin that emerges from the water is scarcely taller than a wavelet.

If you're having trouble envisioning the creature, don't feel alone, for it is among the least familiar of whales. Lacking the size or showiness of more celebrated relatives such as the humpback, the minke is lucky if its image gets included in a book about oceans or the animal kingdom. The irony is that, besides being the most common whale near Great Britain, the unassuming, little-known minke happens to be the most abundant baleen whale in existence. It may be the most plentiful whale of any kind.

I had grown curious to discover how the odds of sighting one might change if I were simply to pick some places on the coast and look long and intently. My companion in this experiment was Thom Gordon, a Scottish sailor and naturalist who had filmed sperm whales in the Azores. We were having just enough success to surprise ourselves. For example, I spent more than an hour scanning a bay alternately swept by sunshine and squalls without a glimpse of a minke, but then picked up three that even a vigilant observer could have missed: two swimming separately, their backs dark as the waves and exactly the same height, and one breaching so far out that the splash was hard to tell from whitecaps the wind had whipped up.

Toward dusk, we made our way to a fishing village to ask about lodging and were directed to a small guesthouse. The proprietor was named Linda Johnson. When Thom mentioned what we had been up to, she invited us into the parlor for tea, asking, "And how often do you get to hold a whale?" Her tone made it plain that this was not a question but the prelude to a minke tale of her own.

Johnson said that folks knew she owned a wetsuit, so when a minke stranded nearby, they telephoned her to come help. As she scrambled down to the shore, she saw the local veterinarian already on the scene. The other thing she noticed right away was blood, for the animal was thrashing on the rocks in just inches of water. "The whale was sixteen feet long but only a baby," Johnson recalled. "And, oh, it was so frightened. You can tell from the eyes. You could just see that it didn't know what was going on." Her palms swept up from her lap to stroke the air while she continued: "You just automatically try to soothe it, running your hands along the skin. It was lovely and all soft and silky smooth. We got a hessian [tarp] underneath it. With five of us on each side, we tried to turn the baby to face out to sea. But each time we let go, it would fall onto its side."

Johnson regarded each of us over the rim of her teacup and sighed. "We had to wait for the tide to lift it," she said. "We told the whale that it was going to be okay, and we urged it along. Come on. Come on. And once there was enough water and it had its balance, off it went. It swam almost out of sight. Then it came back in, and we were worried it would go onto shore again. But it swam away, and we decided the animal just came back to say Thanks and Cheerio, you know?" Johnson ended her story by saying, "That's when we started to worry the poor thing might be going to Norway next."

Most people are aware that whales are still being hunted today. Practically everyone seems to have an opinion about it. Yet few are clear about which kinds of whales are being taken, or where, or by whom. The killing of minkes for profit by Norway and Japan represents most of the harvest of whales worldwide at the moment. Therefore, people arguing over present-day whaling are mainly talking about minkes, whether they know it or not. These whales may not be especially charismatic, but their lives are as fascinating as any species's and past due for a turn in the spotlight.

Closely related to blue, fin, sei, and Bryde's whales, the minke is the littlest member of the Balaenopteridae family, better known as rorquals. Like its more gargantuan relatives (except humpbacks, the oddballs of the rorqual group), it has small flippers to go with its small dorsal fin, a relatively slender body shape, and grooves that allow the mouth and throat to expand when gulping prey. The nose is somewhat more pointed than those of its kin, a trait reflected in both the scientific name of the northern minke, *Balaenoptera acutorostrata,* which means "sharp-snouted rorqual," and its common names, pikehead, little piked whale, and sharp-headed finner.

As a rule, minkes are slate or brownish gray with white undersides. Some populations show white bands on the upper side of their flippers. Most also have creamy streaks slanting up from fore and aft of the belly toward the center of the back on each side. I think of these chevrons as racing stripes, because, as the spear-tip nose also suggests, minkes are very fast whales.

Any resistance to the flow of water past a whale's body creates turbulence, which acts as a drag on speed. Whale skin is porous and absorbs water, which binds to oils in the outermost layer. As a result, a whale on the move is surrounded by a very thin film of liquid, and liquid moving past other liquid creates the least possible amount of resistance. Vibrations from the turbulence that does develop are partially dampened in the permeable skin. Moreover, as the animal's speed increases, the underlying blubber layer is believed to form slight ripples that break up swirls of turbulence before they begin to act as a drag. Minkes rival the swiftest whales—blues, seis, and orcas—and may be able to outrace them all by a fraction, reaching twenty-one knots (twenty-four miles per hour) or more.

The minke's other superlative is its sheer numbers: there may be as many as half a million of them. Pan-oceanic, this whale is found speeding throughout every corner of the globe. Experts recognize separate North Atlantic and North Pacific populations of *acutorostrata* by minor but distinctive color variations. A third type, seen mainly around Australia, is marked by broader chevrons plus additional white on the flippers' undersides. Whalers named it the dwarf minke, though it is in fact the same size as the others and considered a form of *acutorostrata*. However, on the basis of recent genetic work, taxonomists now tend to classify other Southern Hemisphere populations as *Balaenoptera bonaerensis,* the antarctic minke whale, a second species, distinguished by an absence of white on the flippers.

Following the sun—and the food that proliferates as daylight lengthens—the majority of minkes make their way toward high latitudes over the warm months. Some go no farther than temperate waters. Others swim on to roam the very edges of the polar ice caps. While a few may be found over deep bottoms, the animals are more often encountered between the outer edge of the continental shelves and shore. Many appear to do most of their feeding very near coastlines. As autumn progresses, they migrate back to warmer climes. That's the general assumption, anyway, though no one can point to specific winter ranges.

Two minkes marked in the Antarctic with barbed metal discovery tags (placed on various species by whalers hoping to find
out where populations went) were killed three thousand miles
north near Brazil during the winter. The appearance along the
African coast of minkes with a golden tinge of diatoms growing
on their skin—a sign of having spent at least a month in polar
waters—was taken as further evidence of migration from antarctic feeding grounds. A minke from the Southern Hemisphere
was found stranded on a Texas shore near Corpus Christi. On
the other hand, minkes have been observed during the antarctic winter at the edge of the southern ice pack and during the
Northern Hemisphere winter off Norway, England, and Alaska,
among many other places. There are hints that some reside
year-round in the Mediterranean and that others remain in the
tropics. Despite this mixture of locations, molecular biologists
have found a greater degree of genetic difference between northern and antarctic minkes than between Bryde's and sei whales,
implying that populations of the two minke species rarely, if
ever, mingle.

Researchers are beginning to fill in the rough outlines of minke
natural history with provocative details, some of which could
reshape debates over whaling before long. Present-day whaling
falls into two categories: subsistence and commercial. Natives in
Alaska and Russia's Far East go after a few of the bowhead whales
that feed at the edge of the arctic ice pack. Other indigenous
northerners take belugas and narwhals. The Makah Indian tribe
on the Olympic Peninsula of Washington state recently revived
its longtime practice of lancing gray whales that migrate close
to the coast. Minkes and a few northern bottlenose whales are

harpooned by residents of the Faeroe Islands, a self-governing community that lies due north of Scotland but is overseen by more distant Denmark, and some islanders in the South Pacific and Indonesia continue to chase species up to the size of sperm whales.

Only a small percentage of the subsistence hunters still rely solely on muscle-powered boats and weapons rather than engines and guns. They nevertheless consider the pursuit of whales a worthy tradition in itself. And even where the modern era has made alternate sources of nutrition readily available, certain societies continue to prize whale meat and fat as important ancestral foods. In deference to such cultural values, these harvests are exempted from international regulations designed to protect cetaceans. The bottom line is that the hunts remove only a small number of animals from various populations each year.

Commercial whaling is, and always has been, something else again: the commoditization of gigantic wild mammals for markets far removed from the local environment. It amounts to a predator-prey relationship in which shifting regulations based on monetary and political desires replace natural checks and balances. Applied to each great whale species in turn, this regime proved a stimulus for runaway slaughter to the verge of extinction in every corner of the globe.

Trying to become more familiar with the whaling business, a German sea captain named Meincke supposedly went voyaging aboard a Norwegian vessel back in the nineteenth century. En route, he spied what the other sailors knew to be a pikehead and declared it to be a blue whale. In other versions of the story, Captain Meincke earned a reputation on his own boat for always exaggerating the size of the whales he saw. Either way, other

whalers were inspired to start calling the most diminutive rorquals Meinckes. Between mispronunciations and loose transla-
tions, this became minkes, and the name spread.

While some small, shore-based fisheries did go after minkes
in various parts of the world, commercial whalers wouldn't deign
to chase a prize so small, especially since it held no special stores
of blubber, fine oil, or other premium products. And then suddenly, after being ignored for centuries, the little rorqual named
for Meincke's mistake became the most sought after of all the cetaceans, because nothing larger could readily be found any more.
It was worth chasing even through the risky waters of faraway
Antarctica, where the whaling fleets began taking three thousand
to seven thousand per year in the late 1970s and early 1980s.
Before this late burst of attention could seriously deplete the minke's numbers, though, the International Whaling Commission
(IWC) finally issued its worldwide moratorium on commercial
whaling, in 1986.

IWC membership is open to any nation willing to adhere to
the Convention for the Regulation of Whaling, an international
treaty formulated in 1946. The countries that signed on now number sixty-six. One of them, Norway, lodged a formal objection
to the new ban and insisted on exercising its sovereign right to
continue hunting whales within its own territorial waters. Every
IWC member nation is allowed to take such an exemption, the
only real deterrent being the pressure of international opinion (or,
in Mongolia's case, the fact that it has no seacoast).

The Norwegians were always an exception to the rule that
commercial whalers bypassed minkes for being too small to
bother with. Having chased the *vagehval*—Old Norse for "bay
whale"—close to the nation's shores for generations, they began

combing the North Atlantic for them once stocks of the larger species were played out. During the half century between the 1930s and the 1980s, Norway was taking about 2,000 minkes there yearly. The record, in 1955, was 4,500. Norwegian whalers severely curtailed their harvest for a while following the 1986 ban, but they have been steadily raising it for more than a decade to the point that it is now over a thousand animals annually.

Japan chose instead to take advantage of a loophole in IWC rules that allows a nation to kill some whales in order to provide specimens for study. Calling it scientific whaling or a research harvest, the Japanese, like the Norwegians, steadily increased their self-allotted quota over the years. Eventually its fleet was harpooning scores of minkes in the North Pacific and 440 in antarctic waters each year. Then, in 2005, Japan announced its intention to more than double the Antarctic minke harvest, to 935 whales. And expand the scientific whaling of sperm whales, fin whales, and Bryde's whales—the rorqual closest in size to minkes—begun in recent years. And initiate scientific whaling of humpbacks.

Until just recently, experts said there may be as many as 760,000 minkes in the Southern Ocean, another 200,000 to 250,000 in the North Atlantic, and tens of thousands more in the North Pacific. The estimate for the Southern Ocean has since been reduced to around 250,000. Still, since the commercial kill amounts to just four-tenths of 1 percent of the estimated global population of a half million or more, the question is inevitably raised: Why all the fuss? Some might answer that the token level of the for-profit harvest is proof that it is not an economic necessity. Or that one more whale killed by an industry whose track record demonstrated a total unwillingness to limit its rapacity while vacuuming the grandest of lives from the planet is one whale too many. Many see the yearly killing of some 2,000 minkes unabashedly being used as a wedge to reopen the door for commercial whaling of all the great whales as populations improve, a prospect that could become reality sooner than the public suspects.

While raising its own hunting quota on minkes, Norway has been pushing the IWC to permit the killing of a number of other whale species. Its example has encouraged Iceland and Greenland to follow a similar path. As for Japan, the flesh of minkes rendered for "research" all ends up in the country's fish markets and restaurants, which helps explain the nation's lack of interest in nonlethal techniques that could provide the same biological data. For instance, Japanese officials insist that they need to cut open stomachs to examine what whales are eating, even though DNA techniques now allow a thorough determination of a whale's diet merely from small samples of the dung it leaves floating on the surface. Like the politicians' practice of soliciting contributions from lobbyists while claiming that money never influences decisions, scientific whaling is an open ruse. It is a way for Japan to subsidize its whaling fleet while lobbying other nations to help lift the general moratorium. The Japanese have even arranged special loans and business deals for countries that have little involvement in whaling in order to win their votes as members of the IWC. So far, Japan is only taking relatively minor numbers of whales other than minkes for the purpose, they say, of assessing populations and reproductive rates. That the country will soon declare that its studies prove these species can tolerate a substantial commercial harvest is a foregone conclusion. And so is the prospect that, as long as the IWC vetoes such hunts, Japan will simply keep raising its "scientific" whaling quotas and stretching them to include still more species.

Thus, those two thousand minkes annually hauled aboard whaleboats symbolize a much larger issue that the world is going to have to confront not long from now. I made an effort to meet people involved with the taking and selling of minke whales in both Norway and Japan and tried to better understand their views. It didn't change my opinion that commercial whaling trivializes magnificent lives, brushes aside widespread human sympathies, and undermines our sense of wonder at creation every time the sea turns red. But this chapter is not aimed at justifying anyone's bias. The goal is to open more windows onto the life of this wide-spread, populous, yet modest little whale—the commoner—upon which so much hinges.

You can count on a few fingers the number of people who have really delved into the daily habits of minkes. One such observer is Jonathan Stern, who, along with Elie Dorsey and Rus Hoezel, studied the whales in Washington's Puget Sound for the better part of two decades. I arranged to meet him and photographer Flip Nicklin there one recent July. Waiting in line at the dock in Anacortes, Washington, for the ferry to San Juan Island, I got out of my car to stretch in the sun. A fellow two lanes over emerged to do the same. He struck me as a cross between a pirate and a hard-core rocker recently retired to pursue beachcombing: long whit-ish hair, thin on top, silver nautical ornament dangling from one ear, sandals, and an expression that told me he was probably not thinking about any of the same things as the other people in line. Even before I saw his car's Texas license plate and remembered that Jon Stern taught at Texas A&M University, I felt certain that this was my whale guy.

Walking over with a hand extended, I introduced myself, exchanged a couple of pleasantries, and said, "Would you mind telling me what the heck a Reynolds number is?" At the end of his e-mails, Jon always appended a quote to the effect that, when life becomes a drag, one should seek a higher Reynolds number. While the incoming ferry maneuvered in the distance, he started enthusiastically explaining a concept in physics having to do with laminar flows and turbulence relative to the movement of objects immersed in liquid. Even if pirates did discuss such things, they wouldn't use as gentle a voice as this man's; perhaps I'd misjudged. But professor Stern *had* played in a rock band, I soon learned, and he still indulged in pretty serious jam sessions on guitar.

Once on San Juan Island, we rented a small open boat at Snug Harbor and motored out into Haro Strait on the island's west side. Within minutes, we had to slow down to avoid a group of whales. It was the J pod of resident orcas, containing about thirty members. In what has become a daily summer scene, they were accompanied by at least a dozen commercial whale-watching boats large and small. Hundreds of passengers lined the decks, hooting and snapping photos while the captains steered courses parallel to the black-and-white animals, trying to keep at least one hundred yards distant as required by U.S. marine mammal protection guidelines.

As ever, there was the odd private boater who couldn't resist roaring up to the whales so the driver's friends and family could hoot and snap photos closer than anyone else. Also as usual, an inflatable from the volunteer group known as Soundwatch soon arrived to herd the yee-hawers aside. Rather than threatening to report them, the whale guardians would patiently explain the intent of the rules and hand informative literature across the gunwale. The killer whales themselves merely continued rolling on their way, veering here and there to chase salmon, splashing and rubbing against one another, and occasionally leaping from the waves to applause from all sides.

This kind of star power has become the basis of a multi-million-dollar regional industry. It supports not just the tour boat owners and crews but local hoteliers, restaurateurs, and shop owners from Seattle to Victoria and Vancouver, British Columbia, not to mention artists throughout the Pacific Northwest who produce killer-whale-themed paintings, pottery, T-shirts, cards, and trinkets. Looping around the cavorting orcas, Jon turned with a rueful smile to say, "Around here, the animal I study is 'the other whale.'" After a pause, he added, apropos of nothing I could imagine, "Let me know if you smell overcooked broccoli."

Whereas killer whales rise high from the water when they surface to breathe, minkes show comparatively little of their top sides, and for a much shorter time. Their low, diffuse spout is easy to overlook unless it appears against a dark background or conditions are calm and humid enough for the spray to hang in the air like smoke. Nearing the southern tip of the island, I finally spied blows because the water droplets briefly broke the light into a spectrum, creating wisps of rainbow adrift in the breeze. I never managed to locate the source, and I lost sight of the blows as our angle to the sun changed. But when we circled, I did catch a whiff of broccoli steamed beyond its time.

Stern saw me react and nodded. "That's it," he said. He was referring to the aroma of minke whale breath: once inhaled, never forgotten. When we lost track of that, he turned to the whale seeker's strategy of last resort, which is to shut off the engine and float along listening for the blows. In between the cries of gulls, we heard a big breath farther offshore. It came from the direction of Salmon Bank, where a submerged dome deflects currents upward, forming what Stern termed a topographic upwelling. The rising currents mixed with surface currents to create a confusion of waves that became more and more pronounced as the tidal flow through the Strait of Juan de Fuca reached full strength.

In marine systems, swirling energy promises a concentration of food. Flocks of skittering, plunging birds made sections of Salmon Bank look like they were about to come to a boil. Most of the divers were rhinoceros auklets, which are related to puffins, murrelets, and other stubby-winged seabirds collectively known as alcids. With feet set so far back that their bodies stand almost upright when on land, alcids are sometimes described as the northern counterpart of penguins. The auklets surfaced with young herrings draped from their beaks like tinsel, then pattered heavily across the water in preparation for takeoff. Guillemots, another alcid, joined them in airlifting fish back to young in nests, while glaucous-winged gulls wheeled and swooped down onto the surface, seeking herring of their own. Like the tidal rips I scanned in Scotland, Salmon Bank seemed a prime spot to spy a minke's back, and it wasn't long before we did.

From the way the birds spread out, we could tell that the herring were moving in a fairly loose group. The minke was lunge-feeding on them, making openmouthed passes along the surface. It would arise in a rush, and Stern's challenge was to snap identification photos during the brief time the animal was in view. If the whale sounded instead, he would just pick a lively looking section of current, kill the engine, and sit quietly, listening, look-ing, sniffing, playing a hunch as to where the next sequence of lunges might begin.

By Stern's reckoning, there were no more than a score of minkes around the San Juan archipelago. And since offspring born over winter somewhere to the south had already separated from their mothers by the time they reached these islands, nearly all his observations were of solitary animals. He had figured out how to tell them apart through a combination of fin shape, variations in the light-colored streaks running up their sides, and the inevitable scars and nicks that whales accrue. In doing so, Stern discovered that some, if not most, of the animals he documented each sum-mer were the same individuals returning year after year.

Juvenile herring seem to be the minkes' favorite food in this area, followed by the small fish known as sand lance. The whales naturally seek out the densest schools, including what fishermen call herring balls or bait balls. These are groups forced into espe-cially tight, teeming clusters by gulls striking at them from above while diving alcids, dogfish sharks, salmon, or all three hunt them from below. A good way to find a herring ball is by watching for a particularly frenzied crowd of birds. Don't be surprised to see the birds suddenly all fly clear of the water, closely followed by the sharp front end of a pikehead that has risen straight up through the huddled fish, for Stern thinks that many of the whales also use the birds to locate bait balls. How they do this, he isn't sure. Is a minke's eyesight sharp enough to pick out distant flocks? Or do the whales somehow hear the birds' cries or detect the general commotion from underwater?

Some of the minkes Stern recorded for at least two years in a row fed exclusively on fish schools concentrated by birds.

Consisting mainly of fry, which congregate close to the surface, these represent a rich food source, but it is a patchy, ephemeral one and can sometimes be engulfed in one gradual pass. Other minkes Stern kept track of were exclusively lunge-feeders. They tended to take longer dives and hunt schools at greater depths, driving them upward against the barrier of the surface in order to concentrate them prior to making rapid passes through the core from one side or another. For a whale that learns and remembers the most rewarding locations for finding schools, they become a somewhat predictable food source. But the minke has to expend a lot of energy rounding up the fish by itself. That's the trade-off between the lunge-feeding technique and the bird-association feeding technique, and it appears that certain minkes adopt one over the other.

Stern also noticed quirks such as the tendency of one minke called Ed to always land on its back after breaching, whereas Bubbles always landed in a belly flop. Just finding a minke and keeping up long enough to identify it is difficult; picking out variations in behavior is like batting .400 in major league baseball. Yet Stern was able to document enough to suggest that individuality extends well beyond the animals' physical characteristics.

Stern's father served as third mate on large oceangoing vessels. One day, he brought six-year-old Jon a book on whales and dolphins. Not long afterward, the boy heard that a ship had been disabled by a collision with a whale. "It was a ship my dad had been on—a huge luxury liner," Stern told me. "I said to myself, that's a really big boat; I want to learn more about these animals." People come to the study of whales by unique routes in life. But those researchers dedicated enough to keep following whales (or for that matter, other large, intelligent mammals) advance along

a common path: The better they get at looking, the more differences they detect from one animal to the next. They uncover a
range of temperaments and of habits, some learned from mothers and companions, others likely acquired as a result of experience. These idiosyncrasies in turn make the whales easier for us
to relate to and thus more compelling. Once we have a sense of
real individuals out there living particular lives, their sphere of
existence never again seems quite so alien as we had imagined
it to be.

The next day was almost a repetition of the previous outing
but with smoother seas beneath a high overcast. We started the
boat trip by slowing for orcas—the resident L pod, this time—and
their escort of tour boats on our way to look for "the other whale."
As soon as we reached Salmon Bank, a feeding minke appeared
on cue. The whale was so zoomy, and it changed direction so often, that getting ID photos of both its sides took most of an hour.
From the dorsal fin's shape and a long scar on the left side, Stern
felt confident that it was an animal he had first documented in
the San Juans twenty years earlier. "That would be Tribbles," he
said. "I saw it four years ago, three years ago, and the year before
last as well."

Drifting along while we waited for the whale to surface again,
we came upon a bait ball six or seven feet in diameter. Glittering
like the mirrored orb over a disco dance floor, the writhing mass
of small herring was under assault by auklets, cormorants, gulls,
dogfish sharks, and harbor seals. One seal lolled smack in the
middle, performing slow somersaults while waving its head from
side to side, browsing contentedly on compacted fish. Then the
birds took to the air as one, the seal shot to one side, and Tribbles
emerged maw first from directly below.

"These are not monster baleen whales nailing huge swarms of krill or whole shoals of fish," Stern said. "They are small whales working hard, swimming fast, covering a lot of water to get very, very localized food. Most bait balls around here are less than a meter in diameter." Three days later, we found Tribbles at Hein Bank, an upwelling half an hour from Salmon Bank by boat.

Focusing on three places—California's Monterey Bay, the San Juan Islands, and Johnstone Strait between northern Vancouver Island and mainland British Columbia—Stern and his colleagues documented close to sixty individual minke whales on nearly 450 separate occasions. He located one animal in nine different years a total of 37 times. Richard Sears, a blue whale expert, identified Atlantic minkes by photographs and found twelve returning to the same part of the Gulf of St. Lawrence over a six-year period. Such records led Stern to conclude that minke ranges—at least those of the coast-hugging summer residents—somewhat resemble the home ranges of land mammals, with individuals showing a fidelity to particular geographic locales and specific sites within them year after year.

This is where the minke's speed, agility, modest size, and the ecological niche the whale fills as a result join forces with individuality and learning abilities to maximize survival. The more thoroughly an animal comes to know an area, the more efficiently it can exploit the resources there. Every detail of the submarine topography, tides, currents, and smaller rips and eddies that the whale learns aids in its quest for food. Finding rich sites is good; remembering them is better; traveling straight from one to the next means more time eating and less time looking.

Once within a rich site such as a local upwelling, however, the equation changes. A minke's prey targets are so small and mobile that the whale can't know precisely where to find them based on previous information. It has to go into search mode. It appears to do this by cruising through the site in more or less arbitrary fashion. Stern terms it "taking a random walk." The strategy makes sense because the chances of success are roughly equal in every direction at first. Being able to go fast along a heading and turn quickly to start the next traverse helps reduce the time until a payoff. A minke can also refine its search en route. If it favors lunge-feeding, it may begin to herd the fish closer together as soon as it starts encountering schools, creating its own concentrations of prey. For those minkes inclined to let diving birds carry out most of the roundup, the trick is obviously to start paying more attention to whatever clues are used to locate feeding flocks. Stern told me that minkes also take advantage of situations where other marine animals force fish close together. I realized that this was probably what I once saw off the Massachusetts coast at Stellwagen Bank, where fin whales and bubble-netting humpbacks were gorging on a mass of sand lance, and minkes kept scooting in between their giant cousins.

If minkes hunt concentrations of fish by keying in on birds and other predators, there must also be times when the situation is reversed, and the sharp-eyed birds locate thick schools of fish by first picking out minke whale spouts or backs among the waves. Whichever type of animal is following the other, the bird-minke relationship is an intriguing phenomenon, and Jon Stern is not the only one to take note of it.

Before visiting the Isle of Lewis in Scotland, I had stopped on the west coast near the village of Gervais, which lies just east of the Isles of Coll and Mull. In most places, whale-watching operations actively go looking for minkes only when an outing fails to turn up the more spectacular whales advertised; with luck, "the other whale" gets to serve as the consolation whale. In contrast, a handful of companies on the British Isles tout possible minke sightings as the highlight of their marine tours (partly, it must be admitted, because the likelihood of seeing any larger whale there is negligible). One operation, called Sea Life Surveys, was established by a Scot named Richard Fairbairns for the express purpose of combining tourism with minke research. Mindful that Scotland hunted these whales until 1952, and that hunting continues nearby in the Faeroe Islands and Norway, he wanted to increase public awareness of the species while demonstrating ways to collect information that didn't involve killing the subject first.

The drive to Gervais wound past heather and gorse, Scotch pines and silver birches, sheep, castles, countrysides plundered and periodically occupied by Vikings, and finally the sea that carried those Norsemen here. Around the Hebrides, the waters are enlivened by the meeting of cold currents with the warm Gulf Stream pushing eastward across the Atlantic. Local upwellings add to the mix. I began seeing gray seals, harbor seals, and harbor porpoises the moment I left the dock on a Sea Life Surveys tour the next day. Richard Fairbairns's eldest son, Brennen, captained the boat, and Alison Gill, a marine biologist, served as the naturalist. The first thing they looked for when deciding where to go for minkes was "hurries" of birds, as they called the squabbling flocks drawn to a bounty of fish.

No blizzards of wings were in view that morning. However, Gill noticed a loose collection of guillemots, razorbills, and puffins on one span of water. These birds, all alcids, would be diving after sand lance, locally known as sand eels, which Gill said were the minkes' favorite food hereabouts. She felt that the setting held promise, and we turned toward it. Some gannets soared past, folded their wings, and began arrowing into the water. Shortly afterward, we had minkes in sight. The surface was calm and surprisingly transparent, given that waters this productive are usually grainy with plankton. It made all the difference in the world for keeping the whales in view.

As the date was early June, not all the minke calves had yet become independent of their mothers. But when we drew within an eighth of a mile of the first pair that we saw and turned off the boat engine, the youngster didn't hesitate to come over alone for a visit. We could follow most of its progress under the water by the white blazes on its pectoral fins and the cream-colored chevrons running up from its chest like streaks of foam. In no time, the fourteen-foot-long juvenile was circling the boat, making passes close enough that any of us could have stepped off onto its back. On several occasions as it sped by the hull, the whale rolled onto one side so that its eye seemed to be looking up through the water directly at us. When Gill commented that it was hard to tell who was studying whom, all I could think of was how many times, and with how many different kinds of whales, I had heard someone voice the same feeling.

Aside from a brief spell of weak sunshine, the weather varied between a drizzle and a downpour. Still, the visibility through the rain-flattened water stayed good. We sighted a lone minke and then a second mother-calf pair. Both the female and her offspring swam our way to begin circling the boat. The calf moved close beside us and passed right under the hull through the clear, green sea. I had never had a more perfect look at a minke in its entirety, and it gave me a new appreciation of how sharp, how acute, the angle of the nose truly is and how slender and tapered—how per-fectly hydrodynamic—this mammal's body has become. Because the movement of the flukes can be subtle, the forward progress of cetaceans, whether the size of dolphins or blue whales, can ap-pear almost totally effortless. Even at cruising speed, the torpedo-shaped bodies show so little up-and-down motion that it seems as if the animals simply point their noses in the direction they wish to go, and some sort of internal jets or force fields mysteriously power them there.

We passed the next day banging through waves more than high enough to hide any minke's back, but the day after that, we met five or possibly six different whales in the lee of several big islands. Again, some cruised over to engage in what everyone felt amounted to a thorough inspection of us. Minkes aren't neces-sarily put off by the sound of an engine: they have been seen bow-riding like dolphins in front of moving vessels. But Brennen Fairbairns told me that, if you have calm conditions and shut down the motor, the percentage of minkes that will approach your boat rises to 60 percent. The majority are juveniles, the age category over which curiosity seems to have the strongest sway.

Sea Life Surveys had thus far identified fifty-six individual minkes, Fairbairns said. Some were sighted annually or nearly so, and one had shown up every year for the past decade. Others reappeared after intervals of a few years. If there is a pattern to minke life in the region, the rudiments look like this: The whales arrive in the Hebrides through the late spring and begin feed-ing among the islands. A number of them may only be pausing en route to points farther north, including Norwegian shores. The rest, seen regularly enough over summer to be considered residents, appear to linger as long as the food remains abundant.

Individuals that have resided among these isles before get some extra benefit from having learned the whereabouts of prime foraging sites. Their tight focus on sand lance may simply reflect the fact that herring, cod, mackerel, and whiting were locally depleted by past overfishing. The population as a whole gradually shifts toward the north as summer progresses, and as the minkes move they start to include more herring in their meals. Observers in Norway report minkes pushing northward through the warm months as well. Those whales switch from a fish diet to one made up of the krill that flourish at higher latitudes.

Minkes plunder krill alongside blue whales in the Antarctic as well. They eat amphipods, which are tinier crustaceans, and copepods, which are practically microscopic. And yet, with the broadest diet of any rorqual, pikeheads are lithe and quick enough to chase down big fish one-on-one. The whales have been found with full-grown salmon, cod, saithe (similar to pollock), and dogfish sharks in their bellies, and some of these species easily reach three feet in length. Witch flounders, glacier lanternfish, and squid are also on the minke menu.

Wide-ranging flexible food habits go hand in hand with the minke's global distribution and robust numbers. No matter how effectively a whale uses knowledge about a particular home range to its advantage, there are times when the plankton blooms fueling the food chain sputter and weaken, and a minke's best option is to move on and adjust its diet to suit the new setting. Where a blue whale has the power and fat reserves to range long distances seeking concentrations of its principal prey, krill, a minke that finds itself running out of one key food source has the option of shifting to another somewhere nearby. This is the advantage of being a generalist rather than a specialist.

Before leaving the Hebrides, I heard of another boat captain involved in minke whale watching and went to pay a call. Ronnie Dyer was supposed to be running a regular ferry service between the coastal town of Arisaig and the Isles of Eigg, Muck, and Rhum. "When I started twenty years ago, I didn't know we even had whales," he told me on the dock beside his ferry, the *Shearwater.* "Once I saw them, that was *it.*" Captain Dyer became so fond of them that he started altering his course to match theirs, and passengers would find themselves arriving more than two hours late. "If we see something great," he admitted, "the schedule goes right out the window. Once, I counted forty whales going over to Eigg Isle. When a minke jumps, it can clear the water completely. I remember we had one jumping all the way to Eigg. It was still going after an hour and a half. Of course, I'll talk to the passengers before we land and arrange for some to take others who will have missed their rides."

Stepping over a mooring line, Dyer told me that the whales come over and check out the *Shearwater* more often than usual when it is towing a dinghy. Nevertheless, the very best method for attracting minkes is simply to place yourself near them, shut off the engine, and wait, he confirmed. "Old-timers on the islands, all they ever saw was a fin and a back," Dyer told me, "and they said, 'Ah, it's only a whale.' I said, 'You've never looked, have you?' Once they go on our boat and look down and see the whole animal with the white patches, even they get excited about it."

Fairbairns had mentioned watching people break into tears upon seeing their first minke. The longer I contemplated this, the more I found myself wondering how many whales that bring pleasure and amazement by the coast of Scotland do end up along Norway's coast while the minke-harpooning season is under way.

Among the scientific publications piled around the office of Lars Walloe at the University of Oslo are his own papers on human cardiac responses, the effects in Scandinavia of acid rain (generated mostly by industry in the British Isles), and the role of bubonic plague in the fall of the Mycenaean empire. His background is in physical chemistry and human physiology, but his career took an abrupt turn after 1986, the year of the international moratorium on commercial whaling, when Norway's prime minister asked Walloe to evaluate the country's whaling program. The Norwegians had just filed their objection to the ban and informed the world that they intended to keep right on hunting minkes. A large part of Walloe's job involved assembling data to counter criticism that the eastern North Atlantic minke population was overexploited, declining, and too low to support any harvest.

"Minkes have provided food for Norwegians since the Stone Age," Walloe told me. "We aren't sure whether people pursued the whales or relied on stranded animals in the earliest days, but we have written records of active hunting as far back as 1100 A.D." He was being conservative. Some interpret writings from hundreds of years before this as solid evidence that whaling was carried out during the Viking era, from Icelandic outposts as well as from enclaves in Norway. "The name *vagehval* refers to catching the whales in a bay or narrow inlet," Walloe continued. "When a minke entered—it was probably chasing herring schools—men would draw nets across to close off the opening. A minke has the strength to go through such nets, but it wouldn't, so the men could row in and harpoon it. This took place along the entire length of the country's coast."

With the advent of steam-powered ships and the harpoon grenade, hunting of the bay whale dropped off because the real money
was now being made from great whales in the open Atlantic and,
later, around Antarctica. Nevertheless, the Norwegians didn't completely ignore small whales. Some sought the northern bottlenose
for the valuable spermaceti-type oil in its head. There were always
a few boats going after minkes as well, mainly for meat but partly
for practice, to hone whalers' skills, Walloe said. Norwegian minke-
whaling picked up again during World War II to compensate for
food shortages, and the harvest increased for years afterward.

By the time Walloe accepted his new post with the whaling program, some authorities calculated that the eastern North
Atlantic minke population stood at just 16,000. Norwegian scientists gathered harvest records and sightings from surveys, mas-
saged the figures with statistical formulas, and at one point came
up with a total of 180,000 for the same region. A whistle-blower
later leaked internal memos showing that politicians had asked
fisheries officials to raise their estimates.

Although this clearly overstepped the boundary separating
science from state propaganda, it wasn't considered a shocking
breach of standards. In the field of fisheries management, inflat-
ing counts, either by consistently favoring the high end from a
range of possible numbers or by picking hot spots with high densities and then extrapolating the results across a much broader
area, has long been common practice. The research is carried out
by scientists working for government agencies, and the agencies charged with regulating the harvest have the same general
goal as the commercial harvesters, which is to keep the volume
as high as possible. All the parties who stand to benefit from
business as usual are quick to criticize a low count as lacking

credibility. They insist that the assumptions behind the statistics are off base; the surveys were too haphazard; ocean conditions changed and the fish temporarily went somewhere else; we don't know enough about the species's biology and are probably just seeing the bottom of a natural cycle; the sea is simply too big, and there are too many unknown factors at play. None of these issues seems to worry the same people when a high count is offered up instead. Given a system so biased toward producing results the industry prefers to hear, it is not hard to grasp why nearly all the stocks of commercially fished species have suffered precipitous declines despite the many bureaucracies supposedly dedicated to managing them.

The fact that every nation treated whaling as a type of fishery from the start and continues to place whales and other marine mammals under the jurisdiction of fisheries agencies today is unsettling. It institutionalizes a deeply flawed, archaic mind-set. Warm-blooded, air-breathing marine mammals, who produce single offspring every one to five years, operate by a whole different set of biological rules than fish, who travel in immense schools and spawn eggs by the thousands. To lump whales and fish together because they both swim in the ocean hardly makes more sense than placing apes with, say, tree frogs under the jurisdiction of a Department of Branch Climbers.

From a historical perspective, it may be understandable that nations sought to deal with the welfare of whales primarily through an International Whaling Commission built upon a fisheries management model of stocks and harvest quotas. But only inertia explains why mammals so highly advanced and evocative and yet so incompletely understood are still consigned to this old scheme when many of their kind are struggling to survive, the bulk of the public has come to perceive the leviathans far differently than it used to, and the whale-watching industry now employs far more people and generates much more revenue than commercial whaling.

Many experts now accept Norway's revised estimate of about 90,000 to 120,000 minkes for the eastern North Atlantic. With the ability to conceive while still lactating, and with a relatively short nursing period of just three to four months, female minkes are capable of producing a new calf ready for life on its own every year. Biologists think that it may be more typical for females to give birth every other year if the food supply is spotty, but when the whales are well nourished and in prime condition, a majority of adult females may indeed bear young annually. This—and the fact that minkes may mature as early as age six or seven and rarely later than age ten to fourteen—gives the species a much higher potential rate of reproduction than larger whales.

However, before you can calculate the *actual* rate of recruitment for a population, you have to figure in the rate of natural loss, and no one has a very good idea of what that might be. Reports of minke remains in the stomachs of sharks and killer whales are common enough to indicate that predators may take a significant toll on this smallest rorqual, particularly on juveniles. Is it safe to assume that there is still a "surplus" left over for human hunters? If so, how large might it be? While harvesting around a thousand minkes annually may not noticeably affect the eastern North Atlantic population as a whole, can the same be said for the portion with home ranges specifically linked to the British Isles and Norway?

The real question for many is: Why would a highly developed, socially progressive country like Norway persist in promoting whaling in the twenty-first century anyway? Science is of little help here, for the answers stem from intangibles such as national identity. Descendants of countless generations of fishermen, Norwegians draw psychological strength from their relationship with the sea and its bounty, which has included whales for as long as anyone can remember. One manager of a seafood-processing plant told me that he was mystified as to why everyone seemed willing to accept whaling as a traditional cultural activity when practiced by Native Americans with speed-boats and two-way radios but not when carried out by native Norwegians. Svend Foyn, who devised the grenade harpoon in the 1860s and adapted the steam engine to whaling boats, is a national hero here. His inventions led to Norway becoming a leading power in commercial whaling, and this in turn gave the nation a sense of greater pride and independence during the period when it was jockeying for power in an uneasy union with Sweden.

Unwilling to give up their harvest of minkes, the Norwegians started looking for ways to curtail the death throes of victims instead. Until 1983, the chief killing instrument remained little changed from the Middle Ages: a metal spear with barbs. The hooks, or backward-facing prongs, were necessary both to keep a wounded target from escaping and a dead one from sinking. In modern times, a small bow-mounted cannon was used to launch the weapon, referred to as a cold harpoon, or cold lance, to distin-guish it from one containing an explosive charge near the tip. The grenade-laden harpoon head that Svend Foyn created, so effective at incapacitating great whales, was costly and liable to damage too much of the little piked whale's meat. Minkes are small enough that even an animal still thrashing violently at the end of a cold

lance could sooner or later be hauled in close enough for the hunters to finish it off with rifle rounds to the head.

Beginning in 1981, Egil Ole Oen, a prominent veterinarian,
was hired by Norway's Ministry of Fisheries to help make the
process faster and more humane. We met on a dock in the town
of Hopen on Lofoten Island, a base of nearshore minke-whaling
operations and a stronghold of Norway's oceangoing whaling
industry during its heyday. Although the island lies about a hundred miles north of the Arctic Circle, which puts it at nearly the
same latitude as frozen Baffin Island, the warm eastward flow
of the Gulf Stream keeps the coast ice-free. Fishing vessels of all
sizes lined the wharves, and I noticed that even the most upscale
houses in town had cod hanging from drying racks in the yard.
Eiders and puffins fished among the waves in the bays and inlets.
The air at the start of June had the cool, wet feel of early spring
farther south. Birch and mountain ash trees were just leafing out
on sodden hillsides of sedge to give the land a tender green fringe.
Farther inland, snows and mists still clung to the sides of black
crags that thrust toward the midnight sun.

Here in the land where Norse gods once battled giants, Oen
and others experimented with high-velocity projectiles, electric lances, injection with compressed gases, and drugs. Certain
chemicals did prove capable of ending a minke's life in a hurry,
but the risk of accidents for people handling them daily was
high, and the potent chemical residues rendered the whale flesh
unsafe for human consumption. This was not the first time
Norwegians employed toxins to take minkes. Oen informed me
that texts dating back to the year 1240 describe using crossbows
to shoot bay whales trapped behind nets. The iron darts were
loosely fitted to the shaft, and the space in between was filled

with tissue originally taken from dead sheep. Introducing this material through a wound would, within a couple of days, leave a whale weak and surfacing frequently to breathe. The men could return then and handily dispatch the animal with lances. They hauled the body to shore and sliced away the flesh around the main point or points of infection, dipping new darts into the rotted tissue to ready them for the next hunt. Questionable cuts of meat farther from the wounds would be tossed onto the water. If they sank, they were edible. If they floated, it was because they contained infected cells, whose breakdown produced gas. Whether or not people understood this, they knew not to dine on buoyant minke steak.

According to Oen, that method of whaling continued into the 1880s. Local doctors finally isolated the infectious agent and sent samples to Denmark. The material lay around there for thirty more years before a scientist reexamined it and identified the still-viable bacteria as *Clostridium.* Strains of this microbe, which causes proteins to putrefy, were known by then to be lethal pathogens that had long affected sheep and other domestic livestock. More recently, they had earned notoriety as the cause of terrible maladies suffered by soldiers wounded in the trench warfare of World War I. The scientist infected harbor porpoises with the *Clostridium* sample. They died within twenty-four hours, and a whaling technique employed for the better part of a millennium was finally explained in full.

In 1984, Oen and his colleagues settled on a harpoon loaded with penthrite to replace the cold lance. Whereas Svend Foyn's grenade harpoon charged with black powder killed by laceration from exploded metal fragments, penthrite is a supersonic explosive used for demolition. It instantaneously begins burning at more than five thousand degrees Fahrenheit once ignited. Rather than dying from the heat, the animals apparently succumb to the shock waves generated by such rapid combustion. Once again, studies of soldiers in wartime provided background information, revealing that many bomb victims died unmarked by shrapnel. It was the force of the blast itself—alternating pulses of high and low pressure—that felled them.

The nervous system appears especially vulnerable to the shock waves' impacts on living tissues. In minkes, the high-energy pulses damage the brain, causing bleeding in its center. "We still don't understand exactly how the blast works," Oen told me. "The harpoon should be detonated in the whale's thorax, and this is very close to the brain. But we have to improve accuracy, because the killing takes longer if the harpoon goes in farther away. We also need it to explode at a certain depth within the whale to be most effective."

Leading the way onto the deck of a boat, Oen showed me the brains that he and a research assistant were collecting to gauge the results of these bombs exploding inside minkes. He suspected that concussion may cause the animal to lose consciousness almost at once. The difficulty lay in proving it. Trying to deduce a whale's final state of awareness from the degree of wreckage in the organ that processes information amounted to a disquisition upon the nature of existence and dying. The brains I beheld were half again as large as human brains and highly convoluted. If they have been shocked so powerfully that they have blood leaking through them, yet the animal's tail is still flailing or its pectoral fins spasmodically jerking, then what is this whale's status? Are observers merely witnessing the reflexes of an animal no longer registering sensations, or is it in agony? How much of the brain must be functioning for a mammal to interpret insults to the flesh as painful? When is a creature in the throes of death effectively brain-dead? Questions like Oen's have also been asked by those who oppose using animals as laboratory subjects for studies that involve traumatic injury, by the people in charge of executing criminals, and of course, by doctors making decisions about patients on life support.

Though solid answers remain elusive, Oen could take comfort in the fact that his efforts to promote the use of the thermal grenade harpoon have resulted in fewer animals being struck and lost, ripping loose from the barbed lance and escaping with mortal wounds. I was told that about two-thirds of the minkes hit with the penthrite bomb in experiments died within one minute and 90 percent within fifteen minutes. Oen also designed a larger penthrite grenade for use by natives hunting bowhead whales in Alaska. In the meantime, he oversaw training tests for Norwegian whalers to improve their accuracy, always emphasizing the need to lodge the harpoon close to the brain. There was just no getting around the fact that a poorly placed shot could be the start of a long, bloody, and probably excruciating struggle. The same week that he was discussing the subject with me, Norwegian whalers were reeling in a harpooned minke when it revived. In its frenzy, the whale battered the boat, causing the mast to break. Two crew members up in the crow's nest came tumbling down with it into the sea, busting the ribs of one man. Then the minke escaped. No sooner did the first reports come out than newspapers around the globe picked up the story and ran it under such headlines as "Don't Get Mad, Get Even."

Constantly refining the thermal grenade's design, Oen sometimes worked closely with a family of whalers on Lofoten Island, the Olavsens. Flip Nicklin and I had been negotiating with various authorities as we sought permission to ship out with a whaling crew in order to see the minke hunt for ourselves and accurately portray the whalers at work. Given the sensitivity of the subject, our U.S. citizenship, and the reputation that Americans had as the most vocal critics of Norwegian whaling, we kept getting politely put off. A few captains said no outright. We considered this a favor, because the alternative turned out to be waiting around indefinitely, only to be fed some new excuse each day. None of this was surprising, but we had originally been led to believe that the Norwegians would arrange a way for us to participate. Our hopes took a sharp turn upward when Oen and Rune Frovik, a public relations representative from a pro-whaling lobby called the High North Alliance, helped put us in touch with the Olavsen family, hinting that we might be able to travel on their vessel, the *Nybrona*.

Like most of the nearshore whaling ships in Norway, the *Nybrona* was of modest size and was used to fish for cod, haddock, herring, and saithe the rest of the year. The Olavsens had been a fishing family since at least the late 1800s. When they took up whaling in the 1930s, they were among the first in their area to rely on the harpoon gun. Other fishermen did the killing mainly with a hail of bullets, lancing the animal only at the end to keep it from sinking. The Olavsens were also among the first to add the penthrite grenade, in 1984. A second generation of Olavsen whalers now ran the *Nybrona*. Olav, middle-aged, captained the boat. His younger brother Jan Odin, who began going out on whaling cruises at age ten, assisted. Another brother used to captain a second family boat but sold it to the crew and now worked as the harpooner on someone else's vessel.

At last, the Olavsens let us on board. The *Nybrona* was still moored in the Hopen harbor, and we were invited only for a discussion over a meal, but it was a start. In light of the fact that someone who adhered to the Don't Get Mad, Get Even, philosophy had scuttled the *Nybrona* around Christmastime a few years earlier, sending it to the bottom of the harbor, the Olavsens were being more than gracious. The meal we were served turned out to feature *hvalbiff*, or whale steak; Flip and I figured we would have to pass some sort of minke-eating test. The meat was fine grained and purplish, with capillaries and iron-rich blood pigments when raw. Cooked, it was tender and tasted like overly rich beef without a trace of the sea. Jan Odin had earlier looked me in the eye with a wry expression and asked, "Do you like Greenpeace?" referring to the best known of the antiwhaling crusaders. He turned while I phrased an answer in my mind, and when he faced me again, he was holding a bowl of green peas. I asked for seconds of *hvalbiff* and then, just to confound expectations, thirds, while Flip discussed the virtues of bowhead and narwhal whale meat he had eaten while camped on the ice edge with Eskimos.

Our tablemates included Siri Knudsen, an observer from the Norwegian College of Veterinary Medicine. She would accompany the Olavsens each time they left port in search of whales. Between thirty and forty boats participated in the annual minke hunt in Norway, which took place during early summer. Every one was required to have a biologist or veterinarian aboard to record the details about each kill, especially the time from harpoon strike until death; collect samples of DNA, blubber, and tissues; and take thorough measurements of the carcass. Knudsen explained that such observers also check compliance with various regulations, the foremost being the quota of minkes assigned each boat. For ships hunting off the southern coast, the allowable take might be two dozen or fewer. That figure could rise to forty for ships in the north, where the minke population is generally denser.

Before a vessel can obtain a whaling license from the Ministry of Fisheries, its shooting equipment has to pass inspection, and the harpooners must demonstrate their accuracy with the cannon. From the *Nybrona*'s cabin, we wandered up onto the deck. Olav's son, Leif Ole, the harpooner, showed me how to handle the cannon mounted toward the bow. I swiveled the barrel back and forth, taking aim at imaginary minkes and trying to sense what it might feel like to time a shot at a big, fast mammal in rolling seas, hoping to strike just behind the brain and shatter its mind. Leif Ole told me, "You can set up a target one hundred meters away and hit a spot the size of a dinner plate every time with this gun. But we usually wait to shoot at a distance of about twenty meters. And the water must be very calm, almost flat." Otherwise, he said, it is hard just to find the whales by their blows, and hitting one becomes far too tricky. "I use the laser sight," he added. "My father does not, only the gun sight. But he almost never misses, and he almost always kills the whale right away."

As Flip and I parted company with our hosts, they promised to keep in touch about the possibility of accompanying them on a hunt. Then we went back into our holding pattern, with frequent trips to the High North Alliance office to see if any other possibilities had opened up. Once there, I often passed the time reading Alliance newsletters, fascinated by the way the articles insinuated that there was something fundamentally wrong about large numbers of whales swimming in the oceans. According to various authors' calculations, minkes were eating so many fish that they threatened to deprive humans of adequate nourishment while undermining the economies of North Atlantic nations. These countries had a responsibility to their citizens and the world to kill more minkes and other whales. Why wouldn't the public open its eyes? The whalers were nobly trying to help keep nature in balance, while the Save the Whales groups were selfish hypocrites willing to twist the facts to their advantage. On the whole, the material was very nearly identical in tone to broadsides I had seen put out by the other side.

My favorite High North Alliance newsletter piece was one ridiculing Jon Stern as a misinformed minke-lover because he had pointed out that most whalers didn't know whether they were hunting a resident population on its traditional range or a transient one migrating through toward a different range. Unless a commercial harvest is widely spread out, he had warned, it has the potential to eliminate localized populations finely attuned to particular areas. The anti-Stern article came complete with a sketch of the man, caricaturing him as a wild-eyed fulminator. Rune Frovik, the lobbyist, was fond of saying that the goal of the Alliance and NAAMCO—the North Atlantic Marine Mammal Commission, formed by the whaling countries of Norway, Iceland, Greenland, and the Faeroe Islands—was "rational utilization." Every time I heard that, I thought it sounded an awful lot like "rationalization," the most highly developed of human talents I had lately seen on display.

In the end, the Olavsens gave Flip and me permission to observe them whaling. The catch was that we couldn't actually be on the *Nybrona* but had to follow at a distance in another boat. Jan Odin Olavsen told me, "Animal rights groups project an image of big, bloody factory ships running down whales, not small family operations like ours going on a real hunt." He went on to explain that even the hunt itself was not really a chase but more like a slow stalk. The strategy was to ease your ship near a minke and then, relying on the species's tendency to approach vessels, let the target come to you.

As agreed, Flip and I shadowed the *Nybrona* in a smaller fishing boat. The hunt was just as Jan Odin had promised it would be. Instead of high drama with a crimson wake, we found the *Nybrona* bobbing placidly amid low swells little more than half a mile offshore as the Olavsens waited and watched, watched and waited. Lofoten Island's greening slopes and snowfields stood in the background beneath a clearing sky. On the opposite side rose the taller peaks of the mainland and the great glaciers that mantled much of the terrain in between. The sea grew smoother by the hour until we could see the silhouettes of mountains reflected here and there. I had to remind myself of the reality: these were ideal shooting conditions. The midnight sun spread colors across the sea's surface like dyes in molten glass. In the wee hours, when the Olavsens said they were going to move on to scout a different area some distance away, we turned our boat for home.

Back in the port of Reine, Rune Frovik told us that the whaling season appeared to be off to a good start, with more than two hundred minkes taken during the first couple of weeks. Some of the results were arriving at Hopen Fisk & Sild As, a processing plant. There I watched the vessel *Brandsholmboen* offload great blocks of purplish minke flesh with a crane. Atli Konraosson, an Icelander working as an inspector for NAAMCO, told me that the average whale killed weighs five to six tons and yields about one and a half tons of meat. The *Brandsholmboen*'s hold contained twenty-four tons from fifteen whales.

The plant manager, Aage Eriksen, said that antiwhalers had set two slaughterhouses on fire a year earlier. Understandably, a sort of siege mentality still hung in the air as he showed us around. The reason for conducting the hunt in May and June was that the arriving minkes hadn't yet put on much fat, and Norwegians like their *hvalbiff* lean. The fattiest flesh, Eriksen said, was near the tail. Although Norway flouts world opinion by continuing to kill whales, it does so strictly within its territorial waters and sells the meat only within its own borders, as called for by international regulations. Eriksen thought it a shame he couldn't at least sell cuts from the tails to the Japanese, who like fattier meat. The maroon slabs he pointed to reminded me that Flip and I had a lot more pieces of whale meat awaiting us, for we were about to move on to Japan.

Western scientists posing as tourists had been making forays through Japanese fish markets to purchase meat labeled as minke. Then they would return to laboratories set up in hotel rooms, where they analyzed the DNA of the tissues. As many as a quarter of the samples turned out to be the flesh of threatened and endangered great whales or of dolphins and porpoises, all supposed to be fully protected, even from "scientific" whaling. Japan has a history of cheating this way.

Flip and I made our own rounds of seafood stalls in Tokyo, concentrating on the famed Tsukiji Market, where an astonishing cornucopia of marine life is set out each morning. From prized bluefin tuna, which bring tens of thousands of dollars apiece from bidders, to lowly sea cucumbers and periwinkle snails, the displays glistened across acre after acre, releasing a tang of salt and ammonia in the city's heart. Given that the great majority of the different categories of organisms known to science are ocean dwellers, the Tsukiji Market adds up to one of the greatest single collections of earthly life one could possibly visit. Except, of course, it is no longer alive.

We weren't doing any sleuthing, really; just casting about for insight into how the consumption of minkes fits into Japanese life. Like Norwegians, the Japanese identify strongly with the sea, perhaps less so from the perspective of wresting a living from it under harsh conditions but more so from the standpoint of savoring its food chain from seaweed bottom to shark fin top. Flip photographed the stalls selling chunks of whale. The meat was pricier than local beef but still cheaper than the marbled variety known as Kobe beef, most of which is imported. I spoke with the owners of other stalls offering packages of smoked whale meat wafers, dried blubber called whale bacon, and crispy whale cartilage—snack food from cetaceans.

Behind one set of stalls was Hiroshi Tanaka, who would soon inherit the little shop from his parents. He told me that whale meat, which he was well aware came from "scientific" whaling, kept rising in price. "It used to be one dollar for a small package of salted whale bacon. Now it is thirty-five dollars, too expensive for me to eat." This kind of inflation was causing Tanaka to lose customers. Attributing the jump to a scarcity of available products, he found himself worrying about both the future of his business and of the whales. "I have a brother-in-law in the United States," Tanaka said. "He tells us we should stop selling whale. I would not like to see an overkill. It is important to keep everything in balance."

Japanese whalers still use the cold lance on minkes. A struck animal's struggles can be prolonged as a crew tries to work it closer to the boat. Once it is within reach, an electric lance is inserted, and the whale is shocked to death. Japanese officials like to portray whaling as an ancient cultural activity in a nation that venerates tradition. In reality, the practice began with the Wada family in the Yokohama area during the 1600s. This was roughly the same time that the Dutch and English took up commercial whaling and three centuries after the Basques of Spain and France started the industry. The Japanese went after humpbacks and slow-moving right whales, usually not far from shore.

For centuries, the Tokugawa shogunate kept the country largely sealed off from foreign influences, and U.S. history books make much of the "opening" of Japan by Commodore Matthew Calbraith Perry and his gunships during 1853–54. Yet American whalers searching for cetacean populations that had not yet collapsed had been visiting for some time before that, putting into Japanese ports for much-needed supplies. Later, the United States and, especially, Norway provided the Japanese with the steamships and expertise needed to establish a more modern whaling fleet. Japan then began building its own boats. But the country's era of long-range whaling across the high seas and into antarctic waters didn't really get under way until the 1930s, when Japan purchased its first Norwegian factory ship to process the giants on site. In the aftermath of World War II, the United States helped reinvigorate the Japanese whaling industry as a fast fix for protein shortages in the crippled country.

I fell into conversation with a passing shopper in the market, an older man, who recalled, "When I was six or seven years old, it was whale, whale, every day whale. At school. At home. I got tired of it." Times have changed almost beyond recognition since then. Far from being a staple in fast-paced, digital, modern Japan, whale has become a specialty food bordering on a luxury item. During our stay in the capital city, Flip and I lodged with his longtime colleague, Koji Nakamura, a renowned underwater cameraman, and Koji's wife, Miyuki. In addition to introducing us to favorite neighborhood sushi bars, the Nakamuras guided us to the Moon Garden restaurant, one of only a handful of dining spots in Tokyo where whale meat is regularly served. Seated on tatami mats next to a pond full of koi, we put chopsticks to strips of lightly braised minke and dipped them in spicy soy or mustard sauce. I kept thinking of how an article in the British weekly newsmagazine *The Economist* described scientific whaling as a cover as thin as the slices of sashimi that a researched whale inevitably becomes.

I was curious to see a more exotic offering that I had heard about: thin slices of cetacean lips, referred to as whale whispers. Kujira-Ya, or House of Whale, in the Shibuya district sounded like a good place to find some on the menu, but I had no luck. The owner, Tanahashi Kiyohiko, complained that it was difficult enough to buy ordinary whale meat in sufficient volume to hold prices down. A poster on the wall above my seat implored me to Support Scientific Whaling. As I sampled minke dishes and conversed with Kiyohiko about the business, he excused himself for a moment and returned with literature produced by the government-funded Institute of Cetacean Research. He also gave me handouts from an organization calling itself the Beneficiaries of the Riches of the Sea. The latter contained poignant testimony from a mother who claimed that her daughter was allergic to all protein except that of baleen whales. Won't you please help this poor girl by lobbying for whaling, the brochure asked? It went on to suggest that eating whale meat had been shown to alleviate dizziness and obesity as well as a spectrum of allergies.

The institute's pamphlets broadened the theme I had heard in Norway, which was that whales were gobbling an unfair share of the fish in the sea. The big, greedy beasts were purported to be consuming five times the tonnage of marine resources that humanity was. Nearly all the figures cited were based on extremely questionable estimates of whale numbers and daily food intake. The term *marine resources* includes whale food as tiny as copepods and krill, making any direct comparison with human food largely irrelevant to begin with. Yet as the paragraphs rolled on, the propagandists gradually substituted the word *fish* for *marine resources,* creating the illusion that for every herring or tuna or whatever variety a human most enjoyed, the whales were hogging five. Why, common sense told the reader that eating more whales would provide more of those tasty fish for everyone, a win-win situation for humans and obviously a more efficient way to utilize the ocean as a whole. Elsewhere, I saw a Japanese poster that depicted the planet with a rain of fish dropping off its sides and funneling down into the maw of a colossal whale below—for anyone who had missed the point in print.

The moment I stepped out of the House of Whale, I was swept up in a shoulder-jostling flood of humanity that makes Japan one of the leading consumers of fish. And, like almost every other country with a major fleet, it is badly overharvesting commercial stocks in a free-for-all on the high seas. Just as the International Whaling Commission chattered constantly about setting meaningful harvest quotas the whole time the great whales were being massacred, the nations of the world are all wind but no sail when it comes to setting limits on fishing beyond their own territorial waters.

After taking a leading role in wiping out a third of a million blue whales in the Southern Ocean within half a century, Japanese whalers continued to take some blues illegally. They were still at it, as DNA testing of meat in the markets confirmed. Yet the industry position was that the minke population around Antarctica was not only burgeoning in the blue whales' absence but also monopolizing so much of the available krill that this was keeping blue whales from recovering. So if you care about endangered blue whales, for goodness' sake eat more minke. Japan's minister of fisheries went so far as to publicly deride minkes as "cockroaches of the sea." When it came to rationalizing minke hunting, the Japanese made the Norwegians look like amateurs.

Masaki Sakai, employed by the Japanese embassy in Washington, D.C., brought up the fact that people kill all kinds of animals and asked me if it wasn't true that Americans shot species such as cougars and grizzly bears "just because they enjoy it." Yes, of course, I answered. "We are not killing whales for joy but to eat," Sakai noted, "so we cannot understand why there is so much concern over whales. The resource is coming back, and commercial whaling is sustainable. It would increase the food supply. It could help with the hunger of the world."

These were well-reasoned points. But when Sakai concluded with "There is no reason not to kill them," I found myself shaking my head at the telephone. Keeping up the pretense that the validity of whaling is simply a matter of numbers—that, once those rise to a specified level, we can extract a percentage of populations each year without undue harm—obscures an enduring truth. It is that our humanity is defined in part by the moral decisions we make. Sooner or later, we are going to have to address those hard choices between the convenience of treating animals as commodities and our ethical responsibility toward sentient beings. Whales could be the starting point. In light of how little we really understand about cetaceans, and of how markedly our perception of them has been changed by what we have discovered thus far, it seems literally demoralizing to lobby for returning all the species that are no longer imperiled to the category of goods to be reaped from the seas.

I suspect that, deep down, we know which way we are supposed to go. Despite my different forays into minke dining, I never considered ordering a meal of whale apart from my role as a journalist. I'm not really comfortable eating anything that huge and mysterious, least of all when it might very well be smarter than I am.

Animal intelligence is an open-ended subject. We can scarcely describe how our own brains work to store memories, make decisions, or formulate new ideas. Trying to define how smart a whale is may be a pointless exercise. The only indisputable fact is that cetaceans have impressively large brains. Toothed cetaceans, including dolphins and porpoises, meet or exceed most tests for high animal I.Q. Although baleen whales may be equally bright, they are too big for problem-solving experiments in a controlled environment. Their brains are big as well: that of a blue whale may weigh three times as much as an adult human brain. Those heaps of interlacing neurons are doing something, thinking something. But are these animals brilliant? Or are they—as I've heard some scientists guess—more on a par with familiar hooved animals? Ungulates gave rise to the cetaceans, after all, and remain their closest relatives. Could a minke basically be the mental equivalent of a big, wet, wild ox?

Our tendency is to associate mental agility with carrying out a variety of activities, making things happen, trying different maneuvers, and above all, inventing some. That may be a fair standard, but we can't see what whales do during the 95 percent or more of their lives that take place underwater. Second, having limber arms with dexterous fingers ourselves, we relate especially well to creatures that manipulate objects in their environment. But whales lack hands or even a neck. They are working with comparatively rigid bodies shaped like stretched-out footballs. While they can move with equal ease vertically and horizontally, suspended in seamless liquid wherever they go, they aren't exactly built for poking around and diddling with stuff. To the extent that they do, it mostly happens on a scale too large for us to appreciate.

What about communication as a sign of intelligence? Though scientists now locate blue whales by their calls, blue whale expert George Small wrote in 1971 that "no blue whale 'voice' has ever been recorded." People were still saying that about minkes just a few years ago. In their high-latitude feeding ranges, these whales do appear to be relatively silent. But during the early 1980s, more and more minkes began swimming around boats and scuba divers along sections of the northern Great Barrier Reef in winter. The encounters became common enough that some companies added minke watching to their reef adventure trips. Near the start of the twenty-first century, Jason Gedamke, a graduate student working with Dan Costa, a professor at the University of California, Santa Cruz, arrived in that part of Australia and dropped a hydrophone in the water by the animals. He picked up a startling *boi-oi-oing,* which he started calling "Star Wars" because the reverberating sound reminded him of science fiction weapons firing in space. It was so bizarre and un-cetacean-like that he refused to rule out some other sea creature as the source until he had more recordings that he could definitely associate with the passing whales. The *boi-oi-oing* turned out to be a minke voice, and Gedamke went on to identify an assortment of other buzzes, rapid grunts, groans, and growls issuing from the animals. The minkes proved so noisy that he set out an array of fixed hydrophones on the seafloor as a means of tracking the whales' movements in the general area.

I went scuba diving in those marvelously clear waters many times while pursuing a story on coral reefs. Though my timing was off for meeting minkes there, I was able to get together with two marine scientists—Peter Arnold, from the Museum of Tropical Queensland, and Alastair Birtles, of James Cook University—who had logged many an hour in the water with the animals. This sort of adventure was becoming increasingly popular, and Arnold and Birtles were helping the Great Barrier Reef Marine Park Authority develop guidelines for the activity so that it wouldn't conflict with sanctions against harassing marine mammals. Their solution was reasonably simple: you weren't to scoot around after the whales with scuba gear, but you were free to get in with your face mask and snorkel, float while holding on to a rope behind a drifting vessel, and let the whales come to you. Being minkes, many would, yet the arrangement left up to them the choice of how often and how closely to interact.

Somewhere out on the world's longest reef, far from shore or any town, people were designing ways to behave with discretion in order to avoid possibly disturbing passing minke whales. And somewhere else, Japanese boats prepared to steam by Australia en route to cold-lancing minkes in the Southern Ocean. I couldn't get the dichotomy out of my thoughts.

Birtles told me that a couple of years earlier he had been in the water with more than two hundred minkes over the course of the season. "The average group size was two or three near the reef and closer to six in open water," he said. "We've had the count build up to twenty-five at a time." On prime feeding grounds, you might find several minkes near each other as they pursued the same big school of fish. Whalers sometimes reported scores of minkes together amid huge concentrations of antarctic krill. Otherwise, the whales were thought to be largely solitary apart from the brief mother-young association. The documentation of noisy groups traveling together and checking out people along the northern Great Barrier Reef has opened a window upon an entirely new aspect of their lives.

Birtles told me that the average encounter he recorded lasted about an hour. The currents in that area are strong. To stay near people, the whales had to keep actively swimming. Their level of interest had to be high. It wasn't unusual to have some minkes stay two or three hours. One minke that Birtles observed hung around for eleven hours. What was going on in that individual's brain? Fish will pause in their travels to scrutinize you. The least bright cow in a pasture may wander over to have a look, as might a big wild ox. But eleven hours? Possibly calling out messages in its newly discovered otherworldly voice? And Masaki Sakai can say flatly that there is no reason not to kill them?

One good reason not to kill such animals has nothing to do with empathy for whales. It stems instead from sheer human self-interest. After analyzing more than a hundred samples of whale meat from restaurants and shops across Japan in 1999, Japanese toxicologists announced that half the specimens held concentrations of dangerous heavy metals such as mercury. The meat. also contained organochlorines such as dioxin and PCBs, known to cause harm to the nervous, endocrine, reproductive, and immune systems in mammals. Like seals and sea lions, minkes often feed fairly high on the food chain, gulping the big fish that gulp smaller fish that gulp krill-size plankton that gulp smaller plankton. At each of these stages, or trophic levels, pollutants from a large number of food organisms can become concentrated in the single organism digesting them. The process is termed *bioaccumulation.* According to the Japanese researchers, some minkes were storing enough contaminants to pose a serious health risk to a human eating just a few ounces of blubber. A separate study revealed higher-than-normal levels of brain and heart damage among children in the Faeroe Islands whose mothers had eaten whale meat, primarily minke.

Spokespeople for the whaling industry downplayed such findings, emphasizing that whale meat carries lower levels of contamination than the blubber does. That's true, but harmful contaminants work their way through the bloodstream before they are taken up by the liver or stored in the blubber layer. Most tissues contain some lipids, and lipids are what bind to the chlorinated hydrocarbons. Any cut of minke should carry the warning label "Caveat emptor": Buyer beware. Due to prevailing currents, wind patterns, and the cold temperatures that keep chemical compounds from breaking down into less damaging forms, pollutants tend to collect in high latitudes, which is where minkes and most larger whales can be found during their summer feeding season. Health departments already urge consumers to limit their weekly intake of many popular fish, from tuna to halibut, because of concerns over their mercury content alone. In the Great Lakes region of the United States as well as in the Arctic, health problems and abnormal development during early childhood have been attributed to eating fish laden with chlorinated hydrocarbons.

Every marine mammal in the seven seas is burdened with worrisome loads of toxins these days merely because it has no choice but to eat seafood. Human cultures tied to ocean food chains in the Arctic have the same problem. This is a terribly sad thing to think about. And it's disappointing that the whaling industry can't bring itself to just put away the lances and say, Okay, we're tired of fighting world opinion in order to promote the consumption of creatures that we now know may harm the health of whoever dines on them. We're done.

Small, fast baleen whales have been chasing fish around for tens of millions of years. The minke (along with the rarely seen and poorly understood pygmy right whale, which averages just under twenty feet in length) is the modern version. All the other rorquals are somewhat more specialized as well as larger, leaving the minke its niche as the modest-size generalist. Ecologically, this has been a tremendously successful lifestyle, one that made minkes ubiquitous along the continental shelves, shores, and ice edges of much of the globe. By a quirk of fortune, the niche proved equally beneficial to the species throughout centuries of commercial whaling. Relative to its slaughtered kin, the whale that hardly anyone paid much attention to emerged more abundant than ever. This suddenly transformed the littlest rorqual into something quite different—a target, and a test case for the price other whales may have to pay as soon as they start to become common again.

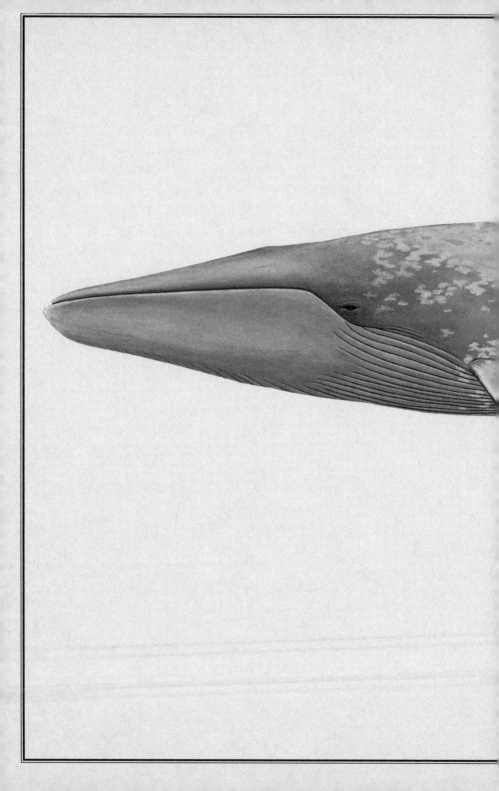

THE GIANT
BLUE WHALE

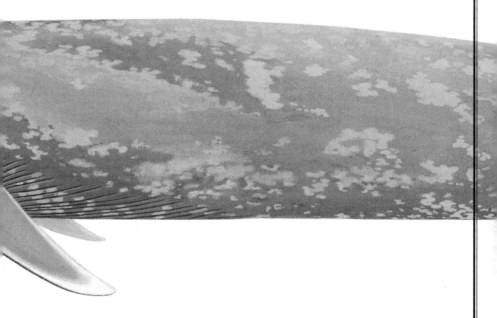

T hroughout most parts of marine ecosystems, key nutrients such as iron and nitrogen are in short supply. They are quickly taken up by the life-forms that proliferate in the sunlit upper reaches of the water column, known as the photic zone. As the organisms die, their bodies sink, along with the chemicals incorporated into them, leaving the surface depleted. Rivers and streams deliver new supplies from the land, but a large share of these also settles onto the seafloor, often still encapsulated in silt. Although people speak of the wealth of the sea, it is important to realize that the sea, on average, is not all that rich. It's just that some portions are fabulously bountiful, especially where waters well up from the depths and carry the nutrients that have been collecting there back into circulation.

During the warm months, high pressure systems develop over Alaska and force air toward the south. These prevailing winds drive ocean currents the same direction. The harder the gusts blow, the more actively the currents flow down North America's Pacific coast. Coming from the north, the waters are chilly and sink beneath warmer layers to run along the seafloor, roiling its sediments as they go. Where the flow meets submerged ridges or seamounts or begins swirling over a canyon, the cold waters may be forced up toward the surface. There, the dissolved minerals and organic chemicals contained in the chilly current spark an explosion of microscopic algae, collectively called phytoplankton, which are eaten by the smallest animals, termed zooplankton, which multiply rapidly in turn—becoming more fuel for a food chain that can culminate in prodigious concentrations of larger organisms. Much larger.

The fog moved in streams and patches, gilded at the edges, with sunlight roller-coasting on the open ocean swells in between. Cruising along in a boat from one clearing to the next was like being ushered through curtains onto a succession of brilliant blue stages where performances were in progress. Here, hundreds of common dolphins leaped in synchrony and competed for the lead, riding our bow wave. There, heavy mist parted to reveal groups of sleek young sea lions going airborne together just like the dolphins, arcing from wave to wave. The next opening was a whirlwind of phalaropes, the most seagoing of shorebirds. Flocks hovered and skittered along the surface to peck at swarms of the shrimplike crustaceans known as krill. Hundreds more phalaropes were floating, buoyed by the extra air that these sandpiper relatives trap within their feathers. Pirouetting as many as forty times a minute, each worked at creating a small vortex to concentrate the krill before dabbing into the swirl. In another scene upon another stage, pink-footed shearwaters were gathered over the krill, and brown pelicans plunged between them like volleys of big darts to scoop fish hunting the krill from below.

We were somewhere near San Miguel, the most northwesterly of the Channel Islands, just forty miles south of Santa Barbara, California. But there was no horizon to fix upon, no landform to orient by, only more veils of gray softly ebbing and billowing, sliding across the undulant sea. Adding to my sense of dislocation, the breeze was chilly and the upwelling currents as cold as if we were probing far northern seas. I was somewhere I had never been before on a water planet, exploring: that was all I felt sure of. It was enough, because the place was filled with marvels. Then we passed into another bright clearing, and three blue whales swam through.

Their blows shot three stories high in columns that spread downwind to become sheets of mist, as if it were the whales that had been making this fog. No sooner did a fresh spout rivet our attention with a blast like the roar of a factory pipe than an enormous bulk would begin to appear beneath it. The body would rise, lengthen, and rise some more—pale gray with a blue tinge where sheets of water ran off the sides, dappled with sea-gray spots—and go on surfacing until it loomed broad and glistening as the top side of a submarine. And every time I told myself that this had to be the peak, that the manifestation was finally complete, the whole seamless immensity emerged higher and longer. Even when the leading part of the body angled down to reenter the waves, more of the whale was still coming up into view, now too thick and long to compare with anything I could think of before the back came rolling forward, bringing into view an unexpectedly small dorsal fin toward the rear and, after a while, a very wide, flat tail that planed upon the water, lifted slightly, and then was at last gone.

At the time, I was reporting on a different subject and had not thought about devoting chunks of my life to following in the wake of whales every year. I'd encountered other whales, and each experience was a revelation of sorts. But the surfacing of a blue whale was an out-and-out thunderclap. *This* was Leviathan. Twice the size of other great whales I'd been near, it was too big to anticipate and too big to fully recall afterward—too much to hold in the mind. I wouldn't be able to picture another until I came upon it, and I found myself strongly compelled to do just that.

The blue whale was first scientifically described by a Scot, Robert Sibbold, traveling the inlet called the Firth of Forth near Edinburgh in 1692. That whales weren't definitely identified as mammals until the following year shows how far our understanding of such creatures lagged behind what was known about land animals. During the next century, the blue whale was formally classified by the father of scientific nomenclature himself, Carolus Linnaeus. So scrupulous in their cataloguing of species, taxonomists aren't above occasionally giving one a ridiculous Latin label, perhaps just to see if anyone else is paying attention to their obscure labors. Linnaeus seems to have set some sort of standard when he named the blue whale *Balaenoptera musculus,* knowing that *musculus* means "little mouse."

Some taxonomists have since divided blue whales into three subspecies: *Balaenoptera musculus musculus,* the northern blue whale, assumed to migrate between arctic or subarctic feeding sites and tropical breeding areas; its somewhat larger counterpart in the Southern Hemisphere, *B. m. intermedia,* said to follow a similar pattern, feeding in the high latitudes around Antarctica throughout the austral summer and retreating to tropical climes over winter; and *B. m. brevicauda,* the smallest subspecies, rarely longer than eighty feet as an adult, believed to stay year-round in the warm waters of the Indian Ocean and possibly other areas in the Indo-Pacific region. However, there remains considerable disagreement over the divisions within this species, and the debate will likely continue until more genetic analysis is completed, along with a thorough analysis of the calls made by various populations. Moreover, *B. m. brevicauda,* sometimes labeled the pygmy blue whale, is held by many to be a suspect category, for it was initially proposed by Japanese whalers to justify harvesting what they claimed was a separate, newly discovered stock of blue whales.

Whatever form they take, the geographic variations of this "little mouse" happen to be not only the largest of all mammals but also the most colossal beasts ever to appear in the history of life on Earth. You might have heard some of the superlatives: how a blue whale's tongue is the size of an elephant and its heart is as big as a car, pumping sixty gallons of blood per minute, or how a human child could toddle upright along the aorta. An infant blue whale is twenty-three to twenty-seven feet long. It gains nine to ten pounds an hour while nursing fatty milk with the consistency of runny cheese until, by the age of six or seven months, the baby has almost doubled in length and increased its weight tenfold, to twenty-five tons. By one year of age, it will be fifty-five feet long. Amazingly, whalers slicing up pregnant females harpooned in Antarctica found some carrying twins.

Counting annual layers in the waxy plug of the inner ear yielded an age of at least fifty years, and possibly one hundred, for one blue whale specimen. Some may live well beyond that. The average adult female—the larger of the two sexes—taken by whalers measured almost 90 feet from nose to tail. Quite a few carcasses spanned nearly 100 feet, and although some people suspect their accuracy, there are records of 108, 109, and even 111 feet. No one ever devised a means to weigh something so vast except in pieces, with most of the body's fifteen thousand pints of blood missing, having flooded away to stain the sea. Nevertheless, a fair estimate for a very large, live individual with a feeding season's worth of stored fat might be as high as 150 or even 200 tons. That exceeds the weight of several of the hugest dinosaurs combined. Or as George Small put it in his seminal book, *The Blue Whale,* "A large female . . . can lose 50 tons while nursing a calf and still weigh twice as much as [the Jurassic behemoth] *Brachiosaurus.*"

The animal's call, a low-frequency moan, is the loudest sound any organism produces. It is issued at 185 to 190 decibels, beyond the noise level a human being can produce with any object. Considering that every decibel expands the effective range of a sound by 25 percent under ideal conditions, it is possible that blue whales communicate across entire ocean basins. Hydrophones can detect blue whale calls about half that far. Whether the animals themselves can hear one another at such distances, or whether they pay attention if they do, is unknown. Perhaps their range for communication is only a few hundred miles. Still, it is intriguing to think that blue whales may have been using the equivalent of satellite phones—or at least of regionwide cell phone coverage—since long before our ancestors started walking erect.

When a blue whale is feeding, the lower jaw sweeps out until it is at a ninety-degree angle to the upper jaw and its curtain of baleen. In a fast-moving animal, this radical opening, sufficient to bring the massive body to a sudden halt, constitutes the most powerful biomechanical action known. The mouth and throat are ribbed with fifty-five to eighty-eight expandable pleats running from the lower lip to the navel. They allow a blue whale to gulp as many as seventy tons of prey-laden seawater at a time, changing the body's shape from supersized torpedo to titanic polliwog. At that stage, a temporary weight exceeding half a million pounds for the largest blues is not out of the question. Now envision one breaching. I don't know anyone who has seen adult blues come completely out of the water during a vertical leap, but they will rise halfway out or more. The chance to see five stories of blue whale sticking into the sky with another four or five stories still in the water is reason enough to take to the *hwaelweg,* which is Old English for "whale way," one of countless names for the sea.

Nature, the original bioengineer, is tirelessly at work expanding the scope of life, fashioning possibilities where none existed before. The evolution of a hoofed land dweller the size of a miniature hippopotamus into the entire suite of streamlined ocean roamers we call whales makes a sensational case in point. A curiously related example of natural selection's inventiveness was recently plucked by the robot arm of a submersible from a canyon

eighty-five hundred feet deep. Described in a scientific paper by
Robert Vrijenhoek of the Monterey Bay Aquarium Research
Institute, this thing from the dark depths of inner space isn't
science-fiction scary like the abyssal fish that seem to be life-sup-
port systems for outrageous sets of fangs. *Osedax,* as the new species was named, doesn't even have a mouth, much less teeth. Nor
any digestive organs. It is a pale, finger-length cylinder coated in
mucus, with a crown of red plumes and a base of coiling, green,
rootlike projections. Almost as strange, the body is always female
and has hundreds of nearly microscopic males living inside her
slimy sheath.

Scientists weren't even sure at first what category of animal
they had in hand. DNA analysis eventually showed it to be most
closely related to certain tubeworms that live around the edges
of deep-sea vents. Discovered not too long ago themselves, those
organisms protect their bodies with hard casings and use feathery structures around their mouths to sweep in chemosynthetic
bacteria, which feed directly on sulfur- and iron-rich chemicals
spewing from molten cracks in the spreading seafloor. That's
one way to find opportunity far from the sunshine that powers
food chains almost everywhere else on Earth. But what does
the tubeworms' soft, mouthless, gutless relative, *Osedax,* subsist
on at the cold, lightless bottom of the ocean? Apparently, this
worm relies on bacteria too, though it doesn't eat them. It hosts
colonies inside the tissues at its base and absorbs their waste
products as food.

In other words, the new creature is actually a fusion of two—
a joint venture, or symbiosis, made odder still by the fact that the
bacteria specialize in feeding on the skeletons of whales that sink
to the bottom of the sea. Long after scavengers have stripped the

last flesh from a carcass, *Osedax* somehow finds its way there and attaches so that the microbes in its base can penetrate the bones. This is a richer feast than it sounds like, because whale bones tend to be packed with an unusually high quotient of lipids, or fats—around 60 percent.

As each cetacean reached the end of its lifespan, its body would come spiraling slowly down into the gloom, league after league, ever deeper and ever darker until—Whoomph!—it landed in an explosion of long-undisturbed silt. When the cloud from the impact finally settled, the otherwise largely barren bottom would be graced with a stockpile of organic compounds large enough to alter the local topography. The fall of bodies probably took place at a fairly regular rate for millions of years. Now imagine an instant of geologic time during which flayed carcasses and cast-off parts came down from whaling boats like a hailstorm, along with many a whale that thrashed loose from a harpoon mortally wounded. Then imagine the years afterward, when fresh corpses became scarce because the supply of live great whales had almost run out.

Among the first to become rare were the right whales, which got their name for being the "right" whale to hunt. Stout, blubbery, and slow moving, they frequently feed along the surface, often fairly close to coasts, and they conveniently float after being killed. By contrast, blue whales can race along at close to twenty knots and cover a mile out of sight between one set of breaths and the next. For centuries, whalers could only watch them swim by—watch and dream of the profits to be rendered from those humongous bodies. The invention of grenade-tipped harpoons during the latter half of the nineteenth century made it easier to incapacitate great whales. But you still had to be able to catch up to them, and the blues were too quick and powerful to be chased down either by sail or oar power. Steam-driven ships finally changed the odds to a point where the biggest, fastest rorquals—sei, fin, and blue whales—began to disappear from both the North Atlantic and North Pacific under intense hunting pressure.

Inevitably, the industry made its way to the harsh but teeming seas around Antarctica, beginning around 1909. As the industrial era advanced, powerful diesel engines were added to the fleets, followed by enormous factory ships for processing and storing catches from the hunter boats. During the 1930–31 season, whalers were able to take 29,400 blues from the Antarctic in a single season. After World War II, the U.S. effort at reconstruction included providing expertise, equipment, and encouragement for Japan to step up its harvest of great whales. By the early 1960s, it was getting hard to find full-grown adult blues in Antarctica. The average length of females taken in the yearly hunts, now dominated by the Japanese, had shrunk to seventy-three feet; between 50 and 80 percent of those killed had not even had a chance to mature and reproduce their kind.

Any livestock owner in the world could have pointed out that slaughtering both breeding females and their adolescent replacements is a certain way to reduce a herd to zero, fast. Yet the whalers' response to the disappearance of blues was to keep taking all they could while concentrating harder on the next-largest species, the fin whale, which may weigh as much as eighty tons. They proceeded to take nearly 700,000. By the time the estimated fin whale population was down to 35,000 or fewer, the whalers were still killing them as opportunities arose but focusing their efforts on the next-largest species, the sei whale. And the

International Whaling Commission, having already presided over the destruction of species that were easier to hunt, once again did little but aid, abet, and apologize for the industry it was supposed to be regulating. When the first serious proposals to restrict commercial whaling were put forth during the 1960s, it was partly as a result of public outcry but largely because populations of the last great whales to be exploited had already crashed and the industry's cash flow was negative. The whalers—"the undisputed champions of shortsightedness in the history of our species," as leading researcher Roger Payne observed in his 1992 book, *Among Whales*—had mined out the lode.

As of 1965, the documented take of blue whales from the Southern Ocean added up to nearly 330,000. In terms of biomass, this works out, conservatively, to 60 billion pounds, equal to the weight of more than 400 million human beings. During the 1964–65 season, 172 catcher boats from fifteen factory ship expeditions had been able to find only 20 blues to harpoon in the entire Southern Hemisphere. The steepness and suddenness of the decline led an outraged George Small to conclude in *The Blue Whale* that the chances of survival for the giant among giants were "virtually nil." His book was published in 1971, before the Russians admitted that, on top of their official harvest, the former Soviet Union had killed tens of thousands of blues between 1942 and 1975 that were never reported.

Small's poignant farewell to the blue whale helped shape public perception of the animal's condition. His pessimism was reinforced by a continuing scarcity of sightings in both hemispheres. Thus, along with the superlatives about blue whales, you may have heard that only several hundred survive in all the oceans, so scattered that they have trouble finding one another to breed, and that their days are numbered. The paroxysm of destruction that drove this grandest of species to commercial extinction may indeed stand as the ultimate allegory about uncontrollable human greed, wretched excess, or however you want to phrase the matter. And it might very well be true that the entire Southern Ocean holds no more than several hundred. The International Whaling Commission's estimate for the Southern Hemisphere is seven hundred to one thousand. If there are more, no one has lately been able to find them.

On the other hand, actual extinction does not look likely any time soon. Signs of possible recovery have begun to appear in the Northern Hemisphere. Moreover—and it is a joy to be able to write these words, because I was no more aware of the facts than the general public is until I started paying close attention—researchers have even been turning up evidence of unexpected abundance in some areas. They put the numbers for just one particular population at two to three thousand, a higher count than many believed would be tallied anywhere ever again. This is the largest group known in the world today, and it is the one I met right off the California coast.

The Channel Islands are arrayed between 30 and 100 miles from Los Angeles. They might as well be separated by a thousand miles and a thousand years. Southern California's mainland is a palm-lined oasis of trendy urban culture. The Channel Islands are windy, weathered, steep, and spare. Most of their acreage is national park, which in turn lies within the 1,658-square-mile Channel Islands National Marine Sanctuary. Though the area is undeveloped, it is hardly uninhabited. On parts of the islands, California sea lions, harbor seals, elephant seals, pelicans, storm petrels, penguinlike Xantus' murrelets and Cassin's auklets, and other colony-breeding wildlife form cosmopolitan throngs of their own. And a few steps beyond the arid terrain begin some of the lushest, fastest-growing forests in the world. You enter through their canopy, parting fronds of bull kelp and giant kelp to sink into an underwater jungle where the seals and sea lions, golden garibaldi fish, and jade-eyed kelp bass fly between vinelike tangles of stalks. The currents flowing into this region, known as the California Bight, come mainly from the north. Funneled by Point Conception, they run into the islands and submarine cliffs. Cold waters come welling up to fertilize the photic zone, and the cafeteria is set.

When I first visited the islands with Ed Cassano, who at that time was the acting manager of the marine sanctuary, half a dozen ships, ranging from a NOAA (National Oceanic and Atmospheric Administration) vessel the size of a navy destroyer to a volunteer's sailboat, were assembled nearby. This flotilla was part of an effort to accomplish something that had not been tried throughout all the decades that blue whales were reaped as a commodity: gather basic data about their ecology and behavior. Information was pitifully scarce. No one was even clear about where the animals went each year after leaving their summer feeding grounds. The consensus was that they headed for the tropics. But to which parts? What did they do there? Our enduring fascination with dinosaurs made me wonder: if the world held no more whales, and they were known only from long-fossilized bones, would people show more interest in figuring out what the lives of the hugest animals of all time were like?

Whalers referred to some types of great whales returning from winter ranges as "dryskins" because they contained relatively little oil. This reinforced the belief that the animals fasted for months on end, drawing down their fat reserves while they waited for the next feeding season to start, but today there are hints that this may not always be the case. We at least know something about what blue whales prefer to eat when they do dine, and their choice makes perfect sense. The largest animal relies almost exclusively upon one of the most abundant types of animal (above the microscopic level). These are crustaceans with the same basic body plan, multiple legs, and long antennae that common shrimp have, and they are known as krill. In every ocean a variety of species are found feeding very close to the base of the food pyramid, on free-floating, single-celled algae. Considered to be among the larger forms of zooplankton, krill are less than an inch long as a rule. The Antarctic krill, *Euphasia superba,* is a notable exception at two to three inches. Oceanographers found it thriving throughout an area four times the size of the United States at densities reaching thirty-five pounds per cubic yard in spots. Russian biologists once reported a single swarm that they estimated at 100 million tons; the greatest single concentration of life yet located, it surpassed the total yearly fish catch by people around the world. Even if that estimate was too high—and it probably was—the amount of animal biomass available in the form of krill comes across as stupendous.

Algae to krill to giant whale is one of the simplest and most efficient of all food chains. It means that blues are only a couple of steps removed from dining directly on sunlight. They scoop in two to perhaps four tons of krill daily. The researchers gathered in the Channel Islands wanted to put together a snapshot of the foraging strategies involved by simultaneously mapping the whereabouts of krill swarms, tracking the whales' movements, charting their dive patterns with the help of time-depth recorders—the first ever attached to blues—and deploying hydrophones to record any vocalizations the giants made.

For part of my visit, I rode along on an old fishing boat retrofitted for science by Don Croll and Bernie Tershy of the University of California, Santa Cruz. To say the craft had a lived-in feel would be generous. The cramped wheelhouse was a jumble of instrument wires, student assistants, drying clothing, and notebooks next to the remains of dinner from the night before—or possibly a couple of nights before—and laptop computers whose monitors danced with bands of color highlighting the krill swarms detected by instruments scanning the depths with sound. In its anarchic way, everything was prepped for gathering crucial data. When wind and chop and fog prevented that, what did the scientists do? Dude, they went surfing. This *was* California, after all. Locating a point off a lonely island where the swell made totally excellent waves, Croll and Tershy unlashed their boards from the boat's roof and passed the day on the breakers' slopes, kicking out from the curl at the last moment before their ride slammed into the ragged volcanic rock on shore. We camped on the island at night, laying out sleeping bags on the sand beneath the stars.

As weather permitted, the team found the whales swimming between specific sites where the krill were most concentrated and ransacking them with marvelous efficiency. During daylight hours, the majority of krill kept to a depth of four hundred to six hundred feet. These crustaceans weren't feeding much down there, Croll said, judging from the empty stomachs of specimens scooped up in a net. This and the fact that they sought out breaks in the submarine terrain, sticking close to ledges, made him

suspect that the krill stayed at that level mainly to avoid diving birds, fish that school in the upper water levels, and other
predators. But the whales would plunge more or less straight
down into the cloud of crustaceans; four hundred to six hundred
feet, remember, is little more than four to six body lengths for a
blue giant. According to the time-depth recorders, the blues then
moved up and down through the krill swarm, an indication that
they were taking repeated gulps before surfacing, straining the
seawater out through their baleen plates in between. Such active
hunting again belied the popular conception of baleen whales
swimming placidly around with their mouths open, gathering a
continuous meal. Tershy thought that, instead of speaking of them
"grazing" plankton like an herbivore, it would be more fitting to
compare blues feeding on krill to swallows or swifts swooping
back and forth through an insect swarm.

The krill begin eating when they rise at night to the surface, where the phytoplankton is thickest. Since many consume
mostly diatoms—single-celled, golden brown algae encased in
silica armor—Tershy liked to say that the krill come up to fill
their bellies with glass. The krill also seek out the upper levels
because the warmer temperatures promote faster body growth,
maturation, and development of the next generation, visible as
eggs cradled among the multiple legs on the lower abdomens of
females. As dusk descended and the krill started coming up, the
whales switched to lunge-feeding along the surface. Racing into
the midst of a concentration of prey, a blue would raise its head
while rolling onto one side and opening its jaws in a great sweep
that sent waves washing outward and usually brought the giant
to a full stop. Very often, lunge-feeding blues roll completely onto
their backs and carry out their scoop with bellies facing the sky.

We could see the surface effervesce as the little crustaceans tried to escape the disturbance they detected hurtling toward them.

In September the next year, I was back among the Channel Islands, this time with Bruce Mate of Oregon State University's Hatfield Marine Science Center, his wife, Mary Lou, and research associate Barbara Lagerquist—the same team I accompanied in Hawaii to learn about wintering humpback whales. As was often the case, Bruce's primary goal in the field was to get satellite-radio tags on animals so he could begin monitoring their travels. And as usual, his tools were an inflatable speedboat; arrows tipped with a barbed, detachable transmitter; a crossbow to fire them; and a system of straps and buckles to steady him in the bow of the boat while it pounded through the waves. But instead of making the long round-trip from shore each day as he had in the past, Bruce and the crew were working from a mother ship, a seventy-plus-foot yacht donated for a fortnight by an Oregon timber and steel magnate who had taken an interest in the research.

In complete contrast to my time with Croll and Tershy, this was five-star living aboard an elegant floating hotel complete with a husband-and-wife staff who ran the ship and prepared meals. The weather was less hospitable. Winds from the north blew unrelentingly between twenty and thirty-five knots per hour. We still tried to go out in the inflatable each day, more to feel that we were doing something than out of any real hope that we could find and tag a blue whale in what Lagerquist, the skiff driver, described in mariners' terms as lumpy seas and Bruce called just plain snotty. Our little craft climbed one side of the waves, literally chugging up steep, moving hills, then surged and swooped

down the other side like Croll and Tershy on surfboards. When
we turned the opposite direction and drove into the waves' faces,
we angled up so sharply as we nosed over the top that we were
concerned an extra blast of wind against the underside might flip
the inflatable end for end.

A number of researchers I've met suffer bad backs and aching
joints from years of banging over the waves. Bruce had his share
of whale-chaser's ailments. They weren't getting any better as we
kept up the search. To scout far enough to locate a blue whale
in the first place was rough; to catch up to it, we had to leap and
slam through the lump at a punishing pace that was never quite
enough to bring us into firing position before the whale finished
its sequence of breaths and sounded again.

We were soon weathered out of fieldwork completely. When
we tried to find a spot to hole up for the night, fierce winds
pushed the big mother ship right out of a bay, dragging its anchor. The yacht's owner arrived with his wife to spend a few days
watching the scientists at work. All we had to offer were listless
people writing up notes and, in Bruce's case, preparing profes-
sional papers while waiting for a break in conditions. Everyone
agreed that going out to chase blue whales in the kind of waves
galloping past would be futile. Still, the unspoken rule that you
never know for sure unless you try hung heavily in the air of the
yacht's posh living room. In the end, the team decided to head out
for another session on the water. What the hell; maybe some blue
whale would randomly surface right next to the skiff.

The waves were no more than six or seven feet high, but
they came with only short intervals between them, and they were
steep enough that some were curling over at the top. As the little craft punched through the corrugated water, Bruce reinjured

an old rotator cuff tear in his shoulder. His only comment was, "Sometimes I remind myself that if this stuff was easy, somebody would already have done it and know the answers." Although the physical beating I took was minor by comparison, I suffered from an excess of imagination. The farther we proceeded out of radio range of the mother ship, the easier it became to envision us clinging to an upside-down inflatable. With their throngs of seals, sea lions, and elephant seals, the Channel Islands have a well-deserved reputation as great white shark territory. We passed blue sharks on the surface, along with the occasional fins of other types I couldn't identify. It seemed the only big cetacean in the vicinity was a male killer whale, whose six-foot-tall dorsal fin sliced between wave crests in the distance.

Our time in the field was coming to an end. But one of the final days dawned clear and calm, as if the weather of the past two weeks were a fever that had broken. Scarcely a ripple of wind marred the sea's surface. It rose and fell in long swells like glass hills with dolphins crystallized inside them. Skimming along, scanning the horizon for blows, we located fifteen or sixteen different blue whales during the course of the day. One had bottlenose dolphins riding its bow wave. Where the whales emerged above the water, they took on a grayish cast. Slipping below, they turned the color of sapphire or shimmering turquoise or a robin's egg. The blue of this giant is not a pigment. It is a consequence of the way sunlight travels in water and reflects back up from the whales' mottled gray skin—an optical illusion of sorts, but no less captivating as a result. Similarly, one of the whalers' names for these giants, sulfur-bottoms or sulfur-bellies, came not from a color in the skin but from the diatoms that sometimes coat the light underside, most heavily in polar regions.

We gave chase sixty times, maybe seventy. Even when Lagerquist gunned the engine and drew close enough that we could see a whale's tail beating underwater, we could also see how, with just a couple of quickened strokes, the animal was able to power ahead out of range. Bruce needed to be parallel with the main part of the upper body to properly tag his target, and he was within milliseconds of pulling the crossbow trigger on two or three runs, if only the animals had kept to their pattern. Some veered aside. Many settled for just one or two breaths instead of the usual three or more while swimming near the surface. Others shortened whichever breath they were in the process of taking and immediately dove the moment we roared close. We could tell from the tilt of the tail that the angle of descent was a steep one, which meant that the encounter was finished.

The researchers had long since come to terms with being something of a pest to whales for the sake of science. Having nothing to show for it at times was discouraging but nearly unavoidable. In this line of work, you get fantastic days and bad days, and you need to be mentally prepared for bad weeks. The real frustration for the Mates and Lagerquist was knowing how much more information was needed before managers could begin drawing up effective plans to safeguard the most vital portions of the whales' ranges and migration routes.

More than a year went by. I traveled to stay with the Mates at their Newport, Oregon, home and accompanied Bruce to his office at the Hatfield Marine Science Center. He told me that his previous summer field season had gone better. Still, it had taken him, Mary Lou, and Lagerquist five weeks to attach satellite-radio tags to seven blue whales, dividing their efforts between the Channel Islands and the Farallon Islands just west of San Francisco.

"Half the whales we saw looked emaciated," Bruce said. "The vertebrae along their backbones stuck out, they were so skinny. Everyone has been recording higher than usual water temperatures and decreasing plankton this year. Whatever's going on with our sea conditions, it seemed to be taking a toll." One radio-tagged whale swam from near Point Conception, north of the Channel Islands, to a spot two hundred miles out in the Pacific in two days, then turned right around and came back. "Nothing there," Bruce concluded. "Here's an emaciated individual looking all over the place, and it can't find a better food supply. People have no idea how hard these animals work for a living."

One radio had failed early, but the others were still transmitting. They told Bruce that the whales were slowly working their way down the Mexican coast after staying in California waters into September. He expected some on their southward journey to possibly linger by Magdalena Bay on the western side of the Baja Peninsula. This was a hot spot for another type of small crustacean: pelagic red crabs, whose elongated front legs and pincers give them a closer resemblance to miniature lobsters than to crabs. Like krill, they live in free-floating concentrations, and they constitute one of the few other prey items that blue whales are known to eat. Researcher John Calambokidis later told me of watching blue whales lunge into swarms. The crabs, all of a couple of inches long, would flare out their front legs and open their claws wide at the last instant, as if warning the megaton attacker to back off or else.

Scientists already knew from matching identification photographs that blue whales seen as far north as Northern California

over summer would migrate past Mexico in the autumn and return the same way in spring. Bruce's main challenge was to find
where they were ultimately bound for the winter. Since 1993, he
had placed radios on fifty-three different blues. The early models,
affixed to the outside of the body, seldom lasted more than two
or three months, and most of the whales were still moving slowly
southward parallel to the Mexican coast when the devices gave
out. In 1995, however, Mate tracked one animal to an area near the
Costa Rican Dome, situated about four hundred miles out from
the western coast of Central America. Rather than a seamount,
this dome is a mound of strong, upwelling currents more than a
hundred miles in diameter. Tuna-fishing crews and survey teams
from the U.S. National Marine Fisheries Service had reported
the occasional blue whale there during winter. But since the odd
blue was seen in that region at other times too, no one could be
sure that such animals weren't coming to the dome from summer
ranges to the east or west or even in the Southern Hemisphere.
The radio signal provided the first confirmation of a blue whale
from the temperate part of the Northern Hemisphere making a
seasonal migration into the eastern tropical Pacific.

Mate's transmitters were in the cigar-size darts he had devised. They stayed attached better than their predecessors and
kept giving out signals for six months or longer. While I looked
over his shoulder, Bruce tapped a series of computer keys and
downloaded satellite data showing the latest whereabouts of a
right whale off South Africa, a humpback off Alaska, a bowhead
in the high Arctic, other whales of various species, and then the
six recently tagged blue whales. Additional taps called up a map of
surface temperatures for the region between Southern California
and central Mexico, which the satellite had generated by scanning

with infrared frequencies. A different set of wavelengths, set to detect the green of chlorophyll, mapped concentrations of phytoplankton, which would indicate where krill were likely to be most abundant. The blue whales' locations corresponded nicely. More taps on the computer could overlay all this with maps showing prevailing currents and other oceanographic data to predict where the animals might head next.

Here we were again, as on the yacht, sitting comfortably out of the weather with fresh coffee steaming on a nearby table. The difference was that, this time, Bruce was gathering more hard information about blue whales in the space of a few minutes than anyone in a previous generation could have compiled in months or years, no matter how well he or she handled a boat. At last, technology was giving those who seek to understand great whales the means to match the scale and complexity of the animals' lives.

There is another way to track blue whales, and it also comes from state-of-the-art technology. After Bruce introduced me to his Oregon State University colleague Kathleen Stafford, she said, "We've suspected for a while that the blue whales off the U.S. Pacific coast are linked to the eastern tropical Pacific. But the exact locations [for the data-collecting stations] this is based on are secret. We could tell you, but then we'd have to kill you." She was kidding, sort of. The information is collected by the navy's Sound Surveillance System (SOSUS) array of listening devices spread across ocean seafloors to detect enemy submarines, and it comes streaming into a locked room at the Hatfield science center. Stafford and Chris Fox, from the Pacific Marine Environmental Laboratory, operated by NOAA, had special clearance to sort through the encrypted data and analyze particular segments, she for blue whale calls and he for noise created by tectonic events—changes in the earth's crust. The two are stunningly similar.

Much as recordings of bottlenose whale calls have to be slowed down for us to hear them because they are mostly above the range of frequencies our ears can detect, recordings of blue whales must be speeded up to be heard because the animals make their utterances in frequencies almost entirely below our range. Even then, they sound a lot like an earthquake, a volcanic eruption, or some colossal landslide down the slope of a midocean trench—the grumblings of a restless planet. With the whales calling at 185 to 190 decibels and earthquakes resounding at 220 to 230 decibels, the volume isn't all that different either. A blue whale close to a SOSUS hydrophone overloads the sensors so badly that the device can't record anything.

In a sense, credit for discovering blue whale calls probably ought to go to submariners from various navies who were on duty watching their sonar screens and listening through headphones. They kept reporting very loud, repeating acoustic patterns in very low frequencies. The first part sounded like a pile driver, the second part like a gargantuan hum. No one knew what to make of this noise. The concern, of course, was that it came from an enemy who was up to something—piloting a new kind of supersubmersible, maybe, or fashioning a sea-bottom fortress like one of James Bond's archenemies.

What you look for in order to identify a noise as being of human or other organic origin is some sort of regularity, or predictability, in the pattern. However, seismic activity can fool you by coming in pulses or emitting an organized sounding sequence of low tones. The spreading seafloor known as the Pacific Rise is one of the fastest-moving portions of the earth's crust and therefore among the noisiest. When Fox began studying the hot plumes coming out of vents there in the latter part of the 1980s, he asked the navy if he could borrow data from SOSUS. The official reply was, in effect, What's SOSUS? Never heard of it. By 1991, some of the wraps had come off the program, and Fox was given access. Before long, the laboratory at Hatfield Marine Science Center was handling ten gigabytes—10 billion bits of data—per week. It was loaded—or, from a geologist's standpoint, contaminated—with marine mammal sounds. Fox was constantly going to cetacean experts to ask, How about this? Is it a whale call?

Although specialists have continually refined the computer programs used to analyze the sound spectrum of the deepest groanings in order to identify biological sources, there are still a number of bizarre noises that geologists like Fox think must come from whales, and which whale researchers believe arise from geologic events. Seasonally, tropical portions of the North Pacific produce a gigantic *BOING!* that people have been trying to figure out since the 1950s. Explanations range from seafloor bulges to minke whale calls. And then, every once in a while, something down toward the very bottom of the ocean emits a rhythmic sound unlike the noises associated with any known geologic activity, and yet too big and too loud to be from any known creature, including blue whales. That doesn't rule out unknown creatures.

Fox played me a toned-down version of the ultimate growl from the abyss. It was beyond monstrous and left me spellbound. Surrounded by shelf upon metal shelf of electronic equipment humming and blinking as it downloaded more recordings from hydrophones spread around some of the 71 percent of the earth's surface veiled by saltwater, he raised his eyebrows and smiled and said, "Mysteries of the deep. They're still out there."

I left for Stafford's cubicle to listen to the blue whale's voice. Standard pitch, the A above middle C on your piano, is defined as 440 hertz, or 440 cycles of a sound wave per second. We are able to clearly hear the call of a right whale, which vocalizes between 200 and 400 hertz. By contrast, blue whale calls vibrate at the bottom end of the sound spectrum, mostly below 20 hertz. Usually about a minute long, the call has three or more components lasting about twenty seconds each. The first is the pulsing vibration that sonar operators interpreted as a pile driver. Next comes a more continuous sound, the hum, which sweeps downward in pitch toward the end. This is followed by another hum and occasionally more. As Stafford played the sounds for me, her computer screens displayed them visually by charting the wavelengths over time, producing a sonogram.

Once Stafford and others recognized the basic set of low-frequency wave patterns characteristic of blue whale voices and became proficient at distinguishing them from background clamor—separating the signal from the noise, as acousticians say—the investigators realized that they were looking at two versions of the call in the North Pacific. One came from near the Aleutian Islands, Russia, and Japan in the warm months, the other from off the North American coast between Washington and northern Mexico during the same period. This corresponded to the traditional division of North Pacific blue whales into two major groups, the western population, ranging along the Asian coastline, and the eastern population, found off North America's coast. There are at least nine other versions of the call worldwide, and further recordings may assume an important role in defining subspecies and populations.

Going a step further, Stafford discerned three variations of the western Pacific call and additional variations of the eastern

Pacific call. Are these different messages, or are they the vocalizations of different subgroups? If they come from subgroups, are these animals somewhat isolated from one another? That's how differences in human language arise. But hydrophones near Hawaii have picked up both western and eastern versions of the standard blue whale call at the same time, opening the possibility that even the major North Pacific populations meet and mingle in certain wintering sites. Along those same lines, numbered tags placed on blues during the whaling era revealed that animals taken in the Gulf of Alaska had come from the waters off Russia's Kamchatka Peninsula as well as from near British Columbia's Vancouver Island. In 1996, the year after Bruce Mate tracked the radio-tagged whale to the Costa Rican Dome, Stafford firmed up the evidence of a migration to the dome from California waters by following the distinct call of the eastern Pacific population via SOSUS listening stations. However, she also got acoustic evidence of blue whales in the eastern tropical Pacific year-round, reinforcing occasional reports of blues there during the summer months.

Whalers referred to different populations as stocks, and many researchers have continued the tradition. From the standpoint of scientific objectivity, this is not a fortunate choice. *Stock* is a fisheries term. It denotes a commodity that awaits harvest or sale. Today's pro-whaling nations such as Japan and Iceland not only like referring to stocks, but they also tend to define lots of them, the implication being that they could devise a harvest that rotates from one to the next, cropping the most populous while allowing others to rebuild. Nothing of the kind has ever been demonstrated, and no one has ever had anything remotely like a clear picture of the degree of overlap or exchange between populations from different parts of the world, much less between subpopulations within a region. Acoustics may indeed prove to be a very powerful and much-needed tool for resolving the global distribution of blues, especially when combined with DNA studies. But, as often happens with a flood of new scientific information, the situation at first only seems more confusing.

Another summer arrived, and I returned to the Channel Islands once more. I rode out to sea with the man who, more than any other, was responsible for documenting the large numbers of blues currently feeding off U.S. Pacific shores. A tall, lean, self-reliant fellow, he has recorded healthy increases as well for humpbacks and grays, the other great whales most often seen along the coast. His name is John Calambokidis. I think of him as the Good Tidings Guy, though his official title would be head of the Cascadia Research Collective, an independent scientific group that specializes in whale population surveys. The effort consists largely of him setting out alone in an inflatable skiff at every opportunity and roaring back and forth through the waves along invisible transect lines as long as the weather holds. Others from the Cascadia team accompany him at times, and some head out on their own as well. Returning to the office in Olympia, Washington, they dump roll upon roll of film on a squad of interns and volunteers, who then spend weeks, if not months, of their lives poring over the images, trying to identify individual animals.

Humpbacks, the original focus of Calambokidis's surveys, are relatively easy to tell apart due to the unique markings on the undersides of most flukes. Picking out individual gray whales is much trickier. The photo analysts have to look for telling combinations of pigment blotches, scars, and barnacle encrustations, a technique originally developed by Jim Darling, who still divides his time between grays off the U.S. Pacific Northwest and humpbacks off Hawaii. As for blue whales, separating one from the next by the subtle mottling visible across hundreds of square feet on each animal's side tests the outermost limits of human pattern recognition. And human patience. It is like putting together a jigsaw puzzle based on a portrait of pebbles. Or staring at one of those multihued clusters of dots that mask an underlying image until your mind finally sees through the apparent randomness to grasp the connections. Annie Douglas, one of the assistants in the Cascadia office, likened the task to a test where you're shown a complicated picture, then shown a second, almost identical picture and asked what's missing.

When Calambokidis and I met in the Santa Barbara harbor during late May, he had just come from the Olympic Peninsula, where Native Americans of the Makah tribe had decided to revive the tradition of gray whale hunting. The ensuing controversy spawned an urgent need to be able to recognize resident animals, which the Makah had agreed to leave in peace while going after grays that were migrating through. By photographing the area around a gray whale's dorsal hump and comparing the images to those in a printed catalogue, Calambokidis said, the Cascadia team was improving the odds of being able to quickly identify individuals.

Back in 1986, Calambokidis received money for a three-year study of humpbacks. He started spending some of it on a survey flight around the Farallon Islands. Like the Channel Islands, they are a rugged, weather-pounded archipelago encompassed by a reserve—the Gulf of the Farallones National Marine Sanctuary— whose waters are enlivened by strong upwellings of cold, nutrient-bearing currents. "And there was a giant, light, shimmering body just under the water," he told me. "Look! It's a rare blue whale! A little later, it was: Look, another rare blue whale! And another . . . We saw more blue whales than humpback whales, which were pretty common around the Farallons. In 1988, we made an aerial survey from the Farallons to Cordell Banks [another marine sanctuary, about one hundred miles north] and came home with an estimate of two hundred and fifty blue whales."

Extensive aerial surveys off California throughout the 1970s and early 1980s had turned up only a handful of blues. No one knew of a resident summer population. The common belief was that any animals seen off this coast were en route north to polar areas. A lot of people thought that fears about the global total adding up to only a few hundred might be justified. The most optimistic claims were that there still might be eleven to twelve thousand blues, with ten thousand of them in the Antarctic, but those figures were being promoted by die-hard whaling nations hoping to be allowed a modest kill quota. The most recent official reports agree that there are still probably fewer than one thousand blue whales in the Southern Hemisphere, and this is an extrapolation from chillingly few actual sightings. "We believed that the number for the Northern Hemisphere was probably worse," Calambokidis told me. "Then we started getting this incredibly good news off California."

The photo catalogue of known blue whales in the eastern North Pacific has now grown to include more than sixteen hundred. In a typical year, Calambokidis, Jay Barlow of the National Marine Fisheries Service Southwest section, and others were able to identify two to three hundred individuals, and more than 50 percent of them would not have been previously documented.

Such a rate of discovery means two things: First, the population is stable or growing. Second, the actual number of whales out there must be significantly larger than the number catalogued to date. In other words, the California population appears to be perhaps two thousand strong and possibly three thousand on the high end of the estimate range.

What no one is sure about is why this is happening. The old notion that whales off the California coast were bound for the Arctic or returning to the tropics may have been valid at the time. Harpooners killed relatively few blues near California, whereas Canadian and Alaskan whaling stations took a great many. Yet Calambokidis feels fairly sure that most of the blues he is tallying today don't go much beyond California in their northward migration. Sightings off Oregon and Washington are sporadic. One blue was identified near the Queen Charlotte Islands off British Columbia in June, but Calambokidis found that same individual among the Channel Islands twenty-five days later.

There is little doubt that the recent buildup of the population off California in summer is real. The question is, how much of it is due to reproduction, as opposed to a shift in range? This group's rate of increase since the early 1980s appears higher than the species's biological potential; that is, it exceeds the blues' natural ability to multiply through birth and better survival. Therefore, some of the animals must have summered elsewhere in the past. Was it in the arctic and subarctic waters, where blues are rarely found today, or in locales farther offshore? The situation is as puzzling as it is encouraging.

At least the mystery of where these blues winter was finally being solved. For starters, several of Bruce Mate's satellite-radio-tagged animals ended up around the Costa Rican Dome. Then

Calambokidis went there with others from Cascadia. Hundreds of miles out in the open Pacific, he managed to photograph thirteen blue whales and found that eight of them had been identified earlier in California waters. Since only about half the blues he photographed off California during a typical year were previously known, it was possible that all thirteen of those whales near the dome were from the same population. Calambokidis noticed several blues there defecate, and a healthy poop strongly suggests recent feeding. His simple observation therefore questioned the whole premise of these animals fasting throughout winter in the tropics. All this groundbreaking news almost didn't get out, for the big ship that Calambokidis was sharing with a *National Geographic* film crew barely stayed afloat through a hellacious storm on the return trip.

Calambokidis and I cleared Santa Barbara's harbor shortly after dawn and set a course southwest through wisps of fog and five-foot swells. And just that quickly, the realm of serial California cities ceased to exist, and we were on our own in a boundless wilderness. Nearing Santa Cruz Island, Calambokidis said he couldn't read any bottom features with the depth finder because its sonar beams couldn't pass through the krill. They were too thick. With more and more shearwaters, phalaropes, auklets, and gulls assembling around us, I felt sure my marginal luck finding whales by the Channel Islands in earlier years was about to change for the better. It did. The remnants of fog cleared, and we began seeing spouts in all directions.

Several blues were lunge-feeding. I could make out the baleen hanging in a fringe from one whale's upper jaw as it swept its head in an arc to make the most of each open-mouthed pass.

Other blues were diving instead. A few raced along the surface in two's or three's in what was more likely a social display than anything related to feeding. Calambokidis mentioned that, when these most enormous of whales hit a speed of fifteen or sixteen knots, they sometimes start porpoising, zooming at least partially clear of the water.

Several that we were following to photograph let loose explosions of dung—great masses of processed krill that turned acres of sea bright pink. Whether studying jaguars or bats, most of the field mammalogists I've worked with collect excrement because it is a convenient summary of what the subject has been dining on. The result for blues was obviously going to be krill and more krill, but Captain Calambokidis had to find out exactly which species of krill and ordered me to collect samples with a dip net.

On a more refined note, one of the whales we followed was white. Surfacing at a distance, it resembled an iceberg gleaming in the sunlight. Below the water, it glowed like a lamp. The closer we drew, the more light gray spots we could make out on the otherwise milk-colored skin. If it wasn't a true albino—and we couldn't be sure—it was certainly one extremely pale whale. We came upon this individual five different times while scouting for other blues. Commenting that it was the first white blue whale he had encountered, Calambokidis thoroughly photographed the creature, biopsied it with a dart, and collected a skin sample from a postdive footprint for additional DNA analysis. If Pale Whale suffered from any condition related to its absence of dark pigment or from any sort of social ostracism, it wasn't obvious. The animal acted as vigorous as the other blues and fed in the same site as the majority of them. In fact, we soon realized that it was always in the company of a second whale, which had normal coloring and was about the same size—around seventy feet. Both probably still had some growing to do before they reached full adult size. Even so, I wondered whether I might not be looking at the largest white creature ever observed.

The following day brought longer, smoother swells and more blue whales near Santa Cruz Island. We had fifty to seventy-five different individuals in view within a single square mile and more scattered on the crowd's outskirts. The place reminded me of a geyser basin in Yellowstone National Park, with all the three-story-tall spouts going off around us. When we turned off the engine, it sounded like we had drifted into some Brobdingnagian steam factory whose valves were constantly being opened and shut. Calambokidis said that he had never seen blues so concentrated, but then, his sonar was showing a mass of krill below that was more solid than he had ever come upon before either.

For the first time while I was among the Channel Islands, the wind blew more gently as the day wore on. Calambokidis decided to take advantage of the increasing calm to run north for a look around San Miguel Island, where the waters were usually roughest. While the surface did become glassier en route, the swells kept rising until they were nine feet high. I felt like a small creature traversing a deeply furrowed field.

Before long, we were shooting off the top of the swells as though they were ski jumps. I don't know how many feet we traveled before landing, but judging from the high-pitched whine of the propeller spinning free in the air, we had some awesome hang time. As we sped ahead at a pace somewhere between porpoising and the aerial escape mode of flying fish, Captain Calambokidis was complaining that they didn't make hulls like they used to; darned if the last one he had didn't crack after only a few hundred hours.

Never accused of easing back on the throttle, my companion was renowned in whale research circles for barreling off solo, day after day and year after year, straight out into the open Pacific until he was beyond radio range, entirely dependent upon his own resources and the dubious reliability of an outboard engine. The man was covering between five and six thousand nautical miles per year this way. He used to average twice as many, and he did that in a fourteen-foot hull-less inflatable, which is a couple of feet shorter than your average canoe and rides through the waves like a stiff trampoline. I don't believe John Calambokidis is reckless. He just doesn't leave much room inside himself for fear, and it is this quality that allows him to accomplish the work he has done for so long alone offshore.

When Calambokidis finally moved on to a sixteen-foot rigid-hull inflatable boat, his knee and back problems eased somewhat. Now, we were in one that measured eighteen feet, a luxury liner by comparison. But the farther we went, the fewer blues we met. We passed bottlenose and Pacific white-sided dolphins, squid-hunting Risso's dolphins, sea lions, and a blue shark, and then smacked into something at full speed—either another blue shark or one of the giant sunfish called mola molas that bask on the surface. Whatever the object was, it stopped the boat cold, practically stopped my heart, and left me wondering if the hull was still in one piece. It held together, and we pushed on. But San Miguel's waters turned out to be a blue-whale desert. Nor did we find more than a handful elsewhere. It looked as though virtually all the whales in the Channel Islands area were gathered for the time being on one side of Santa Cruz Island over the living reef of krill. We turned back to join them.

Pale Whale was there with its companion from the day before. Calambokidis pointed to a portside blue and said, "See that knobby end on the dorsal fin? That's a familiar whale that I first recorded up north in the Farallons and have seen several times since." Later, when I commented on a swath of white stippling another individual's "shoulder," he added, "That's another old friend, Freckles." Plainly, it wasn't always necessary to drive yourself crazy trying to tease out subtle mottling patterns in order to identify an individual blue whale. Calambokidis noted a third acquaintance, first observed in 1986, by a deep slice in its dorsal fin. Another had most of its dorsal fin missing. The remnant was indented in a way that spoke of a single large bite, yet the edge was so smooth that the damage could have come from a ship's propeller. A fifth whale was easily told by a stalked barnacle that dangled from the backswept tip of its dorsal fin like a Christmas ornament.

We were running at a fairly fast clip—no surprise—when a still speedier blue whale passed directly underneath the inflatable from behind. I imagined us being lifted high and dry on Leviathan's back if it chose to surface. It didn't, and Calambokidis went on to chase a pair of blues to photograph. They ended up on either side of our boat like ocean liners escorting a dinghy. Both came so near that we were practically touching them. For all this species's enormity, my main impression was of how streamlined it seemed—as sleek a shape as 120 or more tons of flesh can be molded into. Relatively speaking, you could almost describe the biggest animals in creation as svelte.

Calambokidis recalled reading to his son, Alexei, who was very young at the time, about how a blue whale's blowholes were big enough for a child to crawl through. Alexei promptly volunteered to do that for his dad. Now seven, Alexei sometimes came along and helped spot whales, take identification photographs, and steer, Calambokidis told me. I commented that this had to be about the coolest thing in the world for a kid that age. Calambokidis nodded and said, "I'm at my age, and I can't think of anything cooler either."

One blue changed course to pass right next to us, then proceeded to circle back and carry out two more close approaches. Calling that animal a "friendly" might be excessive, especially if compared to whales such as the wintering grays in Baja lagoons that swim over to "mug" boats for long periods and allow people to pet them. Then again, "friendly" could be perfectly accurate by the standards of huge, fast-moving blues. Their reputation as being standoffish doesn't necessarily mean that the animals are incurious. Besides the fact that it may be harder for them to interact with most vessels than it is for smaller, more agile whales, there is the legacy of intense hunting to consider. Blues live a long time, and many of those around us might have learned to associate boats with the bloody death throes of other blues, perhaps mingled with calls of panic and pain. Now that a generation with no overwhelming reason to fear us is in the majority and rearing young of its own, reactions may be changing. Fred Benko, who operated a whale-watching boat out of Santa Barbara, told me that a small but growing percentage of the blues he encountered showed a positive interest in his ship, the *Condor*.

One could always argue that "friendlies" are really more intrigued by boat hulls, which are more or less cetacean-shaped below the waterline, or by the sounds boat engines make, than by the people aboard. But while hulls and engines might draw the animals' attention at first, whales are too smart not to be able to separate and respond to the two-legged creatures aboard. When a whale spy-hops or makes a close pass, and you find yourself eye to eye, that eye is fixed on you, not on the hull below. That's how it seems to me, anyway. All I know for sure is that having a blue whale pause in its momentous travels to pay attention to us and our little skiff gave me the sense of being a bug that a person was taking the time to notice on a leaf. I felt equally humbled and honored every time.

Regardless of what they were doing or which direction they were moving when we intersected them, the whales stayed focused around the same locale. The word had gone out about this particular bounty of krill, and all the blues seemed to have heard it. Calambokidis dropped a hydrophone over the side to listen. Back through the speaker came a tremendous racket consisting mostly of high-pitched dolphin discussions and the loud barks that sea lions somehow make underwater. Beneath all the squeaks, chirrups, and arfs throbbed a bass counterpoint so profound that it was as if our instrument were somehow picking up the vibration of gravity itself or the earth's rotation. These were the blue whales' broadcast calls, the same vocalizations I had heard in Kate Stafford's lab. While scientists will no doubt be speculating for years about the role of such communications, Calambokidis and his Cascadia colleagues began putting acoustic tags on blues in collaboration with Scripps Institute of Oceanography. They discovered that the two primary calls—the pile driver and the hum—are made only by males, and usually when they were not feeding. But a more variable call is produced by both sexes and particularly during the course of dining.

The scenario would be that feeding excites whales, excited whales give out calls, and other whales, hearing a number of voices emanating from an area, home in on the feast. Although informing other blues about a feeding site means having to share it, researchers don't think that a major krill swarm is seriously depleted by the presence of numerous whales despite the huge bites they take out of it. Rather, the swarm eventually dwindles due to physical factors such as a change in wind patterns, a weakening of the upwelling, and subsequent shortages of nutrients in the upper water levels. Besides, if each individual were to keep the news about a good location to itself, then each would have to find every site on its own, and that would be much less efficient for all. The ability of krill to grow and reproduce in mind-boggling profusion does not make them a uniform, predictable food supply. Swarms are often quite localized, the distance from one hot spot to the next can be very long, and conditions during a given year may or may not yield krill in places that proved bountiful in the past.

As people gaze out at the sea, they behold a panorama that looks the same from one end of the level horizon to the other, and they can't seem to help thinking of the ocean as a gigantic pool that doesn't vary much below the surface either, except to become deeper farther from shore. Actually, neither the water column, the currents, the sea bottom, nor the living communities associated with them stay very constant from one place to the next. The underwater realm can be so varied that a landlubber would do better to envision it as more like a continental landscape with changing terrain covered by a mosaic of meadows, swamps, forests, deserts, and so forth. Habitat differences become extremely important in the management of marine life from shellfish to whales. If we are to effectively sustain those resources, the wide gap between the way experts and the public perceive saltwater environments has to be narrowed.

As long as people tend to view the ocean as homogeneous, nations can cling to the belief that there is always more to harvest somewhere over the horizon, and so the steep decline of commercial fish populations taking place worldwide at the moment will continue. So will that fundamental misconception about the lifestyle of great whales—that they lumber along with their big, baleen-filled mouths open, more or less randomly filtering plankton. Don Croll of the University of California, Santa Cruz, measured the average krill concentration in Monterey Bay and found it to be roughly one one-hundredth of an ounce per cubic foot. That's a higher density than in most areas, but a blue whale would starve trying to strain it from the water. The average concentration around a productive upwelling in the bay was 145 times higher—a lifesaving difference to a mammal with the most gigantic metabolism around.

All the great whales need to place themselves in the right geographic regions during the right part of the year as food supplies peak. To achieve this, they rely to some extent on socially transmitted traditions and knowledge learned from individual experience. Most, if not all, also rely upon some system of mutually beneficial communication to locate feeding hot spots within the region. In the case of blue whales, the final adaptation for exploiting a patchy food source that varies over time lies in being fast and strong enough to readily get from one prey concentration to the next. Some experts surmise that this in itself has been a driving force behind the evolution of giant size in blues.

Naturally, there are other reasons to be big and powerful. An advantage in defending against predators is one; ask any elephant, hippo, or moose. Adding bulk also improves thermoregulation for a warm-blooded animal—up to a point. Heat is stored in the body's mass and lost through exposed surfaces. Large animals have a greater volume relative to surface area than small animals do and thus a greater ability to retain warmth. Being big makes it easier for blues and other whales to feed in and near polar areas. Conversely, the lack of bulk or a well-developed insulation layer in infants may explain why so many cetaceans undertake long migrations to warmer waters to give birth. But the greatest whales are so massive at maturity that it is less of a challenge for them to conserve body heat than to dump the excess generated by muscular activity such as rapid swimming. They can't do it through their skin and the underlying layer of blubber, which together amount to wearing the world's thickest wetsuit. Experts think that whales cope by opening their mouths and exposing the enormous tongue, with its dense network of blood vessels, to the seawater, which is significantly cooler than the animals' body temperature, even in the tropics.

So it looks as though something else lay behind blue whales turning into the most gigantic animals ever, and that factor may have been the nature of tiny krill. The mightier the whales became, the more quickly and efficiently individuals could swim between sites with an abundance of this favored food, the more they could eat once they arrived, and the better they could endure cyclical shortages due to changing sea conditions such as El Niño events by subsisting on stored energy. While the same holds true in part for other large whales, the blue whale's combination of heft and speed remains unmatched by any other ocean roamer. The point is to be able to gobble tons of krill whenever and wherever they are thick and then hustle to the next such setting through however many days and miles of empty-belly seas this may require. Those best prepared to outlast the leanest times leave more descendants—more of their genes—than do slightly smaller individuals who can't take in quite as much food and therefore end up with less energy in reserve. In this fashion, improved survival of the largest translates into greater size for succeeding generations. "It is," as Croll put it, "a continuous ratcheting up."

Don Croll encapsulates blue whale ecology in a scenario he calls "From Wind to Whales." In addition to the kind of upwellings that take place where deep, cold currents run into, say, the Channel Islands or the Farallons, this model includes a related type common along the California coast. Both begin with prevailing winds from the north. But in the second process, the Coriolis effect caused by the earth's counterclockwise rotation tends to push the ocean surface westward, away from the land. Offshore winds add to the push. As the top layers of water move in that direction, deeper, cooler waters are drawn up to replace them. You could watch the principle at work simply by blowing over the edge of a shallow pan of water until a flow starts welling up from below to fill in and keep the surface level.

When I visited Croll in his university office in Santa Cruz, he was clad in more or less the same sun-faded shorts and T-shirt I had seen him wearing on his boat in the Channel Islands. But there was nothing casual about the way he went about analyzing ecosystems. Like Bruce Mate, he used satellite imagery to track the densest concentrations of chlorophyll, representing algae blooms, along the coast and was able to pop up a real-time map of conditions on his computer screen. "We refer to phytoplankton as the primary biomass," he began. "It can respond very rapidly to nutrient availability, doubling in twenty-four hours. Imagine redwoods doing that." The blooms develop in response to upwellings at particular locations and gradually spread southward, following the general movement of currents. Croll samples the krill that start to flourish in response. He does this by dragging a net shaped like a bongo drum through the swarms, collecting different species so he can study their life cycles in detail.

To learn what else shapes patterns in the abundance of krill, Croll relates swarms to environmental factors that were much harder to measure in earlier years. With echo sounders, he can map the krill's whereabouts in relation to underwater topography. His ACDP—acoustic Doppler current profiler—gauges the water's movement at different depths by sending out frequencies tuned to bounce off tiny drifting particles. CTDPs—conductivity-temperature-depth probes—tell him about changes in the water's salinity and heat. An automated high-frequency radar ocean sensor system reveals surface currents by tracking the speed and direction of waves. Remote moorings at a series of offshore sites beam in measurements of wind speed, direction, and ambient air temperature.

If you're a diver, one of the most common forms of floating detritus you see in certain areas consists of the exoskeletons of krill and other crustaceans. Like insects, they shed their old outer coatings and grow new, larger ones as their bodies increase in size. Baldo Marinovich, one of Croll's colleagues at the University of California, discovered that krill have a fascinating ability to undergo reverse molts as well. Under difficult conditions, such as the overheated waters of an El Niño event, the krill may shrink in size as a result of digesting their own protein to subsist. When their old exoskeleton starts to fit like a loose overcoat, they cast it off and grow a smaller one instead.

This year, nothing of the kind was required, for the ocean in the region was cooler than usual and much richer. "We have La Niña conditions, the opposite of the El Niño we just went through," Croll said. "Things are so good, the krill may have three spawns instead of the usual one or two." Describing Cassin's auklets as "feathered blue whales," since they, too, specialize in eating krill around upwellings, he pointed out that these birds were managing to successfully hatch three clutches of eggs on their nesting islands. No wonder Calambokidis and I had practically had to push blue whales aside to get anywhere by boat near Santa Cruz Island this season.

Going from north to south off the California coast, the Cordell Banks, Gulf of the Farallones, Monterey Bay, and Channel Islands National Marine Sanctuaries are all associated with exceptionally productive upwellings, and the blue whales shoot back and forth between them. According to Croll, if enough whales gather in one hot spot, they may even prolong its peak productivity through secondary enrichment. What this means is that the urine and feces from all those huge, feeding animals put enough nitrogen and phosphorus back into the site to stimulate a continuing algae bloom. As summer progresses, currents slow. Upwellings move farther and farther offshore and grow more diffuse. By August, the nearshore part of the "From Wind to Whales" system has collapsed. The locations of blues appear to reflect this, for researchers find them becoming less and less concentrated.

Even as Croll was documenting a banner year for plankton productivity, he and others were aware of an overall decline of plankton in the eastern Pacific since the 1970s. Ironically, he said, this worrisome trend might explain part of the surprising rise in blue whale numbers near the California coast. The decrease in plankton appeared to be most dramatic way offshore, and whales that had been foraging hundreds of miles out at sea may have been moving closer to the mainland in response.

"So is this pile of blue whales we've been finding off California a good sign or a symptom of something that may not be so good over the long run?" Croll asked. "The only other place blue whales seem to be increasing is around Iceland. Why not in the Southern Hemisphere? Why not in the Arctic? We don't know, but the differences between El Niño and La Niña point out how sensitive the whole system is to shifts. El Niño events definitely seem to be developing more often, possibly as a result of global warming." Since he told me that, other scientists have recorded an 80 percent drop-off of the previously superabundant Antarctic krill, *Euphasia superba,* in portions of the Southern Ocean. They say it reflects a general decline in productivity that seems to be related to thinning and shrinking of the antarctic ice cap and an increase of freshwater as a result of the melting. This change too looks like a direct result of global warming. Already, the collapse of krill has led to a parallel fall in the Adélie penguin population, whose diet consists chiefly of *superba.* Other birds, seals, and the rest of the antarctic food chain may be at risk, and the consequences for the blue whales left in the Southern Hemisphere could be even more dire.

The next time I met Don Croll, the professor had relaxed his dress code a bit; instead of the usual shorts, he was wearing loose swim trunks to go with his faded T-shirt. It was March, and we were in a harbor south of the town of Loreto in Baja California, Mexico. Blues were returning northward from their tropical winter range, and some were poking into the Sea of Cortez, also known as the Gulf of California. According to Bruce Mate's satellite-radio transmitters, the gulf also held a few blues that had spent most of the winter right there. Croll took me by skiff out to his research boat, the *Amigo*. We joined his longtime associate Bernie Tershy, a crew of student assistants, and Chris Clark of Cornell University, a leading acoustic specialist investigating the nature and function of whale vocalizations.

Croll put the big boat in gear and pointed it out toward the gulf's desert islands. Nature appeared to be busy illustrating his "From Wind to Whales" productivity model. Northwest airflows prevail in the Sea of Cortez, and at times they develop into strong blows called El Nortes. Even fiercer local winds, known as *chubascos,* can seemingly spring up out of nowhere and turn the usually sheltered waters gnarly in a hurry. They already had on several days since my arrival, and several American biologists would soon die when a sudden windstorm sank their research vessel. In concert with the tides surging in and out of the gulf, the winds generate strong currents. Those running along the sea bottom, which is two miles deep in places, are cold and charged with nutrients. Where they well up, they nurture the same sort of algae blooms and krill swarms seen off the California coast.

By taking acoustic readings and water samples along a grid— a back-and-forth routine Tershy called "mowing the lawn"—the team found the densest krill swarms just downcurrent from the upwellings. The crustaceans were hanging close to ledges on slopes at a depth of 450 to 500 feet, and both blue and fin whales were swooping after them.

"This year is the closest we've seen blues and fins feeding together," Tershy said. "You wouldn't be able to tell which species you're looking at down below by the dive patterns. They're identical." Seen in groups of twelve to twenty here and as many as one hundred elsewhere, fin whales are generally more sociable than blues but quite similar to them in other ways. The rorqual group is a study in speciation as a matter of degree. With the exception of the humpback, all the members of this family, the Balaenopteridae, look like larger or smaller versions of one another. Blues and fins have apparently mated and produced healthy hybrid offspring—blin whales? flues?—a phenomenon first reported by whalers and later confirmed by DNA samples from a few individuals. Further study may turn up hybrids formed from other rorqual combinations. Possible candidates have already been reported by various observers.

Minkes, Bryde's, seis, fins, and blues all share a sleek, elongated form with comparatively small flippers and a small dorsal fin. The larger the species, the smaller that fin becomes in relation to the rest of the body, the farther back it is placed, and the more falcate, or backward curved, its shape. Another trend seems to be that the smaller a rorqual is, the broader its choice of food. For example, thirty-foot-long minkes, the runts of the family, eat fish of many sizes as well as an assortment of crustaceans. Fin whales, the nearest in length to blues, will take small schooling fish and squid; but for the moment, they were matching the blues' total devotion to krill. All kinds of animals were. In the northern Mexico/Sea of Cortez/California portion of the Pacific, the same types of krill that support blues play a key role as food for seven of the top ten commercially sought species of squid and fish, from sardines to salmon and black cod.

Groups of manta rays leaped from the surface like amphibious kites. There were whale sharks in the area, too, going after krill along with the mantas. Other sharks were hunting all the fish drawn to the krill.

Meanwhile, tremendous flocks of winged krill-eaters gathered on the "lawn" we were mowing. Next to the Cassin's auklets—Croll's feathered blue whales—were the loon-size seabirds known as murres, which will descend hundreds of feet below the water to hunt. "Pound for pound, they are the deepest-diving warm-blooded animals on earth." Tershy told me. And where hundreds of eared grebes formed a raft on the surface one moment, nothing but waves showed the next, for these birds dived as a single unit, hunting a particular krill called *Nyctiphanes simplex.* Within another month or so, the grebes would be putting that marine protein to work far to the north, nesting among the reeds on freshwater lakes. Phalaropes, petrels, Bonaparte's gulls, and half a dozen other kinds of birds fluttered about in between whale spouts. I could almost see strands of the food web, spun from deep-moving currents, rising through the surface to stretch skyward in all directions.

All the while, the *Amigo* was towing a complicated sixteen-element hydrophone array. Chris Clark monitored the output, hoping to listen in on both fin and blue whale conversations. The team had mounted other hydrophones on weighted platforms here and there along the seafloor and would hoist them up later to collect recordings. Having detected blue whales making noises other than broadcast calls during social situations, Clark was eager to record more examples. But the blues were being discouragingly quiet. Clark shrugged and said, "They are fairly noisy most other months. They vocalize on their winter range, and they vocalize at the edge of the ice in summer. They call while they're traveling in between. We get amazing blooms of sound around the continental shelf off Newfoundland from midsummer through early autumn, and also off the British Isles. It's this huge, collective groan, the whale equivalent of a pond full of spring peepers."

Clark pointed out that gathering over meals can also be a dandy way to meet prospective mates, and feeding-area vocalizations could be playing a role in that. This scientist possessed an astonishing knowledge of the nature of sound and its permutations in water, such as the way sonic waves bend upward in cool arctic areas and downward in warmer, temperate ones, refracting like light in glass. He knew of a whale Kate Stafford recorded every September that had an unusual fifty-two-hertz hum, and he said he had even heard patterns that seemed as if they must be coming from blue-fin hybrids. He knew enough about whale physiology and ecology to make extremely educated guesses as to the best strategies for communication. Yet, like Jim Darling in his decadeslong studies of humpback songs, Clark found conclusions elusive. Neither he nor anyone else could say what blues are really calling about or why. To borrow Chris Fox's line: Mysteries of the deep? They're still out there. And that's putting it mildly.

Attuned to sounds most people never hear, Clark emphasized the need for the public to pay attention to the problem of underwater noise pollution. "The aggregate noise from shipping in some areas is overwhelming," he declared. "Being underwater is so different from our everyday environment that people can't readily appreciate the potential effects of such sounds on these animals' ability to communicate. It's like back in the days when no one gave much thought to air or surface-water pollution." Consider, too, that virtually all marine mammals depend heavily on passive listening—using the sound waves bouncing around an environment to orient themselves in much the same way that blind people do. Blue whales need this information to navigate in relation to submarine canyons, shelves, and coastlines. From Clark's point of view—or, rather, his listening post—we might want to begin thinking about the ever-growing amounts of noise we dump into the oceans every year as if the sounds were chemicals toxic to marine life once they accumulate to certain levels.

During most of my time in Baja, I traveled with Richard Sears, the French-Canadian researcher who first devised a way to identify individual blue whales, starting in 1979. After reading about field biologists who used whisker patterns to pick out different lions and patch patterns to tell giraffes apart, he tried spot patterns for blues. By 1981, he was getting fairly proficient at it. His main study area was the Gulf of St. Lawrence, on Canada's Atlantic seaboard. Sears started work there by volunteering as an assistant to a scientist studying fish behavior. Busy counting salmon and unclogging fish ladders at dams, Sears didn't know what a blue whale looked like. When he finally crossed paths with one, he wasn't sure what it was. The summer wore on, and his eye improved, and as it did, his interest kept quickening. Then, he said, "on the twenty-second of August 1976, I was looking at finbacks and a blue in the gulf, and I distinctly remember standing up in the boat and saying to myself, 'This is what I want to do the rest of my life.'" The closer his gulf travels took him to Mingan, on the Quebec shore, the more blues he saw. He set up a research base there and has spent the rest of his life doing exactly what he said he most wanted to do.

Each day that El Norte, or *chubasco*, winds weren't threatening, Sears, photographer Flip Nicklin, and I set out in a type of

Mexican fishing skiff known as a *panga*. Light and built for speed, not comfort, it rides like an empty flatbed truck on a washboard road. Whenever Sears heard a whale blow, he would automatically lift his arm to point, lift his chin, and exclaim, "Boom!" sometimes adding comments to himself in rapid French. Like Calambokidis, he had a freewheeling spirit that seemed to find its fullest expression at sea, and he relished every kidney-jolting mile. We covered eighty to a hundred of them a day.

When Sears initially decided to look for whales in the Gulf of California, he had little idea of what to expect. Although whalers had taken some blues off the west coast of Baja, there were only very sporadic sightings of them in the gulf itself. One of the more interesting observations came from Nobel Prize–winning author John Steinbeck in his 1941 work *The Log from the* Sea of Cortez. Writing of travels with his great friend Ed Ricketts, a marine biologist, Steinbeck described cutting through water "soupy" with *Nyctiphanes* krill. He saw daytime surface swarms around Isla Carmen and mentioned that they were associated with feeding blue whales. But at the time Sears began probing Baja, blues were still considered rare throughout the entire region.

"Not only was information scarce and the public convinced that all the whales were going extinct, there weren't that many marine mammalogists," Sears recalled. During his first season in the Sea of Cortez, in 1981, he sighted 20 blue whales. A few years later, he worried that the public might have been right after all, for he located and identified exactly 1 blue whale. The next year, he found 2. But later in the 1980s, he chased down 21. People told him that this had to be every blue whale in the Sea of Cortez. In 1990, he recorded 72 and in other years, almost 80. Lately his counts had fluctuated from as few as 5 to as many as 40. By the time I arrived, Sears had identified nearly 380 different blue whales in this gulf, roughly the same number he had identified in the Gulf of St. Lawrence over the years. Yet while calves made up less than 3 percent of his Atlantic population sample, they added up to 13 percent of the blue whales in the Sea of Cortez.

Sears wasn't sure whether he was seeing an unusually low rate of reproduction in the Gulf of St. Lawrence or if there was some reason females with young avoided that area. He was collecting blubber samples to test a third possibility, which was that toxins were affecting the St. Lawrence whales' health. Those Canadian waters contained high levels of chlorinated hydrocarbons, including dioxin and PCBs, and beluga whales using the gulf were known to be very heavily contaminated. In contrast to the Gulf of St. Lawrence, the percentage of calves in the Sea of Cortez was higher than normal, since they constituted just 5 to 7 percent of the North Pacific population as a whole. Moreover, Sears's biopsies revealed 4 females for every male in the Gulf of California. This led him to believe that females with newborns favored the area as a sort of nursery or kindergarten. Was the attraction the abundance of food available in relatively calm waters? Or less exposure to danger?

In the Gulf of St. Lawrence, Sears used ice scars to help identify individuals. In the Gulf of California, he used marks from killer whale teeth. Worldwide, barely 1 percent of blue whales are observed to have killer whale scars, whereas about 25 to 30 percent of humpbacks bear them. However, one-quarter of the blue whales in Baja were also showing such scars. This didn't imply that they were being attacked here. If anything, Sears suspected, the scars testified to the frequency of encounters with orcas in the open Pacific, which might lead mothers with nursing young to seek refuge in the Sea of Cortez.

Some blue whales almost always fluke, or lift their tails free of the water, before diving. Others hardly ever do. Among the flukers, which present an extra portion of their bodies to view, the percentage of Baja blue whales that Sears found bearing killer whale teeth marks rose to fifty-five. Leaving aside the question of where in the animals' range the attacks actually took place, the marks told him that blues are far from being immune to predation because of their size. At the same time, the wounds' healed-over appearance suggested that most attempts probably happened when the animals were young. Another point of interest for me lay in the simple fact that the population contained flukers and nonflukers, because it was the first line of evidence pointing toward individual variation in behavior. Blues could be as different from one another as elephants or gorillas or household pets tend to be. We simply can't tell, because we aren't able to see enough of what the whales are doing, and we don't know what subtleties to look for in the first place. However, Sears did know of individuals that acted spooky around boats, and others that consistently seemed relaxed. "We have one animal called Nubbin that is so easygoing I could put you right on top of it and you wouldn't bother it," he said.

"I met a Nubbin or Nubbins by the Channel Islands," I told him. "Is this the same whale?"

"I have eighty or ninety matches with whales that Calambokidis has seen off California," Sears replied, "and Nubbin is one of them." Number 382 in the North Pacific whale catalogue, Nubbin had very light, almost pale, pigmentation, but this whale's most distinctive markings were parallel scars from orca teeth and a chunk missing from the left trailing edge of its tail—most likely the result of an orca bite. Sears first identified Nubbin in 1984. A frequent visitor to the Sea of Cortez, Nubbin had been document-ed there twenty-two times since by Sears. Later, Sears recognized the same whale in an old photo taken by a NOAA scientist near Southern California's San Nicolas Island in 1971.

"That's probably what we'll find as the years go on: that some come here regularly and others only occasionally," he said. This was what he was finding in the Gulf of St. Lawrence, where about a quarter of the blue whales he had identified formed a core group that he could count on showing up nearly every summer. While a percentage of the St. Lawrence animals remained until late fall, others exited the gulf and were seen offshore during summer in such places as Davis Strait and The Gully, where I had spied several while chasing northern bottlenose whales. Although the cold-season range of North Atlantic blues remains unknown, they have been seen in the Caribbean during winter. One traveled into the Panama Canal on the Atlantic side in 1922. It was machine-gunned to death as a hazard to shipping.

Sears has documented a few blues in the Gulf of St. Lawrence in winter months nosing through thin pancake ice and soft "grease" ice. Others have been recorded during winter off Iceland. In the Pacific, occasional winter sightings came from California and from as far north as the Aleutians. Then there were Bruce Mate's satellite-radio locations from Baja throughout the winter to take into account, because the waters of the gulf get very chilly. It looks possible that more than a few blue whales in both the North Atlantic and North Pacific populations continue to forage well outside the tropics for some portion of the cold season.

One day, we motored from Loreto past Isla Carmen, on past Isla Montserrat, and came upon a huge adult blue with strongly contrasting dark and light spots and a distinctive notch in its dorsal fin. Sears said it was a whale he had seen in many previous years; then, almost in passing, he mentioned that he had observed a white whale in the Sea of Cortez during 1997. He described it as a fully grown adult. Maybe, I thought, it was Pale Whale's parent. It wasn't. When Sears and Calambokidis compared photos and notes, the realized that they had seen the same white animal. It was seen again as recently as 2005.

Sears's assistants radioed to report a solitary young blue hanging around their boat. When we met up with them, the whale was still there and it at once made a wide loop to come over and visit our *panga*. Possibly a recently independent yearling, it was barely forty feet long, the smallest blue whale we had yet seen aside from babies with their mothers. Instead of appearing bright blue when submerged, it looked almost light green because the water was so loaded with phytoplankton that it had turned jade. The whale made seven more passes over the next half hour, some within ten feet of the *panga* and two beneath it.

Sears said, "The more I see blue whales, the more I sense that they are, or can be, inquisitive and playful. I don't know why, but I see them breach more often here than anywhere else." As if to add an exclamation mark, the young blue made a partial breach in the distance. "Perhaps it's more that the animals were heavily hunted and their behavior is changing now, like we've seen happen with gray whales." I thought of the mother gray that once swam over to a group of visitors while I was in Baja's San Ignacio Lagoon on the peninsula's Pacific side. She submerged, rolled onto her back, then rose in such a way as to place her baby on her belly and lift it into the air next to the skiff. As one, the humans broke into applause and started telling this whale how beautiful her little one was. Less than a century earlier, whalers were calling this species the "devilfish" and spinning sagas of grays chasing boats and sometimes busting them into pieces. The part that wasn't often told was how the men in those boats commonly went about killing the big adult females in Baja's breeding lagoons. They found it easiest to harpoon the babies first and leave them thrashing at the end of ropes in order to draw in the mothers.

Earlier in the day, Sears and I had passed a group of 150 common dolphins, three fin whales together, a Bryde's whale, a gray, then more fins. And while we were watching the curious young blue whale, a humpback spouted in the distance. Sea lions, brown pelicans, and Xantus' murrelets competed for our attention. Porcupine fish, sometimes called blowfish, bobbed along the surface like prickly fishing floats, which meant that they had recently inflated themselves in reaction to attempts by predators to snatch them. On the land, chain cholla cacti and paloverde trees stood against a background of rust-colored cliffs, while the Sierra de la Gigante Range rose five thousand feet above sea level to the west, forming the backbone of the Baja Peninsula. The afternoon gave way to an evening sky of incandescent yellow—a quality of light I remembered from earlier trips to Baja and have seen nowhere else—over a sea darkening to cobalt with electric purple ripples.

John Calambokidis carried out full-throttle gun-and-run reconnaissance across thousands of square miles. Don Croll and Bernie Tershy took a high-tech route toward understanding the ecosystem, dunking thousands of dollars' worth of instruments into the saltwater to extract information. Sears, with his shore-based, go-out-and-have-a-look-around routine, practiced an old-style natural history: he spent a lot of time in familiar places waiting to see what would happen. As with many of the best naturalists, he was motivated in good part by a sense of adventure, which requires high expectations in the face of the unknown. He kept his overhead down and had even figured out a way to cover some of the costs through ecotourism, taking a small number of visitors along in his crew's *pangas* for a few days each field season. It was one more way to keep doing what he had said he wanted to do with the rest of his life.

This more intimate approach to studying blue whales appealed strongly to me, especially since the Sea of Cortez is one of the most intimate settings in which one could possibly study blue whales to begin with. Here, far-wandering giants, typically found some distance from shore, cruise so close to cliff walls and the points of islands that you could just about study them without stepping off solid ground. From a boat's deck, it sometimes looked as though cacti were sprouting from a blue whale's back instead of from the rocks behind it. The land was so sere, so sparsely inhabited, that the contrast with the fertile, life-stirred sea was unfailingly sharp, strange, and lovely.

After leaving Loreto for Isla Montserrat on a different day, we were soon surrounded by big groups of bottlenose dolphins. Fin whales, brown boobies, and brown pelicans all escorted us at different times, and frigate birds swooped down to steal fish from paddling fleets of cormorants. In early afternoon, we were closing the distance to a blue whale sighted from afar when Sears punched the air with a fist and shouted, "It's Nubbin!" By now I was counting on him to lift his arm, point, and say "Boom!" any time any whale surfaced to spout. The gesture was almost unconscious, as was the smile of satisfaction that spread across Sears's face as we drew near to this old acquaintance.

Sperm whales had been sighted by fishermen not far away, and on our return to Loreto a group of two dozen short-finned pilot whales surfaced. They had saddles of light gray pigment on their backs and big melon heads, and they reared and snorted like a herd of horses as they went rolling by. Bottlenose dolphins joined the pilot whales. The two pods swam diagonally across one another's paths. Both started to lob-tail and breach. The pilot whales turned the water to froth. By comparison, the bottlenoses seemed weightless, leaping effortlessly and reentering with scarcely a splash, as if the surface were a soft membrane that parted to admit them. Yellow Baja evening light spread over the mountains in the distance. By the time it grew too dark to make out the back of the one dolphin still keeping company with us, the prow of our boat was moving through phosphorescent plankton that glowed when agitated. We struck sparks all the way home.

On a morning that brought too much wind for us to venture from land, Sears and I paid a visit to Fernando Arcas Saiz at a museum he had established in Loreto. Staffed by volunteers, it promoted education, research, and conservation in association with Parque Marino Nacional Bahia de Loreto (Loreto Bay National Marine Park), established in 1996. Sears had helped support its formation and regularly exchanged information with Saiz, a former sportfishing guide who had turned to ecotourism with whale watching as the highlight.

"We talked to people in town, owners of hotels, concessions, taxis—everyone—to get support for this park," Saiz told me. "The rule is, no more commercial fishing by net-dragging or trawling. Only eight to ten families still catch fish here with gill nets. In a few years we hope to have no nets at all. We want to protect marine life, and we are also looking for ways to help fishermen who use hooks and lines survive."

Despite its generally pristine appearance, Baja is home to a large enough fishing industry that its commercially valuable species have been seriously overharvested. Once-abundant populations of sharks had been especially hard hit by the fishing crews. While some of the biggest cetaceans seemed to be making a comeback, the smallest of all, a little porpoise called the vaquita, weighing just 60 to 120 pounds, measuring four to five feet long, and known only from the northern Sea of Cortez, was on the verge of extinction. Too many had drowned in nets sweeping the gulf for fish and shrimp.

A unique array of plants and animals developed over thousands of years on the desert islands in this gulf, yielding a great many species and subspecies found nowhere else. Since the communities held few, if any, native land predators, many of the islands' birds nested and roosted right on the ground. The flora and fauna alike were now at risk from introduced species, namely, feral rats, house mice, cats, dogs, and goats escaped or purposefully let loose from boats. The highest rates of extinction in the modern world have been on islands, chiefly because the land areas are so limited that alien predators or competitors overwhelm native life-forms before they have a chance to find refuges or adapt. On the *Amigo,* I discovered that Croll and Tershy had a project under way to protect the islands through an organization they helped found: Island Conservation. It was mostly a matter of trapping and removing non-native animals with the assistance of a small staff, local volunteers, and the cooperation of Mexican resource agencies. Compared to the techno-wizardry these researchers practiced at sea, the island work was unsophisticated, unexciting, and mostly thankless. They did it anyway because it was essential. As Croll said, "The real endangered species in this area are not big whales but noncharismatic island mice, endemic lizards, and plants. You can't stand by and watch them vanish just because they aren't well known or popular."

The comment made me realize anew how much I enjoy being around whale people, and not only because they are insatiably curious. They want to help the natural world flourish, an urge that grows readily out of their quest for a better understanding of how that world operates. You have to be willing to expend incredible amounts of time and energy in the attempt to learn about whales, knowing full well how few solid answers you may be able to get in return. To head out each day also requires genuine courage, because the ocean's powers are so awesome and mercurial, and safety is so far away. The other reason I like hanging around these folks—interpreters of satellite images and squawks from submarine-detection hydrophones, krill lifestyle experts, code-breakers of dot patterns on identification photographs, helpmates to marine parks, and would-be saviors of obscure Mexican mice and wildflowers—is that, because there are so many more mysteries than answers, you never know where the study of great whales is going to lead.

In November of that year, I telephoned Bruce Mate to catch up on his work. He had tagged thirteen blue whales with satellite radios over the summer in just four days among the Farallon Islands. The animals were already working their way south down the Mexican coast. Yet the week before I phoned, Mate said, one blue shot twelve hundred miles offshore, heading northwest in the direction of the Aleutian Islands. Several whales Mate had marked the previous year traveled an average of seventy-two hundred miles before their radios gave out, after four to eight months. He wondered how far the latest batch of on-the-air blues would journey.

"There must be a reason these animals have big brains," he told me. "Maybe they have maps in them. They need to know how to get to various places at intervals when they are producing truly great food." The locations are spread along thousands of miles of convoluted coastlines—and among millions of square miles of open ocean. How do the whales find such spots? Do they navigate by the calls of other whales and the reflections of different sounds off submarine features? How many clues must blue whales learn and remember over their long lives in order to be successful at finding food, mates, and whatever else they need? Do their memories of clues work like mariners' charts? Throughout their multi-million-year reign, dinosaurs proved that you don't have to have a big brain to go with a big body. But a blue whale most definitely has both. The combination allows it to operate on a scale that can take up a good part of a hemisphere and maybe more.

Blue whales are a peerless definition of living large. We have stopped killing them and many of their relatives, and our knowledge about their existence is rapidly mounting with the help of new technologies. From here on, the giants' survival may depend upon our ability to interpret subjects that are bigger and more complex yet—the oceans themselves and the human activities that now affect them at every level.

Cetacean Taxonomy at a Glance

Class: **Mammalia**

  Order: **Cetacea**

    Suborder: **Mysticeti** (Baleen whales)

Family:		
	Eschrichtiidae—	gray whale
	Balaenidae—	bowhead whale
		North Atlantic right whale
		North Pacific right whale
		southern right whale
	Neobalaenidae—	pygmy right whale
	Balaenopteridae—	northern minke whale
	(Rorquals)	antarctic minke whale
		pelagic Bryde's whale
		coastal Bryde's whale
		pygmy Bryde's whale
		sei whale
		fin whale
		blue whale
		humpback whale

    Suborder: **Odontoceti** (Toothed whales)

Family:		
	Kogiidae—	pygmy sperm whale
		dwarf sperm whale
	Physeteridae—	sperm whale
	Ziphiidae—	Baird's beaked whale
		Arnoux's beaked whale
		northern bottlenose whale
		southern bottlenose whale
		Cuvier's beaked whale

Blainville's beaked whale
strap-toothed whale
ginko-toothed beaked whale
Andrew's beaked whale
Gervais' beaked whale
Hubb's beaked whale
True's beaked whale
Longman's beaked whale
Stejneger's beaked whale
Sowerby's beaked whale
Hector's beaked whale
Shepherd's beaked whale
pygmy (or lesser) beaked whale
Gray's (or Japanese) beaked whale
Mesoplodon species A
Perrin's beaked whale (classified in
2002)
spade-toothed beaked whale

Monodontidae— narwhal
beluga

Delphinidae— killer whale
false killer whale
pygmy killer whale
short-finned pilot whale
long-finned pilot whale
melon-headed whale
bottlenose dolphin
Indo-Pacific bottlenose dolphin
short-beaked common dolphin
long-beaked common dolphin
spinner dolphin
striped dolphin
Atlantic spotted dolphin
pantropical spotted dolphin

	Atlantic white-sided dolphin
	Pacific white-sided dolphin
	white-beaked dolphin
	northern right whale dolphin
	southern right whale dolphin
	Heaviside's dolphin
	Fraser's dolphin
	Hector's dolphin
	Commerson's dolphin
	Risso's dolphin
	Peale's dolphin
	black (Chilean) dolphin
	hourglass dolphin
	dusky dolphin
	rough-toothed dolphin
	Clymene dolphin
	Atlantic hump-backed dolphin
	Indo-Pacific hump-backed dolphin
	Irawaddy dolphin
	snub-fin dolphin
	tucuxi
Platanistidae—	Ganges River dolphin
	Indus River dolphin
Pontoporiidae—	La Plata dolphin (franciscana)
	Yangtze River dolphin (baiji) (declared extinct in 2007)
Iniidae—	Amazon River dolphin (boto)
Phocoenidae—	Dall's porpoise
	Burmeister's porpoise
	spectacled porpoise
	harbor porpoise
	finless porpoise
	vaquita

How to Get Involved

Adopt an Orca
P.O. Box 1233
Whangarei, New Zealand
Phone: 64 (09) 4343 043
www.orca.org.nz
Killer whale conservation and research in the Southern Hemisphere.

American Cetacean Society
P.O. Box 1381
San Pedro, CA 90733–1391
310–548–6279
info@ACSonline.org
The oldest nonprofit whale conservation group, founded in 1967.

Cascadia Research Collective
218 $^1/_2$ W. Fourth Avenue
Olympia, WA 98501
360–943–7325
www.cascadiaresearch.org
Research with special emphasis on humpback, blue, and gray whales.

Center for Whale Research
P.O. Box 1577
Friday Harbor, WA 98250
orcasurv@rockisland.com
Killer whale studies in Puget Sound, Washington, with opportunities
for volunteer work through the Earthwatch Institute.

Center for Whale Studies
P.O. Box 1539
Lahaina, Maui, HI 96767–1539
Long-term studies by Debbie Glockner-Ferrari and Mark Ferrari focusing
on humpback whale behavior.

Earthwatch Institute
>3 Clock Tower Plaza, Suite 100
>P.O. Box 75
>Maynard, MA 01754
>800–776–0188, 978–461–2332
>*info@earthwatch.org*

Expeditions linking volunteers with wildlife field research projects around the world.

Hawaii Whale Research Foundation
>P.O. Box 1296
>Lahaina, HI 96767
>*www.hwrf.org*

Humpback whale social behavior research, with volunteer opportunities.

Hebridean Whale and Dolphin Trust
>28 Main Street
>Tobermory, Isle of Mull
>Scotland PA756NU
>44 (0) 1688 302 620
>*whaledolphintrust.co.uk*

Locally based conservation through research and education.

Mingan Island Cetacean Study
>378 Bord de la Mer
>Longue-Pointe-de-Mingan, Quebec, Canada G0G 1V0
>418–949–2845
>*mics@globetrotter.net*

Research, education, and guided expeditions.

Natural Resources Defense Council
>40 West Twentieth Street
>New York, NY 10011
>212–727–2700
>*nrdcinfo@nrdc.org*

Conservation through political and legal action on national and global environmental issues.

Ocean Alliance
> 191 Weston Road
> Lincoln, MA 01773
> 800–969–4253, 781–259–0423
> *www.oceanalliance.org*

Conservation and advocacy, founded in 1971 by the leading cetacean researcher Dr. Roger Payne.

Oceanic Society
> Fort Mason Center, Building E
> San Francisco, CA 94123–1234
> 800–326–7491, 415–441–1106
> *www.oceanic-society.org*

Research, environmental education, and opportunities for volunteering.

OrcaLab
> P.O. Box 510
> Alert Bay, British Columbia, Canada V0N 1A0
> *www.orcalab.org, www.orca-live.net*

Killer whale research and conservation, live updates, and real-time whale voices on the Web.

Save the Whales
> 1192 Waring Street
> Seaside, CA 93955
> 831–899–9957
> *maris@savethewhales.org*

Kid-friendly focus on education.

Soundwatch
> 62 First Street North
> P.O. Box 945
> Friday Harbor, WA 98250
> 360–378–4710
> *soundwatch@whalemuseum.org*

Stewardship, education, and monitoring of boats near whales; a program of the Whale Museum.

Straitwatch

P.O. Box 573
Alert Bay, British Columbia, Canada V0N 1A0
250–974–7064
info@straitwatch.org

Canadian counterpart of Soundwatch.

Stubbs Island Charters, Ltd.

P.O. Box 2–2
Telegraph Cove, British Columbia, Canada V0N 3J0
800–665–3066, 250–928–3185, 250–928–3117
stubbs@island.net, www.stubbs-island.com

Educational whale-watching trips off Vancouver Island.

Whale and Dolphin Conservation Society

P.O. Box 232
Melksham, Wiltshire, England SN12 7SB
44 (0) 1225 354 333
info@wdcs.org

A United Kingdom–based group with international chapters working for the protection of cetaceans.

Whale Center of New England

P.O. Box 159
Gloucester, MA 01931–0159
978–281–6351
info@whalecenter.org

Research, education, and whale watching.

Whale Trust

300 Paani Place
Paia, HI 96779
808–873–9600
info@whaletrust.org

Cutting-edge humpback whale research and education.

World Wildlife Fund

1250 Twenty-fourth Street
Washington, DC 20037
202–293–4800
www.worldwildlife.org

Global support and advocacy for marine mammals and other species.